1976

This book kept

BETTY REID MANDELL is Assistant Professor of Social Welfare at Boston State College. She is the author of *Where Are the Children?* (1973) and numerous professional articles, including "The New Conservative: Scientist or Apologist?" and "Welfare and Totalitarianism." She was a member of the editorial board of *Social Work* from 1967 to 1973.

welfare
in america

controlling
the "dangerous classes"

BETTY REID MANDELL

Editor

A SPECTRUM BOOK

PRENTICE-HALL, INC., *Englewood Cliffs, New Jersey*

Library of Congress Cataloging in Publication Data
Main entry under title:

Welfare in America.

   (A Spectrum Book)
   Includes bibliographical references.
     1. Public welfare—United States—Addresses, essays,
lectures.   2. Social control—Addresses, essays, lec-
tures.   3. Social service—United States—Addresses,
essays, lectures.   I. Mandell, Betty Reid.
HV95.W45   361′.973   75–19207
ISBN 0–13–949313–1
ISBN 0–13–949305–0 pbk.

© 1975 by PRENTICE-HALL, INC.
ENGLEWOOD CLIFFS, NEW JERSEY

A SPECTRUM BOOK

1 2 3 4 5 6 7 8 9 10

Printed in the United States of America

PRENTICE-HALL INTERNATIONAL, INC. *(London)*
PRENTICE-HALL OF AUSTRALIA PTY., LTD. *(Sydney)*
PRENTICE-HALL OF CANADA, LTD. *(Toronto)*
PRENTICE-HALL OF INDIA PRIVATE LIMITED *(New Delhi)*
PRENTICE-HALL OF JAPAN, INC. *(Tokyo)*
PRENTICE-HALL OF SOUTHEAST ASIA (PTE.) LTD. *(Singapore)*

contents

Chapter One

**Whose Welfare?
An Introduction**   *1*
Betty Reid Mandell

Chapter Two

**A Radical Critique
of Federal Work
and Manpower Programs,
1933–1974**   *23*
Henry L. Allen

Chapter Three

**Social Welfare and Social Class:
Income, Wealth, and Power**   *39*
Larry Beeferman

Chapter Four

Who Rules the Social Services?   *65*
Betty Reid Mandell

v

Chapter Five

**Social Insecurity:
Welfare Policy
and
the Structure of Poor Families**   *89*
Carol B. Stack and Herbert Semmel

Chapter Six

**The Children
of the "Dangerous
and Perishing Classes"**   *104*
Betty Reid Mandell

Chapter Seven

**Reproduction
and Capitalist Development:
Uses of Birth Control
and Abortion**   *119*
Mie Watanabe

Chapter Eight

Medicine and Social Control   *138*
Barbara and John Ehrenreich

Chapter Nine

**Serving the Rich,
Punishing the Poor:
Welfare for the Wealthy
through Criminal Justice**   *168*
Estelle Disch

whose welfare?
an introduction*

—*Betty Reid Mandell*

Coming to power, they could only conceive of trying to clean up every situation in sight. And so many of the women seemed victims of the higher hygiene. Even a large part of the young seemed to have faces whose cheeks had been injected with Novocain. . . .

. . . there was the muted tragedy of the Wasp—they were not on earth to enjoy or even perhaps to love so very much, they were here to serve, and serve they had in public functions and public charities (while recipients of their charity might vomit in rage and laugh in scorn) . . .

Norman Mailer
Miami and the Siege of Chicago[1]

Why are the recipients of charity vomiting in rage and laughing in scorn at their benefactors? So much service, so much charity—why no gratitude? In fact, why so few improvements? We argue that the people in power have served only in "safe" ways that will not threaten their power. When they serve on boards of directors of social agencies, they allow the professional social workers on the staff to "rehabilitate," "counsel," "educate," and give some money to poor people. But they are not likely to allow social workers to organize a rent strike against a member of the board. Nor are they usually eager to invite recipients of service to join them on the board to share decision-making power. We argue that the kind and quality of the social services people get depends largely upon who runs the society, and for what purposes.

Some people describe the United States and other advanced industrialized countries as "service states." [2] Others call them "welfare states." [3] In a

---

* The author is indebted to Marvin Mandell and Gordon MacLeod for their helpful suggestions in the preparation of this chapter.

[1] New York: Signet Book, New American Library, 1968, p. 35.

[2] Paul Halmos, *The Personal Service State* (New York: Schocken Books, 1970). Adam Yarmolinsky, "The Service Society," in Martin Meyerson, ed., *The Conscience of the City* (New York: George Braziller, 1970), pp. 173–86.

[3] Richard Titmuss, *Essays on the "Welfare State"* (London: Routledge & Kegan Paul, 1969).

complicated technological society, people cannot survive simply by their own efforts; they need the services of other people. Once, in the rural past, the family and village might have been able to care for most people's needs. But those days are past. Except for rich people, the family is no longer the major social insurance system, although family and friends are still a critically important source of social security for most people. Perhaps they are most important for the very poor, who rely on kin when they have no jobs or when their welfare money is used up, as Stack and Semmel show in their article in this book. Policy makers and legislators, in their preoccupation with saving money, often ignore the importance of kinship and break up families. Thus does the state create social insecurity in the name of social security.

What do people in trouble do when their families and friends can't help? They go without help, or they go to a stranger for help. Most likely this stranger is a paid helper, paid either by the person who seeks the help or by a privately or state-sponsored agency. The quality of help a person gets depends very much on the quality of the society he or she lives in, and upon his or her status in that society. We propose to analyze some of the kinds of help that people get in the United States. We shall pay particular attention to who gets what, and why. Some people get "as good as money can buy" (and that is not always very good) because they have the money to buy it; some who have little or no money may get little or nothing. Some people are damaged by "help." Those people could well echo the cry of the farmer's lad (Andres) in Cervantes' *Don Quixote*. Don Quixote sees a farmer beating Andres and stops him. Later Andres meets Quixote again and tells him he received a far worse beating from the farmer afterward because of Quixote's intervention. Andres concludes:

> For the love of God, Sir Knight-errant, if ever again you meet me, even though they are hacking me to bits, do not aid or succor me but let me bear it, for no misfortune could be so great as that which comes of being helped by you. May God curse you and all the knights-errant that were ever born into this world! [4]

Our "ideal" definition of social welfare and social services is broad. It includes any service outside the economically productive sector that enhances people's well-being. Although we include the criminal and juvenile justice systems in our case studies, most criminals and juveniles would probably laugh derisively at the idea of the system being a social service for their enrichment. Despite official rhetoric about "correction" and "rehabilitation" of a juvenile or adult criminal, social control has been the main function of the system, as Estelle Disch points out in her article in this book. She shows that the system has not achieved the kind of social control it seeks, nor has it been very effective in "rehabilitating" people. The problem seems to lie with the larger social system and its structure and values. Herein is the crux of the social service issue. The question is: Should a social service try to fit people

[4] Transl. Samuel Putnam (New York: The Viking Portable Library, 1951), p. 297.

into the slots prescribed by the rulers of society or, if these slots make people miserable, should a social service struggle against the dominant values so that people can define for themselves what makes them happy? There is a constant tension in most of the social services between the goals of social control and the goal of individual happiness.

One's definition of social welfare depends partly upon one's conception of a society's responsibility to its citizens. Before the advent of universal compulsory education in the United States, the rulers of society did not believe that education was a necessary welfare service for all the citizens. Now the Social Security Administration lists education as the country's second largest welfare expenditure. (Health is the largest, with a predicted cost of $116 billion to be spent on doctors, hospitals, medicine, nursing, and other medical services between July 1974 and July 1975.[5]) Although the Social Service Administration views welfare broadly, the general public still thinks of welfare as public assistance—the United States' descendant of England's Poor Law, stigmatized and means-tested. Most people do not, however, think of "Social Security" (Old Age, Survivors, Dependents, and Hospital Insurance) as "welfare." Nor are they likely to view unemployment compensation or workmen's compensation as "welfare," because they are told that they are entitled to these benefits because they worked for them. Still less are people likely to view farm subsidies, oil depletion allowances, or tax write-offs for big corporations as "welfare," even though they involve more government spending than public assistance. The crucial test in the public's mind between the "deserving" and the "undeserving" poor lies in the recipient's relation to the work force. If he or she examined "social security" closely, the citizen who needs to separate the "deserving" from the "undeserving" would find that what purports to be an insurance program is not precisely that. When that citizen retires, he or she will be paid OASDHI benefits from the taxpayer's dollar as well as from his or her own earnings, and will usually receive a good deal more in benefits than he or she has paid. Yet the idea of work-related benefits, even when some of the benefits come from general revenues, exerts a powerful psychological hold on workers. The stigmatization of public assistance helps to keep the worker on the job—any job—rather than to "go on welfare." "Paying your own way" is a deep and pervasive American value. The "freeloader" is an object of contempt. Thus every citizen is assigned a market value, and his or her social benefits are at least roughly computed in terms of that market value. Consequently, one function of social welfare systems is to regulate the poor.[6]

SOCIAL VIEWS OF POVERTY

Throughout the history of industrialized societies, there have been basically two different views of poverty and of the poor. One view blames the socio-

    [5] *The New York Times*, September 15, 1974, p. E 10.
    [6] For a detailed analysis of how this occurs in the public assistance program, see Frances Fox Piven and Richard Cloward, *Regulating the Poor* (New York: Vintage, 1971).

economic system; the other blames the poor. There were some preliterate subsistence societies in the past that had no separate classes of rich and poor, but in all industrialized societies and most agricultural societies today a few people control the means of production and are rich, and a lot of people have no control over the means of production and are poor. During the Middle Ages, when all statuses were relatively fixed and unchanging, people assumed that poverty was ordained by God. The Church cared for those poor people who were not cared for by personal almsgiving. The rich gave to the poor in order to save their own souls, building up credits to assure their entrance to heaven. As mercantilism and industrialism gained force and societies separated more rigidly into rich and poor classes, the rich began to blame the poor for their poverty. They were seldom concerned with poverty as a social illness, and no one thought to study poverty as a sociological phenomenon until about the middle of the nineteenth century. As industrialization proceeded full steam ahead, people valued competition and individual achievement ever more highly. The owners of production spread the word through their media, their elite schools, and their churches that people were poor because of defects in their character. Only a minority held the other view of poverty: that people were poor because the owners of production pay as low wages as they can get away with in order to increase their profit; that capitalism contains built-in vicissitudes which guarantee continual underemployment and unemployment, and periodic economic crises.

PHILANTHROPIC RESPONSES TO POVERTY

The social and psychological roots of altruism and of philanthropy are complex. Some philanthropists give out of guilt, having exploited their workers in order to make their profits. Some give because they have no children to pass their money on to or don't like their relatives enough to pass on their wealth to them. Some give to get a tax deduction. Some give because their religion enjoins them to. Some give to gain social status; some give because it makes them feel good. Some philanthropists have wanted to control their recipients through eternity, as did Mr. Gray, who decreed in his will that the recipients of his money should wear gray, and Cornelius Christmas, who bequeathed an inheritance for bread, coal, and money to be given to the poor yearly only during the week before Christmas.[7] Occasionally a rich philanthropist, understanding the intimate connection between social welfare and the way he makes his money, has sold an honest product while providing generous wages and benefits to his workers. Such a man was the Quaker George Cadbury (1839–1922), who sold pure cocoa rather than the "hair-raising mixture of cocoa, potato starch, sago, and treacle that was the standard commercial product."[8] Cadbury took his religion seriously,

[7] David Owen, *English Philanthropy, 1660–1960* (Cambridge, Mass.: Harvard University Press, 1965), pp. 324, 325.
[8] Ibid., p. 436.

believing it a sin to accumulate vast wealth. He used his factory as a pilot experiment in social welfare, hoping it would provide a model for industry as a whole. His work on the anti-sweating and old age pension campaigns and similar causes "marked him as something of an alien spirit among late Victorian philanthropists and proclaimed his sharp deviation from the main tradition of Victorian philanthropy." [9]

The main tradition of Victorian philanthropy opposed state intervention or collective solutions to anything, either business or welfare. Most Victorian welfare specialists naturally accepted the imperative of a developing capitalism, which needed a free hand and wanted no interference. Looking back from the present perspective of welfare capitalism, some of the Victorian philanthropists seem ludicrous. They seemed so even to some of their contemporaries such as Charles Dickens, who satirized their hypocrisies. It seems funny to us when we read that Charles Loch, director of the London Charity Organization Society, opposed free meals for school children on the grounds that these would give their parents an unfair advantage on the labor market, and would encourage parents to neglect their responsibilities. He even seems a bit out of his mind in his opposition to giving pennies to children: "A penny given and a child ruined." [10] The Charity Organization Society was "seized with panic at the mere mention of socialism." [11] Yet Loch's statements about the relationship of social welfare to private enterprise contain some familiar strains even to a modern ear. The political struggles around welfare issues still center around disagreements regarding society's responsibilities toward its citizens.

Loch believed that poverty could be handled best by rehabilitating poor individuals and families, case by case, through "friendly visitors." These friendly visitors were rich, usually smugly superior and patronizing toward the poor, and usually women with few socially approved outlets for their energies. The Charity Organization Society divided the poor neatly into the "deserving" and the "undeserving," keeping the "deserving" (or the "helpable," as they were later labeled) on their own caseloads, and sending the "undeserving" or "unhelpable" to the almshouses or workhouses run by the government Poor Law. Loch almost refused to admit the existence of unemployment, always putting the word in quotes in his annual reports. "Out-of-work cases are frequently want-to-thrift cases," he said smugly. He advised thrift for the unemployed [12] and believed that looking for a job strengthened a man's moral character. With a perverse logic that is still widespread, Loch believed that unrestricted and unregulated charity *caused* poverty, and he and the Charity Organization Society set out with missionary zeal to attempt to regulate the free-handed charities that, in his view, coddled poor people and weakened their moral fiber. His was the dominant view of

[9] Ibid., p. 435.
[10] Ibid., p. 237.
[11] Ibid., p. 240.
[12] Ibid., p. 242.

Victorian England and Beatrice Webb, one of the founders of the Fabian Society, was decidedly in the minority when she pointed to "a deeper and more continuous evil than unrestricted and unregulated charity, namely unrestricted and unregulated capitalism and landlordism." [13]

The Liverpool Central Relief Society gave grudging recognition, in their 1897 annual report, that some people could not be blamed for their poverty because of irregularity of employment, sickness, or other things beyond their control. Yet they concluded, as did the London Charity Organization Society, that most poverty was due to individual weakness:

> As might have been anticipated, drink, improvidence, and neglect of family obligations, were among the chief causes.[14]

It was harder for Liverpool citizens to ignore unemployment since the depression of the 1880s and 90s had hit Liverpool, a port city with masses of transient labor, even harder than London. To deny unemployment there would have been an Alice in Wonderland exercise. The historian David Owen comments, however, that Liverpool's Central Relief Society was hardly revolutionary in its prescriptions for poverty:

> More friendly visiting, provident dispensaries, encouragement to saving, and personal reformation were the ingredients in the familiar prescription. One might readily infer that if the poor would not drink so much, would use the savings banks, and would wash more frequently, social distress would at least be markedly alleviated.[15]

ORIGINS OF THE SOCIAL SERVICES

We believe, as the author Joyce Carol Oates has said, that "the greatest realities are physical and economic; all the subtleties of life come afterward." [16] So it is with charity and the social services. While charitable benefactors and their deliverers of service may convince themselves that their motives contain only pure undiluted altruism, one must look for the physical and economic realities behind the benevolent rhetoric in order to fully understand the social services. It is not a mean or petty exercise to examine the motives of those who claim to be benevolent because, as Albert Camus said,

> The welfare of the people in general has always been the alibi of tyrants. It serves the further advantage of giving the servants of tyranny a good conscience. It would be easy, however, to destroy that good conscience by shouting to them, "If you want the happiness of the people, ask them what will make them happy." [17]

[13] Quoted in ibid., p. 504.
[14] Quoted in ibid., p. 462.
[15] Ibid.
[16] Cited in a review of Alfred Kazin, "Bright Book of Life," in *American Journal*, Vol. 1, No. 8 (July 3, 1973), 7.
[17] "Homage to an Exile," *Resistance, Rebellion, and Death*, transl. Justin O'Brien (New York: Modern Library, 1963), p. 74.

The charitable givers and their professionals seldom ask the recipients of service what kind of service they want; rather they give what they think the recipients need, according to their own perception of the poor. The way affluent people view poverty and the social class system is closely tied in with their assessments of political and commercial needs. One may see this more clearly by looking at the origins of the social services than at one's contemporary system because objectivity about a contemporary system is often harder to achieve than is objectivity about past societies.

The history of today's social services grows out of the history of poverty and reflects, at least in part, the views of the dominant class about how the working class should fit into business and political needs. Charity hospitals were founded during the seventeenth and eighteenth centuries in England when mercantilists began to worry about England's declining population and the possible loss of manpower.[18] Barbara and John Ehrenreich, in their article in this book, argue that the system of medical care continues to exert social control both through coercion and cooptation of patients, and that the forms this control take are powerfully shaped by the class, sex, and race characteristics of the doctors.

When charities were being formed, Brittania ruled the waves, and "the manpower requirements of Britain's maritime interest were never far in the background when charities for waifs and orphans were projected." [19] Some philanthropists denounced the practice of leaving unwanted babies by the roadside exposed to die as not only inhumane but a waste of manpower for a developing nation and for its colonies.[20] A retired sea captain, Thomas Coram, started the London Foundling Hospital to care for these unwanted babies. The Hospital restricted admission, as private agencies have always done, yet about 37 percent of the babies they cared for died. This was still a better record than the reported 59 percent death rate among workhouse children of the Poor Law. When Parliament passed a law opening the doors of the Foundling Hospital to all comers (perhaps, as one Lord suggested, out of anxiety about recruiting for the Navy), babies streamed in at an enormous rate from all over the country. During 46 months of unrestricted admission, 68.3 percent of nearly 15,000 children died in the Hospital—over 5,500 of these dying before they were six months old. In 1760 Parliament decided that it was too expensive to care for all unwanted babies, so urged that children be apprenticed out of the Hospital as quickly as possible, and the Foundling Hospital restricted admission again.[21] Most legislators have never been eager to spend much money on the poor.

Despite the fact that babies died like flies in the Foundling Hospital, that charity became one of the most prestigious in England. The composer George Frederick Handel donated an organ to its chapel, and gave regular benefit

[18] Owen, *English Philanthropy*, pp. 14–15.
[19] Ibid., p. 15.
[20] Ibid., p. 54.
[21] Ibid., p. 56.

performances of his oratorio *Messiah,* and the artist William Hogarth decorated the walls with his art.

The explicit purpose of the British Marine Society, founded in 1756, was to recruit destitute boys for the fleet and merchant shipping, because England was having trouble with recruiting enough people for its naval war against the French. The founder Jonas Hanway, fired with British patriotism, could hardly be accused of modesty or caution in his vision of the future of the Marine Society:

> British benevolence being thus united with *native British fire,* will diffuse the *genuine* spirit of patriotism through these realms; and we may soon hope to see such *improvements* in maritime affairs, as posterity looking back, will view with *equal gratitude* and *applause.*[22]

England's eighteenth-century manpower needs even inspired philanthropists to save people from drowning through the Royal Humane Society, founded in 1774 and modeled after a similar organization in Holland, where a lot of people fell into canals. The purpose of the Royal Humane Society, to resuscitate drowning people and to teach "the Godlike Art of Resuscitation,"[23] "neatly combined philanthropic and scientific with mercantilist values."[24]

Some philanthropists were touched not only by the sight of abandoned children but also by the plight of the "fallen women" who gave birth to those children. These women were victims of the prevailing double sexual standard which held that men could "sow their wild oats" but "good" women remained chaste. The Victorians' guilt about this double standard moved them to found institutions to "rehabilitate" the "fallen women" (which meant to give them moral and religious instruction and to train them for domestic work), but the philanthropists were not as easily moved to grant the women equality with men. The philanthropists blamed the women rather than the social system, so it followed logically that their prescription for preventing unwanted pregnancies was to change the women's character. This kind of thinking is still pervasive among some social workers today. Women have made progress in the United States today toward winning the right to control their reproductive functions through contraception and abortion. But the population picture is quite different now than it was when British orphans were needed for the Navy. As Mie Watanabe suggests in her article in this book, the victories which women have gained can also be turned against them by governments that seek to limit population, especially certain segments of the population.

Despite the many moralists who charged that providing institutions for the care of unmarried mothers and for the treatment of venereal disease only encouraged such vice and immorality,[25] those institutions were vastly more

[22] Quoted in ibid., p. 59.
[23] Ibid., p. 60.
[24] Ibid., p. 15.
[25] Ibid., pp. 52, 58.

popular philanthropies from the middle of the eighteenth century on than were women's colleges. In the nineteenth century as now, women liberationists agitated for equal education, but when Emily Davies proposed in 1886 that Girton College be founded for young English women, she and her colleagues had a long uphill struggle to get enough money to open the college, and a continuing struggle to make ends meet. Meanwhile the established elite men's colleges, Oxford and Cambridge, were sailing along with large endowments. "Women's education . . . made no irresistible appeal to British philanthropists." [26] Yet,

> among the causes whose appeal . . . benevolent Victorians found most irresistible, were those having to do with the preservation of female virtue or the rehabilitation of those who had lost it.[27]

Societies that are sharply polarized into separate classes are inherently unstable societies, simply because people these days do not tolerate inequality easily. Most rich people resist losing their wealth and privileges, so there is often a continual tension between the rich and the poor. Running through the history of philanthropy and the social services, one can trace several strands of the thread of anxiety the rich feel about threats to their wealth and well-being. The most persistent threat to their wealth is the wages they pay the workers. Every cent given to a worker means a cent less profit. Another threat, always in the background to be feared but only occasionally occurring as a genuine possibility, is the possibility of revolution which might radically change the distribution of wealth. Added to these threats to the wealth of the rich is the threat to their physical well-being posed by contagion from the poor; either the physical contagion of disease caused by unsanitary living conditions or the deterioration of neighborhoods caused by encroaching slums. The flight to the suburbs began in England in the early stages of industrialism.[28]

Most charities and welfare systems began as a response to one or another of these threats or a combination of them. The Poor Law in England and public assistance in America followed the principle of "less eligibility"—that is, that the amount of relief given to the worker should be less than the lowest-paid job available, so that the worker should not be tempted to live off relief rather than get a job. As Larry Beeferman shows in his article in this book, the principle of "less eligibility" is still in effect in the United States. As low as many wages are, public assistance nationwide is still lower. When the relief system deviates from the principle of less eligibility, as it sometimes does in some Northern states these days, public and legislative protests generally center on the amount of the welfare grant rather than on the inadequacy of the wages. Cloward and Piven make a convincing case for their argument that public assistance has served two main social functions: to enforce work norms and to quell civil discontent.[29] The eighteenth-century philanthropist

---

[26] Ibid., p. 360.
[27] Ibid., p. 173.
[28] Ibid., p. 143.
[29] *Regulating the Poor.*

Jonas Hanway pointed out as well as anyone could the relationship between philanthropy and the accumulation of wealth:

> As the true foundation of riches and power is the number of working poor, every rational proposal for the augmentation of them merits our regard.[30]

Every rational proposal, that is, except the equalization of wealth and power. In the late seventeenth century, the English philanthropist Thomas Firmin put the poor to work at flax-spinning.[31] In the early nineteenth century, the London Mendicity Society "set out to break the public of its ancient habit of giving money to beggars" [32] and introduced a labor test.

> At first this consisted of stone-breaking, the classic proof of good faith and hunger on the part of the poor, but later the Society acquired a mill and put its clients to grinding and preparing corn for the bread distributed as relief.[33]

The charity schools of the seventeenth and eighteenth centuries trained girls and boys for the labor market, drilled them in "habits of industry and sobriety," and gave them religious training. Their founders hoped

> to Reform the Lives of a Class of Mankind, which, to the utmost Degree, needed Reformation . . . by beginning early with Children, before any evil Habit has taken Possession of them.[34]

A smug charity lady of the late eighteenth century extolled the social advantages of charity among the poor by pointing out that household servants and the laboring poor were

> useful members of the state, for their services are essential in the greatest degree, to the comfort and convenience of the higher orders of society.[35]

Senator Russell Long, Chairman of the Senate Finance Committee, was no less explicit in 1970 when he berated what he called "professional hoboes on the Federal dole" and complained that he could no longer find anyone to do his laundry! [36] Long was referring to a group from the National Welfare Rights Organization, which had disrupted Senate hearings on welfare and occupied Secretary of Health, Education and Welfare Finch's office.

The seventeenth- and eighteenth-century charity schools contained a built-in contradiction. While philanthropists saw them as training grounds for British industry, they also feared that the workers might get big ideas about their station in life and lose the humility their teachers worked so hard to instill. Most philanthropists wanted submission and gratitude, as evidenced by the opening prayer girls at a charity school were required to recite in the eighteenth century:

[30] Quoted in Owen, *English Philanthropy*, p. 15.
[31] Ibid., p. 17.
[32] Ibid., p. 112.
[33] Ibid.
[34] Quoted in ibid., p. 24.
[35] Quoted in ibid., p. 99.
[36] CBS News, June 11, 1970.

Make me dutiful and obedient to my benefactors. . . . Make me temperate and chaste, meek and patient, true in all my dealings, and industrious in my station.[37]

Welfare institutions for children in the United States today are still concerned with instilling reliable work habits, even though the moral and religious training is usually not as explicit as it was in the eighteenth century. In a recent rehabilitation program for juvenile delinquents, the Provo experiment in Utah (now defunct),[38] the adult counselors did not impose any moral preachments or explicit rules on the boys; rather they created a social situation in which boys were brought in line to stay at their (menial) jobs through the medium of peer-group pressure. The boys were manipulated, but in infinitely more subtle ways than those practiced by the moralists of the early industrial period. The differences between the early charity schools and the modern Provo experiment are rather similar to the differences between the crude authoritarianism used by the early capitalists to control their workers and the "team work" with its peer-group pressure to conform, of IBM, the epitome of post-industrial technological capitalism.[39]

British mercantilists created hospitals for the sick poor partly out of their alarm about the high death rate of the labor force and the loss of working time through illness. An eighteenth-century philanthropist who argued the importance of hospitals neatly calculated that the death of every industrious worker capable of having children caused a "Two Hundred Pound Loss to the *Kingdom*." [40] London residents could not ignore the poverty, squalor, and congestion of a city that had nearly trebled in population owing to immigration during the seventeenth century and continued to increase its population rapidly during the eighteenth century. Poverty breeds illness, and contagious illness can spread to the affluent, so fever hospitals for the control of contagious diseases, especially typhus, were begun in the late eighteenth century. While most charities were supported by voluntary funds in those days, even conservatives admitted the need for state aid for fever hospitals. Among the first private British charities to be subsidized by parish and parliamentary funds were the fever hospitals founded in the late eighteenth and early nineteenth centuries.[41]

Dispensaries for the poor, public health nursing, public bath houses, drinking fountains, and housing for the poor were all inspired by concern about the squalid living conditions of workers. The English Poor Law Commissioners, concerned that epidemics and disease were a major factor in keeping the poor rate higher than they liked, conducted a study of the living

[37] Quoted in Owen, *English Philanthropy*, p. 27.
[38] LaMar T. Empey, "The Provo Experiment: Introduction," in Harry Gold and Frank R. Scarpitti, eds., *Combatting Social Problems* (New York: Holt, Rinehart & Winston, 1967), pp. 371–74; LaMar T. Empey and Jerome Rabow, "The Provo Experiment in Delinquency Rehabilitation," ibid., pp. 375–95; LaMar T. Empey, "The Provo Experiment: Research and Findings," ibid., pp. 395–404.
[39] *The New York Times*, July 29, 1973 Sect. VI, p. 10.
[40] Quoted in Owen, *English Philanthropy*, p. 38.
[41] Ibid., p. 123.

conditions of the London poor in the 1840s.[42] Many of the poor had been displaced from their neighborhoods when railways and new commercial buildings took over inner-city areas. They could not move far from their work, so often lived wherever they could find shelter, in squalid huts or in doorways. (Urban renewal has been going on for a long time.) The private charitable housing projects for the poor were, like modern housing projects for the poor, usually "low-amenity" structures—crowded, unesthetic, and never adequate to the need. They were also, then as now, usually unprofitable to build and maintain and so did not attract private developers until they were subsidized from public funds. So it is today. Some liberal and radical critics of the Victorian philanthropists argued that private charity's housing for the poor was worse than useless, because it gave the impression that the housing problem was being solved, when in fact it was growing to such enormous proportions that only state funds could meet the need. Others argued differently, believing that because the state was not willing to relieve the problems of the poor in any substantial way, private philanthropy set an example for the state to follow when it was ready.

THE "WELFARE STATE" VS. SOCIALISM

Some radicals today argue that most established charity and social welfare systems are counterrevolutionary, in that they drain off workers' discontent by throwing the workers a sop, thereby preventing a large-scale revolution which could radically change the distribution of wealth and power. Although the merits of that argument are debatable, there is no doubt that welfare systems *have* been constructed partly to reduce workers' discontent which threatens to change the economic system. One of the clearest historical examples of this was Bismarck, the Prussian ruler, who was explicit in his vision of a state-supported welfare system as insurance against more radical changes. Bismarck

> was anxious to make German social democracy less attractive to working-men. He feared "class war" and wanted to postpone it as long as possible. . . . He argued explicitly that if the state would only "show a little more Christian solicitude for the working-man," then the social democrats would "sound their siren song in vain." [43]

Bismarck was not a liberal. He opposed shorter working hours for women and children in factories; he opposed any state interference with private industry or agriculture. Yet he initiated disability and old age pensions in the 1880s. He wanted them to be financed wholly out of state funds, so that welfare could be used as an instrument of political control. He

> drew a revealing distinction between the degrees of obedience (or subservience) of private servants and servants at court. The latter "would put up with much more"

[42] Ibid., p. 374.

[43] Asa Briggs, "The Welfare State in Historical Perspective," in Mayer N. Zald, *Social Welfare Institutions* (New York: John Wiley & Sons, 1965), p. 62.

than the former because they had pensions to look forward to. Welfare soothed the spirit, or perhaps tamed it.[44]

Bismarck's use of welfare as an "alternative to socialism" was studied carefully and used as a model in many European countries when they initiated welfare systems.[45]

England's philanthropic and welfare activities set the stage and provided the models for America's public and private welfare systems. England's philanthropic history is replete with examples of welfare being constructed as a bulwark against socialism. The poor seemed much more threatening after the French Revolution. Some of the early nineteenth-century philanthropies were

> insurance against revolution, a means of keeping the populace, if not contented, at least reasonably submissive.[46]

Charity in the nineteenth century "seemed to take on a cautious and calculating, almost harsh, tone." [47] Fears induced by the French Revolution found ideological justification in Malthus, who foresaw a doomsday of population explosion if population was not controlled by restrictions on the sexual urge and the charitable urge. He advocated abolishing all state provisions for the poor, leaving only private agencies to dispense charity to the "deserving poor." He set the stage for the case-by-case investigations of the Charity Organization Society, advising dispensers of charity to check

> the hopes of clamorous and obtrusive poverty with no other recommendation but rags

and to encourage

> the silent and retiring sufferer laboring under unmerited difficulties.[48]

So began the ideological justification for separating the "deserving" (silent sufferers) from the "undeserving" (obtrusive and clamorous). The philanthropists who followed this line of thinking believed in the divine rightness of social classes.

> Distinctions between social classes, scripturally sanctioned and inevitable because of differences in individual talents, were part of the Great Design. To be industrious and tractable was, of course, the obligation of the poor. Not everyone would have discovered in a near-famine, as did Hannah More, the plan of "an all-wise and gracious Providence to *unite* all ranks of people *together* and show the *poor* how immediately they are dependent on the rich." Yet the deference owed by the poor to the rich was a ubiquitous theme in the charity literature of the time. They were to understand that their welfare was more adequately "promoted by the gradations of wealth and rank, than it ever could be by a perfect equality of

---

[44] Ibid.
[45] Ibid., p. 63.
[46] Owen, *English Philanthropy*, p. 97.
[47] Ibid.
[48] Quoted in ibid., p. 98.

condition; even if that equality had not been in its nature chimerical and impracticable." [49]

It was beyond the vision of the eighteenth and nineteenth centuries to deal with the poor as equals.

Even the most devoted and self-sacrificing of those who served the poor never dealt with them on terms of equality, nor did it occur to them to do so.[50]

The Sunday Schools of the late eighteenth century were also a response to "the menace of Jacobism" [51] and the French Revolution. They aimed at

reforming the behavior of the lower orders and implanting in them a becoming reverence for the Christian religion and their social superiors.[52]

Some of the philanthropists of the time were clearly frightened of the poor and their children. They spoke of their "low habits of vice and idleness," and called the children "city Arabs."

In the larger cities the poor were a race of savages, whom nobody knew and who lived in sections which nobody visited.[53]

The first organizations set up to educate children of the poor in England—charity schools, Sunday Schools, and Ragged Schools—all were a response to the social disorganization of a developing urban industrialism. One Malthusian critic of philanthropy, Walter Bagehot, thought it did more harm than good because "it brings to life such great populations to suffer and be vicious . . ." [54] Those who were more sympathetic to the poor, however, saw that private charity was clearly impotent in dealing with large-scale poverty and social disorganization. Frederic Mocatta, founder of the Jewish Board of Guardians, wrote to Charles Loch of the Charity Organization Society in 1886 that in view of the possibility of social revolution it would be to the best interest of the rich to devise some state scheme such as a graduated income tax to relieve the schism between rich and poor. He said apologetically,

"I am aware that such an idea will be called Communism, or Socialism, or that it may be considered as subverting every rule of political economy, but things must not be allowed to remain as they are." [55]

Despite his advocacy of limited state intervention, Mocatta thought "all labour laws, such as the eight hours movement . . . so many absurdities," [56] was fiercely against the London County Council considering working-class

[49] Quoted in ibid., p. 103.
[50] Ibid., p. 104.
[51] Ibid., p. 113.
[52] Ibid.
[53] Ibid., p. 135.
[54] Ibid., p. 167.
[55] Ibid., p. 427.
[56] Ibid.

housing, and thought the idea of state-aided pensions for the aged "a damning heresy." [57]

Although the nineteenth-century rich resisted state intervention, there were some among them who

> could foresee a day when wealth itself would be on the defensive

and these saw philanthropy as an "insurance policy of wealth." [58] In the 1840s, Lord Ashley saw his proposal for working-class housing as "the way to stifle Chartism." (Chartism was the British political movement to win workers the right to vote.) Lord John Russell was less optimistic, believing that the agitated mood of workers in the spring of 1848 boded "an unhealthy season for aristocracy and royalty." [59]

In the 1890s, Charles Booth conducted a major study of the London poor *(Life and Labour of the London Poor)*, in which he concluded that 30 percent of Londoners were living below the bare subsistence level. In the process of doing the study, Booth changed from a "Conservative individualist into a collectivist of sorts." He advocated making the "very poor class" virtually wards of the State, on the grounds that

> if this small and weak element were placed under the tutelage of the State, it would be possible to avoid socialistic interference in the lives of all the rest.[60]

David Owen comments that this was

> a sound enough Tory prescription for avoiding socialism, but few Conservatives of the time would have contemplated social homeopathy on the scale recommended by Booth.[61]

Booth's conservative prescription for the very poor is quite similar to the thoughts of some modern American conservatives, such as the sociologist Edward Banfield, who considers the feasibility of close supervision of the poor in state-sponsored housing projects and rearing some children of the poor in state-sponsored institutions.[62]

England adopted state intervention in the welfare of its citizens much sooner, and on a scale far larger, than the United States ever has. Yet the federal intervention that has been initiated in the United States was largely a response to social unrest. The first large-scale thrust of the federal government in income maintenance was the Social Security Act of 1935, the response of the Franklin D. Roosevelt administration to the Depression. The second large-scale federal thrust against poverty was the "War on Poverty" of the 1960s, the response of the Lyndon B. Johnson administration to the urban unrest created by massive migration of Blacks to the cities, where they were unemployed or underemployed. Roosevelt, architect of the New Deal, was no

---

[57] Ibid., p. 428.
[58] Ibid., p. 470.
[59] Ibid., p. 377.
[60] Ibid., p. 505.
[61] Ibid.
[62] *The Unheavenly City* (Boston: Little, Brown & Co., 1970), p. 246.

socialist; he was an enlightened capitalist seeking to stave off revolution so that capitalism could survive. Neither was Lyndon Johnson, architect of the "Great Society," a socialist. He was rather seeking to dampen unrest and build an urban political coalition so that he and the Democratic party could keep their political power.

Henry Allen's article in this book shows how government employment and work training programs during both the New Deal and the War on Poverty served to prop up the capitalist economic system. The government never intended to provide decently paid work to everyone because a capitalistic system needs some unemployment.

CASTE AND CLASS IN SOCIAL WELFARE

In the early twentieth century, charities began to rely less on volunteer workers and more on paid workers. The majority of both volunteers and paid workers have always been women. Along with teaching and nursing, social service was considered particularly appropriate for women because of women's supposed suitability for nurturant roles. On the other hand, most of the members of the boards of directors and most of the administrators of welfare agencies (including hospitals and schools) have always been men because of men's supposed superior capability in making high-level decisions. Thus a sexual caste system was superimposed upon a class system in the social services. In their articles in this book, Barbara and John Ehrenreich and Mie Watanabe show how the sexual caste system has discriminated against women in medical care and in control of women's reproductive functions. As Watanabe points out, the government has used the Aid to Families of Dependent Children (AFDC) program to exert repressive control over women.

In the United States, there has also always been a racial caste system in the social services. As in all other organizations of society, Blacks, Puerto Ricans, Mexican-Americans, and American Indians suffered discrimination in employment, salaries, and promotions. While both women and minority groups have been underrepresented at professional decision-making levels, they have been overrepresented in the clientele of most social agencies, because they are poor in disproportionate numbers. Estelle Disch, in her article in this book, shows how this works in the criminal and juvenile justice system. My article on foster care and adoption shows how it works in the child welfare system.

Income maintenance benefits such a public assistance, social security, unemployment compensation, workmen's compensation, and private pensions have not changed the class structure of America, as Larry Beeferman documents in his article in this book. The social property is securely in the hands of a privileged few, and no income maintenance scheme has ever been proposed in any legislature that would change that fact. Nor is such a change likely to be proposed, as long as the economy is based on maximizing profits rather than producing for the common welfare.

PROFESSIONAL AND ORGANIZATIONAL IMPERATIVES

As agencies hired paid workers and began to require training for workers, organizational and professional imperatives took shape. Although social agencies began in response to certain social needs, once the organizations took shape, they also developed needs of their own, not necessarily in tune with those they were set up to serve. The needs of the poor, for example, can be defined by the middle class according to the needs of the middle class for jobs and political patronage. Daniel P. Moynihan says that

> middle-class professionals—when asked to devise ways of improving the conditions of lower-class groups—would come up with schemes of which the first effect would be to improve the conditions of middle-class professionals.[63]

Some people have suggested that social workers were given the job of administering the public assistance part of the Social Security Act because the middle class needed jobs during the Depression. Certainly the War on Poverty fattened the billfolds of a good many of the middle class, especially academics. Estelle Disch discusses how staff in the criminal and juvenile justice system perpetuate dysfunctional institutions in order to protect their jobs.

Among the oldest of vested interests in the social services are doctors and hospital administrators. High among the reasons for originally establishing medical schools and other training hospitals were the doctors' eagerness for a place to practice, a clientele (mostly poor) on whom to conduct research, a place to attract, teach, and train medical students, and a place to develop specialty and subspecialty interests. The eighteenth-century teaching hospitals were thought of as

> demonstration laboratories for medical educators and as incubators of medical progress.[64]

The primary purpose of University College and King's College Hospital in England, opened in 1833 and 1939, respectively, "was to provide clinical material for medical students." [65] Perhaps the most powerful factor in establishing specialized hospitals in the nineteenth century was

> the desire of medical specialists to have hospitals of their own or perhaps to transform themselves into specialists by virtue of setting up a hospital, and some of these institutions . . . were hardly more than one-man affairs.[66]

[63] *The Politics of a Guaranteed Income* (New York: Random House, 1973), p. 54.
[64] Owen, *English Philanthropy*, p. 40.
[65] Ibid., pp. 170–71.
[66] Ibid., pp. 171–72.

Some of these one-man affairs profited handsomely from charitable endowments that had been intended for the sick poor.

Medical and hospital professional associations have almost always been in the vanguard of resistance to state intervention in medical care. Richard Titmuss, discussing the political struggle to implement Lloyd George's national health insurance legislation of 1911 in England, says that doctors engaged in a

> Hobbesian struggle for independence from the power and authority exercised over their lives . . .[67]

Richard Harris describes the same kind of Hobbesian struggle in the fight against Medicare conducted by the American Medical Association.[68]

In social work, professionalism has often resulted in overly bureaucratized agencies claiming objectivity while losing their spontaneity and warmth and their accessibility to the poor. This began to be evident in the London Charity Organization Society, whose critics complained that "scientific charity" was

> impersonal, grudging, and wrapped in red tape and that its homilies against indiscriminate and thoughtless charity too often meant no charity at all.[69]

One clergyman described such grudging charity as "the gospel of the buttoned pocket." [70]

Despite social workers' search for professionalism and scientific objectivity, doubts about the efficacy of social work have never been more pervasive and deep, even within the profession, than in recent times.[71] Casework agencies may be giving useful help to some verbal middle-class clients, but few people argue for their large-scale effectiveness with the poor, and counterculture youth seldom patronize most of them voluntarily. One of the oldest and most prestigious family service agencies, the Community Service Society of New York City, a descendant of the Charity Organization Society, has recently discontinued doing casework in favor of broader community involvement.

LABELING THE CLIENTELE

I have a hunch that if a sociologist had studied the socioeconomic status of the "deserving" and the "undeserving" as they were labeled by the early

---

[67] R. M. Titmuss, "Health," in M. Ginsburg, ed., *Law and Opinion in England in the Twentieth Century* (Berkeley, Calif.: University of California Press, 1959), p. 308.

[68] *Sacred Trust* (Baltimore: Penguin Books 1970).

[69] Owen, *English Philanthropy*, p. 215.

[70] Ibid.

[71] See, for example, Joel Fischer, "Is Casework Effective? A Review," *Social Work*, 18 (January 1973), 5–21; and Noel Timms and John Mayer, *The Client Speaks: Working Class Impressions of Casework* (Chicago: Aldine Publishing Co., 1970).

Charity Organization Society, he or she would have found that the "undeserving" contained a disproportionately large number of the class that Karl Marx called the "slum proletariat" or the "lumpenproletariat" (unskilled laborers). The "deserving" were usually described as industrious in the literature of the time, and I suspect that that group included mostly unemployed skilled manual workers and white-collar workers. The same kind of class divisions occurs in agency labeling procedure today. The "multiproblem" or "hard-to-reach" family is more often than not the family of the unskilled worker living in the slums. The clients that agencies deem most "helpable" by the agencies' forms of intervention are most often skilled or white-collar workers. Thus there is a two-class system between the clients of private agencies; a two-class system between private and public agencies; and a two-class system in public welfare. The "lumpenproletariat" of public welfare receives AFDC, Medicaid, General Relief, or Supplemental Security Income (SSI), while every citizen whose work is included by law in work-related OASDHI benefits receives "Social Security" retirement benefits or Medicare. The benefits given by Social Security are very low, but the recipients feel more dignity in receiving them than do public assistance recipients. In the criminal and juvenile justice system, there is a two-class system determining who gets caught and prosecuted and who goes free.

The division made by the Victorian philanthropists between "deserving" and "undeserving" were but crude forerunners of the labeling and categorizing of needy people that was to come. Most societies do not say, "Everyone who needs help, of whatever kind and for whatever reason, is entitled to the highest quality of help without stigma or prejudice." Rather, most societies have gradually separated out categories of people for special help. Some categories are considered more deserving than others, depending on the particular cultural norms and taboos of the society. Today, for example, a Buddhist monk in Thailand with shaven head and eyebrows and bare feet performs a sacred mission when he takes his begging bowl into the community. The almsgiver who puts money in the monk's bowl performs a holy act. At the same time, if a barefoot man or woman in ragged clothing begs for alms on Skid Row in an American city, most people regard him or her with contempt and give money—if they give at all—grudgingly. Only deeply committed religious people such as the Catholic Workers consider such giving to be a holy act.[72]

Public welfare in England and America began in the workhouses, the almshouses, and the debtors prisons. Everybody was thrown in together: able-bodied debtors, cripples, the mentally ill and mentally retarded, children, the aged, the unemployed. Because pauperism did not evoke as much public sympathy as some other kinds of misfortune, reformers began to relabel separate categories of people in order to get them out of the almshouses. Thus "paupers" were relabeled as "insane," "lame," "blind,"

[72] Michael Kirwan, "36 East First," *The Catholic Worker*, July–August 1973, pp. 4, 7.

"orphans," "aged." [73] This process of "deviance labeling" later distinguished between "delinquent" and "dependent," the higher-status label. "Dependent" is the twentieth-century replacement for the label "orphan." Black children are more apt to be labeled as delinquent, and placed in institutions for delinquents rather than in institutions for the dependent and neglected, or for the emotionally disturbed. Both the label and the institution the child gets frequently depends upon fortuitous historical circumstances rather than the needs of the child.[74] Estelle Disch discusses the labeling process as it affects criminals and delinquents. The research facts keep coming in on the adverse effects of labeling.

Once people have been labeled, other people are likely to see them in stereotyped ways that fit the labels. Rosenthal provided a striking example of this by showing that teachers expect children to live up to their labels and insure that they do. Among a roughly similar group of children, the ones labeled "late bloomers" did indeed bloom, and the ones labeled "slow" did indeed stay "slow." [75]

Dr. David Rosenhan conducted a study in which eight normal researchers feigned insanity and obtained admission to a total of twelve mental hospitals. To gain admission, they all told the same story—that they heard strange voices that said "empty," "hollow" and "thud." Otherwise, they told the truth about themselves. Once in the ward they stopped faking their symptoms. All were diagnosed as schizophrenic at admission, and discharged with a diagnosis of schizophrenia "in remission." The length of hospital stays ranged from seven to fifty-two days, with an average of nineteen days. Commenting on the massive errors that psychiatrists probably make in diagnosing people, a *New York Times* article said,

> The tragedy . . . is that labels do not go away. A diagnosis of cancer that has been found in error is a cause of celebration," he [Rosenhan] said, "but psychiatric diagnoses are rarely found in error. The label sticks." [76]

The label sticks and stigmatizes.

A survey of attitudes of 800 private psychiatrists showed that they prefer to work with neurotics, personality disorders, transient situational problems, and psychotics. Few psychiatrists are interested in working with the mentally retarded, alcoholics, addicts, sociopaths, or cases of chronic social inadequacy. Such patients will be bounced from agency to agency and will wind up in a state facility.[77] The psychiatrist Robert Coles writes that

---

[73] Andrew Billingsley and Jeanne M. Giovannoni, *Children of the Storm* (New York: Harcourt Brace Jovanovich, 1972), pp. 31–33.

[74] See, for example, Scott Briar, "Clinical Judgment in Foster Care Placement," *Child Welfare*, 42, No. 4 (1963), 161–68.

[75] *Pygmalion in the Classroom; Teacher Expectation and Pupils' Individual Development*, Holt, Rinehart & Winston, N.Y., 1968.

[76] *The New York Times*, January 21, 1973.

[77] A. C. Brown, "Psychiatrists' Interests in Community Mental Health Centers," *Community Mental Health Journal* (Fall 1965).

the poor neither know about us [psychiatrists] nor can they afford our expensive care. And often we do not know about the poor and seem little concerned about getting to know them.[78]

Jane Mercer's study of labeling as it affects retarded children showed that lay people in the community are less quick to label a child retarded than are representatives of formal organizations, particularly public school officials. The label falls most readily on non-Anglo children, a phenomenon Mercer called "institutionalized Anglocentrism"; it is

> particularly pronounced in those public institutions established for the purpose of promulgating and enforcing the public norms of the core culture; the public schools, law enforcement agencies, welfare and vocational rehabilitation agencies.[79]

Mexican-Americans and Blacks labeled retarded are less deviant than Anglos so labeled; they also have higher IQs and fewer physical disabilities than labeled Anglos.

TOWARD A ONE-CLASS SYSTEM

It goes without saying that the poor will get less of everything, including social services, than will the rich. This will be true as long as there is a separate class of poor people. Yet there are ways to equalize social services and reduce the stigma attached to receiving a service designed specifically for the poor. Richard Titmuss formulated an "iron law of welfare": services for the poor are poor services. That is why some welfare specialists argue for universal services for the entire citizenry rather than for special services for the poor. Services that are also available to the middle class are better services simply because the middle class has more political and economic power to obtain good services.

This is easy to see in public education, where schools in poor neighborhoods have poorer facilities and less money. The current political struggle to equalize revenues for suburban and inner-city schools is a thrust in the direction of obtaining equal social services. The open admissions policy of City College of New York City was forged through a political struggle for equality. (Although Black and Puerto Rican people led that struggle, the policy actually benefits proportionately more poor White students than minority-group students.)[80] Medicare for all people over 65 covered by Social Security was an opening wedge toward universal health insurance. The means-tested program for the poor, Medicaid, is subject to the political vicissitudes and indignities that shape all categorical public assistance

[78] "Psychiatrists and the Poor," in H. H. Meissner, ed., *Poverty in the Affluent Society* (New York: Harper & Row, 1966).

[79] Jane R. Mercer, *Labeling the Mentally Retarded* (Berkeley: University of California Press, 1973), p. 121.

[80] Timothy S. Healy, "New Problems—New Hopes," *Change*, 5, No. 6 (Summer 1973), 27.

programs. Old Age Assistance, a program for the aged poor, was a stigmatized program; "Social Security" retirement benefits are not stigmatized because they are universally available. Because Old Age Assistance was federalized in 1974 as Supplemental Security Income (SSI), it may carry less stigma under the aegis of the Social Security Administration, yet the stigma remains in any means-tested program. Low-income housing projects in the inner city are by law "low-amenity" structures and are stigmatized. The struggle to build scatter-site housing or to subsidize rent or home ownership for the poor in middle-class suburbs is a thrust toward greater equality in housing.

A word about our selection of topics is in order here. We have not attempted to discuss all the social services; that would be too large a task for one book. We have selected topics with which we are most familiar and which are critically important today. There are other equally important topics that cry out for more attention, such as the plight of the aged and the handicapped who have been tossed aside by society; or children, whose liberation has barely begun. However, we believe that our frame of reference is equally applicable to all the social services and to all the categories of those who are considered marginal people in society today.

a radical critique of federal work and manpower programs, 1933–1974

—Henry L. Allen

All the chapters in this book share a common assumption—that in this society the welfare of working-class people is secondary to the welfare of the rich, and that social services are constructed in a way that will not seriously threaten business goals. We believe that what is good for General Motors (or agribusiness or the doctors) is not necessarily good for the country. In this chapter, Henry Allen shows that some things have not changed very much since the nineteenth century. The goal of business is still to maximize profits, and human needs are secondary. Government work programs in the Depression were never intended to employ all those who needed jobs, and the work training programs of the 1960s proceeded on the nineteenth-century assumption that the poor, rather than the economic system, were to blame for their plight. As in the nineteenth century, the programs functioned as the "insurance policy of wealth."

Federal work programs and the income maintenance programs of social security and public assistance were begun at the same time in the Depression, and work and welfare policies have been interrelated since then. As Carol Stack and Herbert Semmel point out in their discussion of AFDC, the 1935 Social Security Act provided assistance for those categories of people whom legislators assumed to be outside the labor market: children, the aged, the disabled, and the blind. The others, especially able-bodied men, were supposed to earn their own money. *Supposed* to earn—that is the catch. There are gaping chasms between reality and official rhetoric. No legislation has ever been passed in the United States to guarantee a job to everyone who wants it.

Mie Watanabe later discusses unemployment as it relates to business needs. Businessmen consider some unemployment desirable, because a fully employed work force would drive up wages and reduce profits. The government prevented this during World War II, a time of nearly full employment, by extracting a no-strike pledge from labor leaders. The high levels of unemployment that prevail in the United States today would be politically dangerous in European countries where workers are more militant and historically less inclined to believe that theirs is a classless society which offers equal opportunity to all.

Henry Allen closes with a question that many people are asking today: Can the economic system continue to be patched up with palliatives, or are more profound changes essential?

Over the last forty years the role of the federal government in dealing with the continuous problem of unemployment has changed along with the changing conditions of the economy. Whatever the form of federal intervention during that time, from massive work relief to social service-oriented programs, unemployment remained one of the more obvious failures of the capitalist system. This chapter will explore the various reasons for the failure and weaknesses of the various government efforts in coping with the problem of the inability of people to secure productive work in the most productive economy in the world.

From the Works Projects Administration and the Civilian Conservation Corps of the New Deal to the Manpower and Development Training Act and the Job Corps of the 1960s and early 1970s, federal work programs were designed to resuscitate either a totally ailing economic system or localized pockets of depression. The need to sustain private ownership of the means of production was the common assumption underlying all the programs. The federal government intended to restore the system to order and to make it function more effectively by working through, in conjunction with, or alongside the business class which controlled resources and labor. Federal intervention in unemployment that would challenge the control of labor by private enterprise was never envisioned. Substitution of production for use and of public ownership of the means of production rather than private control for the profit of a few received no serious consideration as a solution for the enduring problems of unemployment.

Through its policies the business class had created a situation in which millions of people were without jobs. They either would not or could not ease the resultant unemployment crises. The federal government was the only instrument capable of carrying out strategies to deal effectively with unemployment. Perceptive and "progressive" businessmen understood this fact and welcomed federal programs as no threat to their domination of the economy. Without federal intervention business could not have remained free to control a system in its own interests. The fact is that this intervention, often disguised as reform, almost always benefited the business class. Opposition to the reforms meant continued deterioration of the system, an unthinkable alternative to be avoided at all costs. It was feared that the alienation and anger of the unemployed, the victims of this breakdown, would lead to ever greater demands for radical change. Something had to be done before demands evolved into militant action that fundamentally threatened the continuance of the capitalist system.

The Depression of the thirties and the urban rebellions of the sixties were met politically in the only manner logical to those who held political and economic power. There had to be sufficient reform and impact in the programs offered to give a large proportion of the unemployed a minimal level of assistance. Even with the reforms the basic contradictions of capitalism remained intact. Extensive poverty continued to rub against fantastic wealth; the distribution of economic power meant that political equality remained more myth than reality; and the possibility of rewarding work for all eluded fulfillment because the system needed unemployment and cheap labor.

Whether the government was providing jobs, job training, or job placement, federal work and manpower programs perpetuated structural inequities in the labor market. Despite pronouncements and legislation to the contrary, racism, low pay, and anti-unionism marked the actual operations of the programs. Their endurance reflected the fact that all these efforts at putting people back to work operated within the requirements of the existing system.

The basic continuity of these programs over the last forty years, their political aims, their relations to business, and their limited impact should provide us with an understanding of why unemployment and underemployment continue. The root causes of the situation have never been attacked. Instead the troubles of the time have too often been laid to rest at the feet of the powerless, as if they had created their own misery. The solution too often proposed was for workers to become better prepared to compete against one another for jobs and economic security. That solution, as we shall see, was no solution at all.

THE NEW DEAL

The gigantic Roosevelt experiment of "relief, reform, and recovery" showed a definitely new bias to a controlled and humanized capitalism as contrasted with the brutality of laissez faire. But the necessary conclusion seems to be that no such compromise with a decaying system is possible.[1]

Although the Civil Works Administration and the Federal Emergency Recovery Act preceded the Works Progress (later Projects) Administration, the WPA became the central government agency dealing with work relief during the Depression. When it was established in 1935 its goal was to remove 3.5 million people from the relief rolls and put them to work, leaving at least another 10 million still unemployed. The economic and political thinking which limited the actual number of people who were to be put back to work was part of John Maynard Keynes' theory, best described as pump priming. Injecting the work force with a measure of productive work and wages would have a snowballing effect of the rest of the economy. The

[1] John Dewey, in Introduction, p. vi, of *Challenge to the New Deal*, Alfred M. Bingham and Seldon Rodman, eds. (New York: Falcon Press, 1934).

business class would begin to regain confidence to invest its capital, bringing more of the unemployed back to work and getting the economy moving again.

The federal government never abandoned that Keynesian principle. As a result, unemployment never went below 7 million until the beginning of World War II. The government never made any effort to provide jobs for all the jobless. The WPA was viewed as a temporary measure to endure until the business class regained control of the situation.[2] Full employment, if it came at all, would result from the government doing whatever was necessary to see the business class through the latest in a series of breakdowns and crises in the system.

The WPA employed an average of approximately 2 million people at any one time. This resulted from gearing the work relief program not to the actual job and economic needs of the unemployed, but to the policy of pump priming as a technique to restore private enterprise. If the federal government put 2 or 3 or 5 million people back to work, it could have put another 10 million back to work. While this was possible in strictly economic terms, it was not possible politically, for "Congress never seriously considered increasing the size of the WPA to provide work for all."[3]

At least three major reasons accounted for this political limitation on the size of the WPA. First, WPA projects were legislatively designed to be noncompetitive with private industry.[4] Although this intent broke down in segments of the construction industry, it generally meant that WPA projects were barred from certain areas of economic activity, especially in the production of prime necessities—food, shelter, and clothing.[5] While those necessities were denied in large part to many millions of people, unemployed workers who could have produced those necessities for themselves and their families remained idle. The "democratic" system enacted legislation preventing them from meeting their real needs.

Second, if government work relief were too extensive, it might "threaten the private enterprise system itself."[6] The ability of the government to eliminate unemployment would present a severe challenge to business-class control of the labor force. Both in periods of crisis and noncrisis, the jobless would come to expect government activity to provide those jobs. Because a certain level of unemployment was necessary to capitalism, the system could not afford full employment. The potential for conflict was too dangerous if the unemployed could rely on their government for rescue from the failure of

[2] Alden F. Briscoe, "Public Service Employment in the 1930's: The WPA," in Harold L. Sheppard, Bennet Harrison, and William J. Spring, eds., *The Political Economy of Public Service Employment* (Lexington, Mass.: D. C. Heath, 1972), p. 97.

[3] Ibid., p. 102.

[4] Arthur Burns and Edward A. Williams, *Federal Work, Security, and Relief Programs* (New York: Da Capo Press, 1971), p. 2.

[5] Ibid., p. 5.

[6] Frances Fox Piven and Richard A. Cloward, *Regulating the Poor* (New York: Pantheon Books, 1971), p. 82.

the system. Because the Depression was a "temporary problem," any permanent government commitment to eliminate unemployment would be a success the business class could not afford. Third, employing all would have cost more money. To get the money, the government would have to tax workers heavily to pay for the wages of the unemployed, because corporations surely would not have borne the burden. This would have been difficult politically.

At its height the WPA employed no more than 31 percent of the unemployed.[7] This statistic takes on meaning in relation to the political constraints on federal intervention in the economy. If the WPA "was deliberately barred from an organic relationship to the economy in which it operated"[8] then the relief efforts of the New Deal would have to be carried out "without interfering with the 'natural processes' of the market."[9] Complete relief of the human suffering that resulted from the system's near collapse would have conflicted with preservation of the system itself. Enough jobs would be provided so that both political tranquility and the economy would not totally disintegrate, but not so many as might threaten private control of the economy.

While the WPA did provide a modicum of relief from human suffering, it functioned primarily as an agency for maintaining political stability and of capitalist restoration. When the economy recovered periodically and the situation appeared to be improving, levels of WPA employment went down correspondingly. For instance, in 1937 only 1.5 million persons were working for the WPA when the economy seemed to take on life. The appearance of life turned out to be a false pregnancy. When the Depression worsened again in 1938, the WPA employment figure jumped to 3 million.[10] Throughout the Depression as the business cycle went up and down, a general policy took hold of employing no more than one-quarter of the unemployed.[11]

The legislation which established the WPA was amended in 1939 to stipulate that a worker could remain on the WPA payroll for a maximum of eighteen months, at which point he/she would be fired. The reason for this is clear. Because only one-quarter of the jobless were put to work, there was a need to rotate the available jobs within the large pool of unemployed. The explanation for this "American roulette" was the need to prevent workers from becoming dependent on government jobs, thereby creating the impression that these jobs were only one step above the relief rolls. Because the Depression was still viewed by business and government as temporary in 1939, it was anticipated that those workers dismissed from the WPA would soon find jobs in the private sector. Yet only 12.7 percent of those terminated in 1939 found other employment that year.[12] The rest either found them-

[7] Briscoe, "Public Service Employment," p. 102.
[8] Burns and Williams, *Federal Work, Security, and Relief Programs*, p. 3.
[9] Piven and Cloward, *Regulating the Poor*, p. 95.
[10] Ibid., p. 112.
[11] Ibid., p. 98.
[12] Ibid., p. 113.

selves on the relief rolls or forced into jobs which often paid less than WPA wages.[13]

WPA wages themselves failed to provide even a minimally decent standard of living in most of the country. Wage levels were set above the amount paid on relief, but generally lower than the prevailing wage paid for comparable work in the private sector. The principle at work was for the unemployed to choose work over welfare (although only a minority actually had that choice) and to take a better-paying job in the private sector when such a job was available.[14] This again shows that the WPA was a temporary mechanism geared toward assisting the business class, rather than an agency committed to solving the harsh realities of poverty resulting from forced unemployment. Organized labor consistently argued for the institution of the prevailing wage on all government work relief projects as the only guarantee against undercutting the wages of those in private industry. In practice the government held to the payment of security wages (what people needed to survive) rather than the prevailing wage, even when the prevailing wage was officially a part of WPA policy.

There were minimum and maximum security wage rates set, varying with occupation and region. In the South the minimum ranged from $21 per month to a maximum of $31 per month, while the rates in the Northeast went from $40 to $94 per month.[15] This wage policy not only perpetuated gross inequities in terms of living standards but also was simply insufficient to achieve what the government considered an "emergency" standard of living, especially for those on the lower to middle part of the scale.[16] Using the government's "emergency" standard, they were earning between 39.5 and 76.8 percent of what they needed. Between 1935 and 1939, as the rate of inflation increased, matters worsened. In 1941 the average WPA wage was $58.79 per month, an actual decrease in the wage rate because of inflation. Nor was there any provision for increasing the wage according to family size. As Harry Hopkins, administrator of the WPA expressed it, "I believe that all families should receive the same wages regardless of their size. That is my idea of pay." [17] On the whole those who were fortunate enough to secure government work relief were only slightly better off than those on the relief or welfare rolls.

When the infrequently enforced official policy of the prevailing wage was abolished in 1939, massive walkouts and strikes occurred in 37 states. In July, 1939, 123,000 WPA workers struck. Although they had legal guarantees of their right to organize into unions of their own choosing, WPA officials from Harry Hopkins on down believed it was unnecessary for them to unionize. Using this logic, the WPA refused to bargain with any union which had

[13] Donald S. Howard, *The WPA and Federal Relief Policy* (New York: Russell Sage Foundation, 1943), p. 167.

[14] Ibid., p. 165.

[15] Ibid., p. 160.

[16] Ibid., table, p. 178.

[17] Ibid., p. 172.

organized WPA workers.[18] The reaction of the government to the wave of strikes that hit WPA projects nationally was predictable. Hopkins maintained, "there is no such thing as a strike on a relief job," leaving workers to wonder just what it was they were doing if not striking. Roosevelt voiced the same sentiment when he declared, "You cannot strike against the government." [19]

The pattern of government actions against these strikes became clear when it moved to fire any WPA worker who missed five consecutive days of work. Even though this regulation was not designed to break strikes and had hardly ever been used previously, in some areas it was an effective means of forcing workers back onto the jobs—at lower wages. The government also emphasized that strike activity was not only ill-conceived, but also illegal.

The Justice Department moved against the strikers in Minneapolis, one of the centers of strike activity, where a progressive and strong union movement had established itself in the early thirties. In February 1940, 162 WPA strikers were indicted on charges of criminal conspiracy in connection with strikes in that city. Ultimately 32 people were convicted and 14 received jail sentences of from 30 days to 8 months.[20] The trials represented "the direct and conscious policy of the White House. The whole machinery was set in motion by President Roosevelt." [21] The trials in Minneapolis were designed as a lesson to millions of workers on federal work relief programs: strikes against the government would not be tolerated. The trials and convictions served "notice on WPA workers that they had better take quietly and submissively the pay cuts and decreased appropriations the future holds in store for them if they want to keep out of the federal penitentiary." [22]

The trials were clearly political, carried on not in the interests of justice, but in the interests of preserving government control over workers, in much the same manner of the business class. Paternalism and repression conjoined in the response of the government to the strikes. It was wrong for workers to strike because they should show gratitude to the hand that fed them; if they did strike, they must understand "that such a strike against government . . . verges on revolution." [23] The federal government and the WPA mirrored the official stance of capitalism toward workers and strikes.

The racial policies of the WPA also worked to preserve the status quo of Blacks and other minority peoples in the United States. The operation of the Federal Emergency Relief Administration, which administered all local relief until the WPA took over in 1935, set the policy precedent. Because the design and actual implementation of work projects was administered on the local level by the established political machinery, racial discrimination was an inherent part of early relief efforts. The following letters to the NAACP magazine, *The Crisis*, illustrate this:

[18] Ibid., pp. 218–20.
[19] Ibid., pp. 222–23.
[20] Ibid., p. 225.
[21] Dwight McDonald, in *The Nation*, February 3, 1940, p. 122.
[22] Ibid., p. 123.
[23] *Newsweek*, July 17, 1939, p. 43.

. . . . , Miss.
22 March, 1934

N.A.A.C.P. Gentlemen: In reply to yours of the 8th Inst. to making reports on conditions that exists against our people under the N.R.A. and other relief agencies in this City. I will say that they are very bad. One of the cases is that of a man of our race about 65 or 70 yrs. of age with 8 in family. his name is . . . . . He was threatened with arrest for pressing the relief agency for assistance. He wanted food for himself and family. He is in bad health, Miss . . . , who is managing the relief here is the one that threatened to arrest him because he insisted on them to give him food. Later she became vexed at him and taken him in her Machine to a Pecan Factory, and offered him to the management for 60¢ a day. Which he refused and told her that that Factory was not working according to the Code. Mr. . . . has been refused assistance on Two occasions that he applied. From the same office. He has also been registered with the Government Re-Employment Office since the first opening, and up to now has not had a days work. He has a wife, a mother-in-law 77 yrs. old and no job, no relief, he has not had work for 3½ years.

. . . .

. . . . . , La.
April 3, 1934

DEAR SIR: Only few line to ask you to do something for us down hear in Plaquemines Parish. We have report to the E.R.A. and they dont give us any work and dont gave relif to the colored peple. so kindly got in tutch with Washington. See why they dont gave us work and done wont to give relif down hear in Plaquemines Parish. Miss Marjorie Rickey is Parish Director. Bad place to recave mail. No work to make a living, no money to leave. this will bee all for today kindly do this faver for us. From

. . . .[24]

The WPA was a measurable improvement over the FERA, primarily because relief efforts were much more centralized under the WPA, somewhat mitigating local racist practices. Yet Black unemployment was double that of Whites in 1933, and that statistic remained constant throughout the New Deal. The WPA never narrowed the gap between Black and White in the area of joblessness. Blacks continued to be the hardest-hit segment of the population during depression. Black and White unemployed were forced to compete for too few jobs, inevitably increasing racial tensions in the country.

Racial discrimination was also rampant on the Tennessee Valley Authority, considered the most progressive social engineering project of the New Deal. "As one studies the operation of the T.V.A., one is struck by the fact that in almost every activity, the Negro is either systematically excluded or discreetly overlooked." [25] The proportion of Black workers on this project, as well as hundreds of others throughout the country, was proportionately smaller than either their percentage in the population or their percentage of the unemployed warranted. A pattern developed of skilled jobs going to White workers while unskilled jobs were reserved for Blacks. In addition to discrimination in hiring, the TVA reinforced housing segregation. Lily-white

---

[24] *The Crisis*, September 1934, pp. 330–31.
[25] Charles H. Houston and John P. Davis, "TVA: Lily-White Reconstruction," in *The Crisis*, October 1934, p. 291.

towns such as that at Norris, Tennessee, were built as "model" towns under the TVA.[26]

The record of the Civilian Conservation Corps was no better. Although the enacting legislation contained the obligatory nondiscrimination clause, there was an "official policy which prevented full participation by Negroes." [27] For instance, while the Black population of Mississippi was 50 percent, Blacks constituted only 1.7 percent of the enrollment in CCC camps in the state. Tremendous pressure and persuasion, especially from the NAACP, was necessary to secure even token participation by Blacks. Once Blacks entered the CCC, strict segregation was the rule.[28] When blacks left the camps, they did so to "become gardeners, . . . or cooks; more were placed by Corps officials as janitors, table-waiters or chauffeurs." [29] The CCC only perpetuated the traditional occupational patterns of Blacks in this country.

One historian has written that "the New Deal failed to solve the problem of depression, it failed to raise the impoverished, it failed to redistribute income, it failed to extend equality and generally countenanced racial discrimination and segregation." [30] It should be added that it also failed to put millions of workers back to work, thereby creating the basis for many of its other failures. In 1936 only 27 percent of the unemployed were restored to jobs by the WPA. By 1940 this was down to 20 percent. The level of funding for the WPA was always inadequate to deal with the massive unemployment that existed.[31] Only as the war in Europe began and defense-related spending boomed did the government shift from direct employment to subsidizing private industry through war and defense contracts. The beginning of war meant the end of Depression and a moratorium of some twenty years on federal work programs.

THE NEW FRONTIER AND THE WAR ON POVERTY

The nature of federal intervention in the economy in relation to unemployment and jobs has significantly changed since the end of the New Deal. No significant job creation program appeared between the termination of the WPA in 1943 and the 1971 Emergency Employment Act.[32] This did not mean the economy functioned perfectly, or unemployment dropped to unnoticeable levels. Instead, the federal government developed a strategy of

[26] Leslie H. Fishel, Jr., "The Negro in the New Deal Era," in Bernard Sternsker, ed., *The Negro in Depression and War* (Chicago: Quadrangle Books, 1964).

[27] John A. Salmona, "The Civilian Conservation Corps and the Negro," in Sternsker, *The Negro in Depression and War*, p. 79.

[28] Ibid., pp. 82–85.

[29] Ibid., p. 90.

[30] Barton Bernstein, "The Conservative Achievements of Liberal Reform," in Barton Bernstein, ed., *Towards a New Past: Dissenting Essays in American History* (New York: Vintage, 1969), p. 264.

[31] Howard, *The WPA and Federal Relief Policy*, p. 570.

[32] William J. Spring, "Congress and Public Service Employment," in Sheppard, et al., *Political Economy of Public Service Employment*, p. 132.

intervention which guaranteed millions of jobs, but did not threaten business-class control of the economy. This was effected through government purchase of goods and services which generated over one-quarter of all jobs in the economy by 1970, primarily in the areas of direct government employment (such as civil servants and bureaucrats) and defense-related expenditures.

The development of this state capitalism, characterized by government subsidization of business, illustrated the failure of the free enterprise system to provide jobs for a significant proportion of the work force. State capitalism enabled private employers to hire workers, which they otherwise could not or would not have done, thus mitigating the continuing dilemma of unemployment. This strategy left the basic structure of the economic system intact.

Unemployment has generally remained at "tolerable levels" since the 1940s—that is, at no more than 6 to 7 percent. "Tolerable" is defined by the policy makers and power wielders in government and business as that percentage which does not present a threat to the continuation of private control of resources and labor for profit. The thrust of government unemployment programs in the last decade has been the continuing assumption that the existing economic system needs no fundamental alterations. The "theory of human capital" which in essence blames the unemployed worker for his low level of skills and unemployability has been the guideline for government policy. "The manpower training programs developed in the 1960's reflected a . . . philosophy toward unemployment and poverty: the concept . . . that these traditions are a direct result of low worker productivity, which in turn results from inadequate education and training." [33] Thus, the Manpower Development and Training Act appeared in 1962, taking as its starting point this "theory of human capital." Work programs now became social service projects where the victims of the system would have their deficiencies rectified.

The failure of the business sector to provide adequate jobs in the economy has in turn been rewarded with millions of dollars in public money flowing into the treasuries of businesses. This is because almost all manpower policy and programs have relied on the business sector to either train or rehabilitate and subsequently employ the unemployed. "In effect these programs constitute training subsidies for business." [34] These subsidies, and the reliance on the private sector to solve problems which it has more or less deliberately created set the basic policy whereby no relationship between the structure of the economy and unemployment was admitted.

The philosophy underlying government manpower programs in the last decade set certain goals for these programs. The first aim was to establish a more efficient process of matching jobs and workers. A plethora of government services arose, theoretically designed to aid both business and

[33] Sheppard, et al., *Political Economy of Public Service Employment*, p. 89.

[34] Howard M. Wachtel, "Looking at Poverty from a Radical Perspective," in *The Review of Radical Political Economics*, 3, No. 3 (Summer 1971), 12.

labor. This goal was predicated on the assumption that a mechanism for creating this matching process would actually eliminate much unemployment, because it was obvious to the planners that the jobs were there. The second goal was to aid the "disadvantaged" in preparing themselves for jobs. This was to be accomplished through a variety of rehabilitation and training programs which would "uplift" the individual and prepare him/her to compete effectively for jobs in the free-market economy. The third goal was to provide for a minimum level of direct government hiring through job creation programs, in a time of an unemployment crisis. None of these goals was designed to deal with the root causes of unemployment. Instead they all revolved around a social service concept which blamed unemployed workers for their plight and offered government services to aid them.

In addition to these enunciated goals, there were important unstated ones as well, related to contemporary political necessities. The rhetoric of the New Frontier, Great Society, and War on Poverty was crucial for both Kennedy and Johnson to secure the Black vote and to curb potential or actual urban unrest. In these urban areas unemployment concentrated primarily, although not exclusively, among Blacks, other minorities, and youth in general. Because there was not a depression situation, except in these areas and among these groups, it was unnecessary to institute WPA-type programs and provide jobs for millions throughout the country. However, some impact in the area of unemployment and poverty was necessary both to ease the simmering urban crises and to lessen the blow of these localized depressions on the economy at large. Again, government intervention over the last ten to twelve years, as in the thirties, was never intended as anything but a temporary bandage to cover a festering wound.

The Kennedy Administration was initially inclined to rely on traditional fiscal and monetary policies to ease unemployment. Measures such as tax cuts or easing credit terms would spur a "sluggish" economy and create an increasing number of jobs. The increase in unemployment during the Kennedy era illustrated the failure of these policies. Although there was growth in the economy, mostly at the top in terms of increased profits for corporations, the unemployment rate rose in the first three years of the Kennedy Administration.

Another reason for increased joblessness was the administration's concern with inflation. Economists who defended the existing economic structure contended that there was an integral relationship between inflation and unemployment, postulating that as the latter went down, the former went up. This was based on the argument that increased spending caused inflation. They argued that a certain level of unemployment was desirable in order to control inflation. This translated itself into a policy of forced unemployment for a certain percentage of the work force. Given this kind of economic reasoning the individual worker could hardly be blamed for not having a job.

The thinking of the Johnson Administration reaffirmed that of the previous administration on unemployment and manpower programs, even though Johnson realized the political expediency for expanding such programs. Secretary of Labor Willard Wirtz, in explaining unemployment among the poor, stated, "The main reason for this . . . isn't the economy. It's the condition and position these people are in—uneducated, untrained, with health problems, police and garnishment records, fatherless children, and so forth. . . ." [35] He went on to speak of "jobs going begging." The logic behind this observation requires a belief that the existing economic system operated more or less perfectly. Then one can blame the victim without ever having to question the real reasons for the conditions Wirtz described. The Nixon approach continued in the same vein. Treasury Secretary George Schultz believed that the "American economy is basically healthy, producing a reasonably good supply of regular jobs." [36]

Schultz' statement made sense to important elements in the business community, who not only agreed with it but also helped formulate such thinking as part of the official ideology of the system. For instance, as early as 1947, the U.S. Chamber of Commerce was saying that the way to deal with unemployment was to "take those measures which will encourage the expansion of existing businesses and the increase in the number of business units. Were all our efforts directed at this objective such unemployment as exists would soon tend to disappear." [37] This recognition of the need for government subsidization of business was cloaked in the rhetoric of free enterprise and liberalism, but the reality was the growth of state capitalism. In effect the federal government has pumped billions of public dollars directly into the treasuries of private corporations in a massive effort to stabilize capitalism.

In the early sixties, when there was official concern over "distressed areas" and "urban blight," the Committee for Economic Development, a think tank for the most powerful business interests in the country, recommended that "the time has come for more conscious efforts to match jobs with workers and workers with jobs." [38] The committee made a series of other recommendations, all of them hewing to the interpretation of unemployment stemming from the need for extending social services to the poor, making minor revisions in the economy, or increasing government subsidies to big business.

The government saw manpower policy as an alternative to fundamental change in the economic structure. Without federal intervention in the economy there was a danger of a collapse. Yet the beneficiaries of the existing system shaped the nature of the intervention rather than its victims. The number and complexity of manpower-related programs in 1974 illustrate the extent and nature of this intervention. The *Digest of Manpower Programs*, a booklet published by the Department of Labor for "administration use only," lists fifty-four different programs, almost all developed since the early sixties.

[35] Spring, p. 135.
[36] Ibid., p. 139.
[37] "A Program for Sustaining Employment," Report of Committee on Economic Policy, Chamber of Commerce of the U.S.A. (Washington, D.C.: 1947), p. 5.
[38] *Distressed Areas in a Growing Economy* (New York: Committee for Economic Development, 1961), p. 8.

They range from employment and training opportunities (MDTA) to manpower delivery systems (Work Incentive Program), from employment techniques and special programs (services to minority groups, older workers, youth) to technical development and analysis (job market information, occupational projections). Although thousands are aided by these programs every year, they are designed to perpetuate a system that leaves many millions more suffering.

AN EVALUATION OF THE PROGRAMS

As late as 1969, in a report prepared for the Office of Economic Opportunity (OEO), the government admitted that it knew "remarkably little about the effects of these [manpower] programs." [39] It was known that the programs had not reduced in any significant way the overall unemployment rate. For every person helped, the natural workings of the economic system produced another unemployed worker. Even those who were put to work found that their incomes were not significantly increased, indicating the marginal type of jobs which people secured as a result of government activity in this area.[40] For instance, those completing MDTA programs had their family incomes raised an average of only $10 per week and six out of every ten were earning less than $80 per week. In effect, the programs did help some unemployed get full-time low paying jobs.[41] MDTA thus produced marketable cheap labor for the economy.

Wage rates paid to MDTA trainees clearly indicated the type of jobs they were being trained for. In 1962 enrollees were earning $1.25 per hour. In 1973 it was $2.76 per hour, hardly a living wage in an urban area. There were also discrepancies in wage rates paid men and women, and Blacks and Whites. In 1973 men averaged $3.05 per hour, women $2.36. White trainees received $2.84 per hour, their Black counterparts $2.55.[42] These wage differentials probably resulted from tracking within the programs, gearing people toward certain occupational classifications on the basis of sex or race. When a person completed an MDTA training program, he or she would then graduate from the ranks of the jobless poor to that of working poor. The self-esteem of the person was enhanced in theory, although little changed in the person's standard of living.

The Job Opportunities in the Business Sector (JOBS) program, initiated in 1968, resulted in a $60 million subsidy to business that provided job

[39] Thomas K. Glennan, Jr., *Evaluating Federal Manpower Programs: Notes and Observations* (Santa Monica: The Rand Corporation, 1969), p. 1.

[40] Simon Rottenberg, "Critical a priori Examination of Manpower Policy," in *South Atlantic Quarterly*, 71 (Spring 1972), 248.

[41] Earl D. Rain, "A Nationwide Evaluation of MDTA Institutional Job Training," in John A. Delehanty, *Full Employment and Opportunity for All* (Scranton: International Textbook, 1969), pp. 375, 382.

[42] Manpower Report of the President, April 1947, p. 53.

training to the "hard-core" unemployed. Those large corporations that participated received an average of $3,000 per trainee. "Many of the 'disadvantaged' hired under the JOBS program would likely have been placed in similar slots even without the subsidies." [43] Thus, the reason for cash payments, termed "inducements to hiring," was unclear, except to increase the profits of the corporations that participated. When it became less profitable to participate, as during the recession of 1970–71, even the subsidies could not induce the businesses to take on JOBS trainees in the face of their need to cut back operations. Whenever the interests of the cooperating corporations dictated, the corporations scuttled the original intent of the JOBS program, which was to make the unemployed "permanent, productive members of the labor force."

The Job Corps, begun in 1964 and modeled after the Civilian Conservation Corps, reflects the same relationship between government and business in attempting to solve unemployment. Aimed toward youth from the inner city, the primary goal was to provide rehabilitation and training so that they could enter mainstream economic and social life. OEO enlisted major corporations, such as GE, IBM, and Litton Industries, to assist the Job Corps. These corporations contracted with the government to manage Job Corps urban centers. The original government intent was to establish a commitment from corporations to hire Job Corps graduates.

In the final analysis the advantages gained by the corporations were much greater than those gained by unemployed youth. Because the centers operated on a cost plus fixed fee basis, they were highly profitable to the contracting businesses. The firms also secured excellent public relations benefits from their "involvement" in urban problems. Some of them engaged in extensive advertising campaigns to publicize their commitments. At the same time Job Corps training program graduates provided a source of semiskilled cheap labor at no expense to the companies. The companies reserved the right to hire or not to hire, often rendering the training program superfluous.

While in training, a Job Corps enrollee earned $33.20 per month, plus all living expenses, free medical care, and a monthly allotment to the family. After eighteen months of training, a graduate could expect to earn no more than the minimum wage. More importantly, the chances of getting a job were not significantly improved.[44] Young people in the program understood this to some degree. No more than one in nine stayed for as long as a year, and the Job Corps had to undertake expensive public relations campaigns to attract people to the program. Advertising could not solve the problems that unemployed youth faced. Neither could it transform an essentially token program into something that would actually change the lives of the

[43] Sar A. Levitan, "Manpower Programs for a Healthier Economy," in Lloyd Ulman, ed., *Manpower Programs in the Policy Mix* (Baltimore: Johns Hopkins Press, 1973), p. 107.

[44] Sar A. Levitan, *The Great Society's Poor Law: A New Approach to Poverty* (Baltimore: Johns Hopkins Press, 1969), p. 304.

participants, let alone the vast majority who could not even be accommodated in the program.[45]

The Neighborhood Youth Corps (NYC), another program in the War on Poverty, differs from the Job Corps in that its goals are much more limited. It is "largely an income maintenance program, offering little training or preparation for work." [46] The real purpose behind the program was to ease the school dropout rate and lessen the rate of juvenile crime. To believe that this could be done by providing make-work jobs at $1.25 per hour stretches the imagination. No pretense was made of getting at the fundamental reasons for the problems the program hoped to solve. It is therefore understandable that neither the Job Corps nor the NYC had an effect on reducing the percentage or the rate of growth of unemployed youth. Neither did it affect the school dropout rate or juvenile crime. Though it is probably true that in certain areas and at certain times the programs offered a margin of assistance creating at least the appearance of progress, they were really a safety valve to ease a crisis situation.

From the end of the Johnson Administration and into the Nixon presidency, two developments were initiated which indicated that even some of the meager gains of the earlier programs were to be taken away. The first was the effort to turn welfare into "workfare" by literally forcing people off the welfare rolls into whatever jobs were available in the economy. The second development was the scuttling of the minimal involvement of the poor in some of the planning of the manpower programs, which had been a part of the OEO philosophy.

The Work Incentive Program (WIN) illustrated the first development. By training and minimally educating welfare recipients, WIN proposed the removal of large numbers from the welfare rolls. With no built-in guarantee of permanent, well-paid work at the end of the training period, it was necessary to establish some coercive aspects to the program, such as categorizing some recipients as "mandatory registrants." Whether the philosophy behind the program was liberal (under Johnson) or punitive (under Nixon), the fundamental approach was the same; those on welfare were somehow to blame for their situation. Remaining in their present state was either undignified or improper. They should be performing productive work for the benefit of society and themselves.

Behind this rhetoric was the reality that out of 3 million eligible people in 1971, only 300,000 were trained. Of these, only 20 percent actually got jobs. The jobs were generally of the dead-end variety that paid little more than what these "newly productive" members of society had received on welfare. Two categories of work that were especially promoted were homemaking aides (a euphemism for servants) and clerical personnel. The fact remains that the jobs simply were not there for those in WIN, let alone for all those on

[45] Levitan, in Ulman, *Manpower Programs,* p. 108.

[46] *Work in America*, Report of a Special Task Force to the Secretary of Health, Education and Welfare (Cambridge: MIT Press, 1973), p. 168.

welfare capable of working. People cannot be forced back to work if there is no work for them; and the lack of employment opportunity is the reason many are welfare recipients in the first place. Yet as more and more people are forced into welfare, the government responds with manpower programs that cannot work. At the same time, the Nixon Administration partly created and manipulated middle- and working-class anger toward welfare recipients, with the poor caught in the middle with no choice at all.

In December 1973, Nixon signed into law the Comprehensive Employment and Training Act (CETA). The novel feature of this program was the complete elimination of any relationship between the federal government and agencies and organizations representing the poor. Since OEO, the poor had been able to approach Washington directly through the Community Action Programs (CAP); this had brought a degree of political power to the poor which they had not previously had. At times it meant increased militancy on their part, because the CAPs provided a mechanism for organization and mobilization. Under CETA, which emerged from the New Federalism philosophy of the Nixon Administration, manpower programs and the funds for them flow directly from the federal government to state, county, and city governments. Under the guise of reform and decentralization, the people affected by these manpower programs will be even more powerless than before. This was the intent of the Nixon Administration. In addition, the level of funding for manpower programs is declining, except for WIN. Depression conditions for the unemployed appear solidly entrenched for the near future.

The integral relationship between unemployment and the existing capitalist economy has never been admitted to by either the government or the business class. Federal work and manpower programs could never succeed in eliminating unemployment, because they all operate within the context and structure of the prevailing system. At best they have been short-term remedies to crisis situations, which will ultimately recur. At worst, the programs have been punitive and coercive, offering only the illusion of change. Until the symbiotic relationship between these programs and the economic system that made the programs inevitable is ended, the possibility of ending unemployment remains elusive. A genuine program to end unemployment will necessarily conflict with the interests of the business class and the structure of the economy as it now exists. Such a program is possible, but it will require far more profound changes in the structure of the economy and society at large.

chapter three

social welfare and social class:
income, wealth, and power

—*Larry Beeferman*

To understand welfare, one must understand wealth and work. On the one hand we see giant corporations and agribusiness amassing profits; on the other we see government supporting these corporations and showing less concern for the underpaid worker and the unemployed. Falling through the cracks, we see millions of poor people, no better off in a relative sense than they were a decade ago. The postwar affluence of American families was achieved largely at the cost of more family members working, because the spendable wage gains of the average worker during the last ten years have been minuscule. As the Queen said to Alice in Wonderland, "Now *here*, you see, it takes all the running you can do, to keep in the same place. If you want to get somewhere else, you must run at least twice as fast as that!"

Estelle Disch shows in another chapter how in the criminal justice system the government protects the rich and not the poor. Larry Beeferman shows here how this works out in terms of government spending and tax policies. Retrogressive tax rates favor the rich, as do the billions of dollars' interest paid to those holding government debt securities. The federal government spends more than eight times as much on the military as on public assistance. State and local governments spend about as much on police and corrections as they do on social welfare, and far more on transportation—most of this on highways, which subsidize the more affluent suburbs at the expense of the cities. Government is clearly more interested in preserving the social arrangements which helped to produce social pathology than in alleviating the symptoms of pathology.

Although only a small fraction of government spending goes to AFDC recipients, these recipients receive the largest amount of media attention, so many believe that welfare recipients cause their economic problems. An analysis of the true state of economic and political affairs is exceedingly complex, particularly because the rich do not reveal as much about their finances and power as do the poor. Yet if we are to understand the true state of social welfare rather than "blame the victim," we must insist on knowing the truth.

The 1960s were a period in which the boils of social wrongs burst with an explosion of pain and anger. Multitudes were spurred to lance the wounds so exposed. Yet others were driven to more drastic prescriptions for the suffering patient. It was one of the more violent episodes in a life shaken by the fevers of the 1930s, the battles of the 1940s, and the chills of the 1950s. The early years of this decade have been witness to soothing calls for patience, of a need to desist from the passions of the past, indeed to retreat even from modest efforts to assuage the ills of the nation. The patient seems mute, more likely owing to a paralysis of will and enervation of spirit than to the comfortable ease of recovery.

We exist as part and parcel of that social being. We experience the vagaries of its existence, its sufferings, and triumphs. It is with that greater social being that our own hopes, wishes, dreams—the greater and lesser prospects for our own existence—are indissolubly joined. As its smallest units (yet its most important ones), it is upon us that its health, well-being, and welfare ultimately rest.

It is social welfare that is our concern—its present state and the prospects for its future. Both require an understanding of its past. All in turn demand a sense of what defines social welfare and how its requirements are met.

For example, social welfare is often identified with the action of governments. But in a society in which the extended family is a viable social unit, there is no need to support the elderly out of a public treasury. A society of self-sustaining farmers—one in which people are not compelled to sell their labor for wages—does not require unemployment benefits for those whose skills are no longer "marketable."

Our society bears the stamp of other experience. It is at its root one of capitalistic production, exchange, and consumption. Human activity is reduced to exchangeable entities—commodities—numerically equated in the form of money. Nothing escapes the terrible leveler which equalizes all by reducing all—food, leisure, labor, even honor—to money. Social life is quantified. It is difficult for author and reader alike to resist the equal but empty exchange of living experience for numbers.

WORK

No, indeed, ours is not that society of self-sufficient farmers which could sustain the Jeffersonian vision of a viable democracy. Rather it is one of wage and salaried labor. The history of this country to the present is witness to the growth of that class of persons who must sell their labor to live—sell their labor to those who possess productive property: mines, factories, machines, buildings, farmlands, etc. Most of those who formerly labored for themselves on farms, in small shops, as skilled artisans, or as independent inventors and producers are today employees of others.[1]

[1] Reich estimates that in 1780, 20% of the U.S. labor force were wage and salaried employees and 80% self-employed entrepreneurs; in 1880, 62% employees, 36.9% entrepreneurs, and 1.1%

The viability of entrepreneurial ventures exists more in the realm of wishful rhetoric than in the world of harsh economic reality. More than one-fourth of all partnerships and proprietorships fail the test of profit.[2] In recent years, a larger and larger fraction of such businesses have shown a loss.[3] Among those who qualify as "successful," a small number garner the largest portion of the rewards of business.[4] Doctors and lawyers, especially, benefit in a proportion far beyond their number.[5] Farmers are the most likely to fail and suffer the greatest losses.[6]

Those who obtain income from the rental of property, or from royalties, patents, copyrights, etc., are reduced to economic insignificance. Such rental income must be supplemented by an imaginary (imputed) one to render it substantial.[7]

Dominating the vast army of workers, the diminishing breed of small businessmen, and the other minor economic actors are those who possess the bulk of productive property through ownership of corporate stock. These people derive income from that property in the form of dividends.[8] It is said that managerial prerogatives are distinct from the rights of stockholders. In earlier periods the two were fused: a capitalist not only owned productive property but also was intimately engaged in administering it. These functions

---

salaried managers and officials; in 1969, the figures were 83.6%, 9.2%, and 7.2%, respectively. See "The Evolution of the United States Labor Force," by Michael Reich, in *The Capitalist System*, by Richard C. Edwards et al. (Englewood Cliffs, N.J.: Prentice-Hall, Inc., 1972), pp. 174–82.

[2] In 1970, 2.72 million of 9.4 million proprietorships and 296,000 out of 936,000 partnerships showed a loss. See *Business Tax Returns 1970, Statistics of Income*, US IRS Publication 438 (10–73).

[3] Between 1961 and 1970, the percentage of failing proprietorships almost continually increased from 21.1% to 28.9%; the percentage of failing partnerships continually increased from 22.5% to 31.6%. *Business Tax Returns 1970* (Washington, D.C.: U.S. Government Printing Office).

[4] In 1969, the top 5% of proprietorships received 24.3% of all net profits; the top 2.6% of partnerships garnered 29.7% of all net profits. See *Statistical Abstract of the United States, 1972*, p. 471.

[5] In 1970, medical-related proprietorships represented 3.7% of all profitable proprietorships, but accounted for 17.9% of all net profits. Those for legal services were 2.1% of profitable proprietorships but obtained 4.6% of all net profits. Medical-related partnerships numbered 2.5% of all profitable ones but received 13.3% of the profits. Partnerships providing legal services, 3.6% of the total, garnered 17.4% of net profits. *Business Tax Returns 1970* (Washington, D.C.: U.S. Government Printing Office).

[6] In 1970, 39.2% of all farm proprietorships failed to make a profit, suffering nearly *half* of all the losses shown by proprietorships. *Business Tax Returns 1970* (Washington, D.C.: U.S. Government Printing Office).

[7] Those who construct the national income accounts consider people who own their own homes as being in a business and renting their homes to themselves! In doing so, they derive an imaginary (imputed) rental income. In 1973, this accounted for about 60% of all rental income. Real rental income was about $10 billion out of a total personal income of over $1,000 billion.

[8] Actually, corporate income is composed of dividends and undivided corporate profits. The latter represent income retained within the corporation for further expansion. Stockholders have title to those acquired assets so they, too, should be considered as income, but are not. In practice, such accumulated profits are reflected in long-term stock prices; if the stocks are sold, then the "hidden" income emerges as a capital gain. During the last quarter-century, undivided corporate profits have averaged *slightly higher* than dividends, though the former are more likely to soar during booms and plummet during recessions. See *National Income and Product Accounts, 1929–1965*, and post-1965 issues of the *Survey of Current Business*.

are now largely separated. The subsidiary managerial functions are now represented by (highly) paid salaried labor. But both are sustained in symbiotic harmony through the persistent drive for profit.[9]

This separation from the actual production process is a further refinement of the capitalist concern with the return on capital, expressed as a percentage on investment. It is now manifest in the form of institutions which loom as large or larger than those corporate entities which actually supervise production.[10] Possession of their financial instruments yields "interest"—the most distilled and "purified" form of profit. Ownership of corporate or government bonds, business loans, consumer and mortgage credit, savings accounts, equities in life insurance policies, pension plans—all breed interest. Net interest paid by corporations now rivals—for the first time since the Depression—payments in the form of dividends.[11]

These sketches give only a shadowy picture of economic power. The light of experience reveals that economic power is nothing without political power, and that both are fused as a total social power, each nourishing the other. Command over production and the work that animates the mines, factories, and offices of the nation is permuted through a tangled web of relationships to power over the institutions which define what is right and appropriate and proper and which reinforce that control. Those relationships are revealed in a hierarchy of power, wealth, status, and income.

INCOME

Despite protestations to the contrary, this country is no closer to income equality than it was a quarter of a century ago. Even government figures leave little room for doubt (see Charts 1 and 2). It does appear that the highest-income groups have suffered some slight losses since World War II. But the most substantial gains were shown by those in the upper half of the income brackets and were actually made at the expense of only those at the very top.

Even these comments do not fully define the situation. There are significant problems in estimating what actual incomes are, for under- and nonreporting are common. But if the net that traps and measures the wages and salaries of workers is fine, the coarser web that should secure the income of the wealthy fails to do so. In 1972, nearly half the missing income was of the sort accruing to the very wealthy: dividends, interest, etc.[12] Consequently,

[9] See, for example, "The New Capitalism," by Robin Blackburn, in *Ideology in Social Science*, Robin Blackburn, ed. (New York: Vintage Books, 1973), pp. 164–86.

[10] See, for example, *Commercial Banks and Their Trust Activities: Emerging Influence on the American Economy* (Washington, D.C.: U.S. Government Printing Office, July 1968).

[11] *National Income and Product Accounts, 1929–1965* and post-1965 issues of *Survey of Current Business*.

[12] For example, an analysis of the Census Bureau survey shows that in 1972, 98.1% of all wage and salary income was included in its estimates. By contrast, only 45% of income from dividends,

CHART 1

Percentage Aggregate Income Received
by Each Fifth of Families

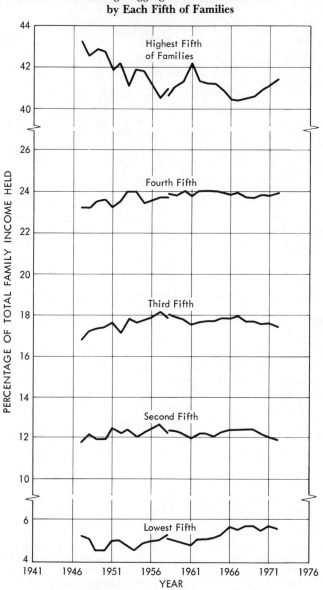

SOURCE: *Current Population Reports*, Series P-60, December 1973, p. 45.

various studies suggest that the income shares of the top 1 percent and top 5 percent groups are several points higher than shown in the accompanying charts.[13]

CHART 2

Percentage Aggregate Income of
Top 5 Percent of Families

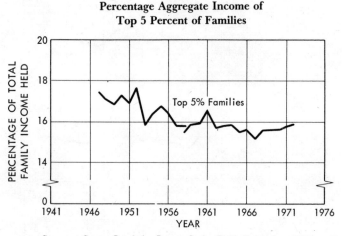

SOURCE: *Current Population Reports*, Series P-60, December 1973, p. 45.

This is still not the entire story. Excluded from the conventional income definition are non-money items and realized capital gains. The first usually goes to low-income groups. It consists of food, clothing, housing, and medical services (e.g., Medicare) given *gratis* by an employer or the government, or food and housing provided by a farmer for his own use. The second accrues to high-income groups. It corresponds to properties (stocks, bonds, land, real estate, etc.) that increased in price and were sold at a profit.

Inclusion of such income would mean gains for both low- and high-income groups. But the latter would benefit much more in absolute terms. Moreover, if one were to include these findings in the distributions of income cited, then

interest, net rental income, income from estates and trusts, and net royalties were recorded. Recorded income was $772.9 billion, whereas the estimated actual income was $857.9 billion. Nearly half of the $85 billion gap, $41.3 billion, was represented by errors in the dividends, interest, etc., category. See *Current Population Reports*, Series P-60, No. 90, December 1973, U.S. Department of Commerce, p. 25.

[13] Several studies that have used interpolation of more accurate income tax return data with the Census Bureau information support this contention. See, for example, *Size Distribution of Family Personal Income: Methodology and Estimates for 1964*, by Edward C. Budd et al. (Washington, D.C.: Bureau of Economic Analysis, June 1973), distributed by National Technical Information Service, U.S. Department of Commerce; "Distribution of Federal and State Income Taxes by Income Class," Presidential Address, American Finance Association Annual Meetings, New Orleans, La., December 28, 1971, mimeographed paper; and *Who Bears the Tax Burden?* by Joseph A. Pechman and Benjamin A. Okner (Washington, D.C.: The Brookings Institution, 1974).

the top groups would very likely show an increase during the 1947–73 period.[14]

TAXES

Now, recall that the income measure we have been discussing *includes* the benefits of various government social welfare programs. The largest of them—social security—basically represents an income transfer program *within* the lower half of the income distribution. It results in a tremendous amount of double counting of income for that group and creates the impression of relative income gains which are, in fact, not real.

It would really be better to see how the blessings of the system "naturally" emerge from private capitalist production. This is not possible, for no such system exists. The action of governments is demanded to sustain it. In 1972, almost 16 million people, nearly 20 percent of the employed work force, were employed by the federal or state and local governments in a civilian or military capacity.[15] Thus, those who earned a living in this way would have to be excluded from the analysis.

Still, one can ask, after all is said and done, benefits and taxes included, what is the effect of government actions on the income of families and individuals? This is difficult to answer because a method must be found to estimate the taxes paid according to income group. We rely here on one such effort which we have modified slightly on the basis of our own assumptions.[16]

In column 2 of Table 1 we have "adjusted money income," derived from the Census Bureau data but scaled up to match the overall more accurate Bureau of Economic Analysis (BEA) totals. Column 4 incorporates estimates

[14] Ackerman et al., have made crude estimates of the importance of capital gains to upper-income groups. Their data show that if such gains are included in the distribution of income then the portion received by the top fifth of families showed only minor changes from 1947 to 1968. Even without the inclusion of capital gains, the top fifth gained in income share from 1969–72. Note also that the overwhelming portion of capital gains accrues to those in the top 1% and top 5% brackets so their relative gains are even more substantial. See "The Extent of Income Inequality in the United States," by Frank Ackerman et al., in Richard C. Edwards et al., *The Capitalist System*, pp. 207–19.

[15] In 1972, there were approximately 13.3 million civilian government workers and nearly 2.5 million people serving in the military out of an employed work force of about 84 million. Of course, many others are employed as a result of government purchases of goods and services. See *Economic Report of the President, 1973* (Washington, D.C.: U.S. Government Printing Office), pp. 220–21, 226.

[16] See "The Taxes We Pay," by Roger A. Herriot and Herman P. Miller, in *The Conference Board RECORD* (May 1971), pp. 31–40. My analysis differs from the one cited primarily in the following ways: (1) I do not include imputed income or retained corporate earnings or employer contributions to private pension and welfare funds; (2) I do not include the effect of corporate profits taxes; and (3) I assume that social security taxes paid by employers and all other indirect taxes (property taxes on business, sales taxes, excise taxes, etc.) are passed on to the consumer in the form of higher costs. The actual allocation of particular taxes to various income groups follows the assumptions of Herriot and Miller.

TABLE 1

Distributions of Income of Families and Unrelated Individuals, 1968

(1) Adjusted Money Income Levels	(2) Number of Families (Millions)	(3) Adjusted Money Income (Billions)	(4) Total Income (Billions)	(5) Total Income Before Govt Transfer Payments	(6) Total Direct Taxes (Billions)	(7) Total Income After Direct Taxes (Billions)	(8) Total Indirect Taxes (Billions)	(9) Total Income After Direct and Indirect Taxes (Billions)
Total	64.31	$619.1	$649.6	$593.9	$124.3	$525.3	$88.4	$436.9
Under $2000	6.36	6.7	9.1	2.5	0.7	8.4	2.0	6.4
$2000–$4000	7.97	24.0	26.7	15.2	2.3	24.4	5.2	19.2
$4000–$6000	8.22	41.2	43.3	34.0	5.2	38.1	7.6	30.5
$6000–$8000	8.94	63.1	65.0	58.3	9.8	55.2	10.6	44.6
$8000–$10,000	8.37	75.4	77.1	71.9	12.6	64.5	11.4	53.1
$10,000–$15,000	14.28	174.6	178.5	169.9	33.4	145.1	24.2	120.9
$15,000–$25,000	7.89	146.3	150.7	145.0	30.9	119.8	17.9	101.9
$25,000–$50,000	} 2.29	62.8	66.9	65.0	16.1	50.8	16.8	44.0
$50,000 +		25.0	32.2	32.0	13.4	18.8	2.7	16.1
				Percentages				
Total	100.0	100.0	100.0	100.0	100.0	100.0	100.0	100.0
Under $2000	9.89	1.1	1.4	0.4	0.6	1.6	2.3	1.5
$2000–$4000	12.39	3.9	4.1	2.6	1.9	4.6	5.9	4.4
$4000–$6000	12.78	6.7	6.7	5.7	4.2	7.3	8.6	7.0
$6000–$8000	13.90	10.2	10.0	9.8	7.9	10.5	12.0	10.2
$8000–$10,000	13.02	12.2	11.9	12.1	10.1	12.3	12.9	12.2
$10,000–$15,000	22.21	28.2	27.5	28.6	26.9	27.6	27.4	27.7
$15,000–$25,000	12.27	23.6	23.2	24.5	24.9	22.8	20.2	23.3
$25,000–$50,000	3.02	10.1	10.3	10.9	13.0	9.7	7.7	10.1
$50,000 +	0.52	4.0	5.0	5.4	10.8	3.6	3.1	3.7

SOURCE: See note 16.

of non-money wages, farm income, Medicare benefits, and net realized capital gains.[17] As noted, modest gains are made at the bottom of the distribution and relatively large ones at the top—at the expense of those in the middle.

Recall now that column 4 includes *all* income from government transfers. (Otherwise the distribution would be as shown in column 5.) These transfers are the result of taxes. People pay taxes directly on their income and wealth and indirectly in the cost of the products and services they consume. Column 6 shows the personal taxes on income and wealth paid to federal, state, and local governments, and individuals' personal contributions for social insurance. The distribution is progressive but not nearly so much as might have been expected. Moreover, because high incomes are greatly underestimated, the effective tax rates may be much lower.

Other taxes create an even worse picture. Over the years, property taxes on apartments and businesses, excise taxes on gasoline, cigarettes, and liquor, sales taxes on consumer products, social security taxes paid by employers but included in the final sales cost, etc., have become increasingly important. These, shown in column 8, amounted to $88.4 billion in 1968, nearly 75 percent of direct taxes. The distribution of these is highly retrogressive.

Two additional income distributions can now be constructed. One—given by column 7—shows what people receive in cash or its equivalent. The effect is a shift of about 5 percent of national income from the top quintile to those below. However, it is what people actually receive in concrete physical terms, in goods and services, that is important. This leads to the other income distribution. It incorporates the effect of the decrease in purchasing power which results from indirect taxes being included in the cost of goods sold. This we call the total net effective income distribution. It is the final distribution after inclusion of transfer payments and direct and indirect taxes. The net result is a shift of less than 4 percent in income share from the top quintile to the rest of the distribution.

Despite this, the top 1 percent of families retained about 7 percent of net effective income, the top 5 percent nearly 16.5 percent, and the top 20 percent about 43 percent. Moreover, these are *minimum* estimates. The actual shares are very likely larger.[18]

Although these statistics are a devastating commentary on the contemporary "welfare state," they lose some impact because they are global in character. They do not refer to particular families or individuals. Now it is

[17] Herriot and Miller use for their estimate of net realized capital gains that supplied by the IRS as part of its "adjusted gross (taxable) income" measure. But only one-half of (long-term) capital gains are taxable. Thus, if one assumes that the bulk of all capital gains are long-term, then one must assume that Herriot and Miller seriously underestimate the income shares of top bracket groups.

[18] For example, if all capital gains are assumed to be long-term and the nontaxable portion included in total income, then the after-all taxes shares of the top 1%, 5%, and 20% of families and unrelated individuals become 8%, 19%, and 44.5%, respectively. Moreover, these results do *not* take into account the underestimation of high-income data referred to in note 13.

true that median and mean family incomes have been increasing. Suppose, however, one looks at the wages of a typical factory worker, clerk, or sales person.

CHART 3

Typical Family and Worker Weekly Incomes

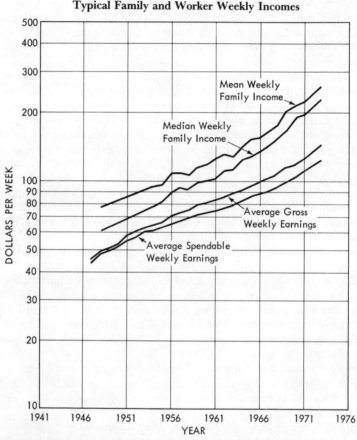

DEFINITIONS AND SOURCES: *Mean and median family weekly income:* Yearly median and mean family income divided by 52; 1948, 1954–69—*Survey of Consumer Finances* (Ann Arbor, Michigan: Survey Research Center, 1960, 1962, 1964, 1966, and 1970; 1970–73); *Current Population Reports*, Series P-60, Nos. 85, 87, and 93.

Average gross weekly earnings and *average spendable earnings:* The average weekly earnings of all production or nonsupervisory workers in private nonagricultural industries before and after social security and federal income taxes. Taxes for the latter refer to a worker with three dependents, 1947–71, *Economic Report of the President, 1973*, p. 229; 1973–74, *Business Statistics*, U.S. Department of Commerce, July 26, 1974, p. 4.

The gap between the average earnings of such workers and mean or median family income continues to widen (see Chart 3). The increase in such earnings appears more modest when one looks at the after-tax (social security and federal) income of a worker with three dependents. Even more startling is how this "spendable" income is translated into "real" dollars after inflation is taken into account (see Chart 4). The gains of the last ten years all but vanish and those for the 1940s and 1950s are a mere whisper of their former selves.

CHART 4

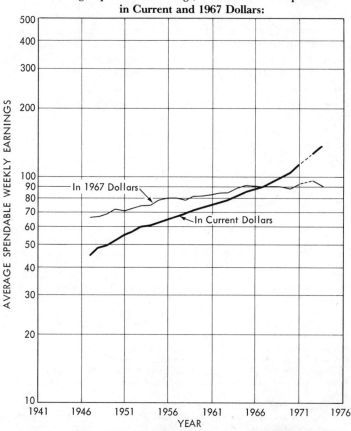

Average Spendable Earnings, Worker with 3 Dependents in Current and 1967 Dollars:

SOURCES: 1947–71, Economic Report of the President, 1973, p. 229; 1973–1974, *Business Statistics*, U.S. Department of Commerce, July 26, 1974, p. 4.

It may be asked, how does one explain this puzzling discrepancy between average family income and the typical wages of a worker supporting a family? A part of the answer is found in the double-counting we mentioned before;[19] however, it must also be in large part because more and more members of families are working. Behind all the figures lies an increased labor demanded of families in order to sustain themselves.[20]

In particular, increasing numbers of women are active members of the labor force.[21] It is appropriate that women have the right to a full role in productive activities outside the home. (Indeed, they are the sole support of many families.) But the fact that such women—and other family members— are driven to it is testimony to the failure of our social organization to provide the vaunted prosperity without exacting onerous and unnecessary tolls.

If the fortunes of those active in the labor force are mixed, then one can only speculate about those who are not. There is an officially established level which defines poverty and provides the basis for much discussion of it. That definition is of dubious merit.[22] But even if one accepts this term, it is obvious that there is an ever-increasing gap between the global or specific measures of family income and what is considered to be a poverty level. If one is compelled to define a minimal "acceptable" standard of living—and that, too, is a notion of questionable value—that definition should be relative to the prevailing average standard of living. But the present poverty formulation rests on an imaginary minimal diet—an unchanging absolute standard —which becomes further and further removed from what might be called typical. It is asserted that a smaller and smaller fraction of the populace lives in poverty, as presently defined. But if the standard of poverty (in money terms) were defined relative to average income in this society, it is doubtful that there would be any decline in poverty.[23]

[19] Recall the discussion about the distribution of income. It was observed that transfer payments accruing to low income families came primarily from taxes on low income families. Census Bureau distributions of income double count, including *both* the transfer payments and income which is taxed away to pay for those transfers.

[20] In 1971, 38.7% of all families had two earners and 14.1% had three or more earners. See *Current Population Reports*, Series P-60, No. 85, December 1972, p. 24. Except for those in the highest income brackets, there is a close correlation between number of earners and mean family income. See *Current Population Reports*, Series P-60, No. 90, December 1973, p. 27.

[21] In recent years, for those families in which both husband and wife worked, women earned an amount equal to 40% of the husband's salary in white families, and nearer to 50% in black families. See *Current Population Reports*, Series P-23, No. 39, December 1971, p. 14. The fraction of all women of working age who are working has steadily increased from 20.4% in 1900 to 43.8% in 1972. See *Economic Report of the President, 1973*, p. 91. From 1940 to 1970, the percentage of married women (husband present) who were working increased from 14.7% to 40.8%. See *Handbook of Labor Statistics 1971*, U.S. Department of Labor, p. 49 and *1969 Handbook of Women Workers*, Women's Bureau, Bulletin 194, U.S. Department of Labor, 1969, p. 26. Moreover, the percentage of mothers who were working soared from 8.6% in 1940 to 38.2% in 1967. See *1969 Handbook of Women Workers*, p. 40.

[22] See, for example, Chapter 2, "The Number of Poor," in *Permanent Poverty, An American Syndrome*, by Ben B. Seligman (Chicago: Quadrangle Books, 1970).

[23] For example, in 1959 median family income (according to the Census Bureau) was $5,417 and the average poverty level for all families was $2,719, or 50.2% of the former figure. In 1970, median family income was $9,867 but the average poverty level for all families was only $3,601, or 36.5% of the former. Using the conventional poverty level, one finds that the number of

Moreover, behind the numbers and figures are real people who live real lives, who have real concerns and aspirations for both the concrete and more elusive pleasures of life. It is difficult to quantify poor or unnourishing food, shoddy or unnecessary goods, the burdens of a totally inadequate transportation system, or the debilitation of the media which often serves us ill. Not only are the material rewards of this earthly existence not shared equally, but the value of even having them is questionable.

WEALTH

The income figures we have presented show that millions of our people are poorly clothed, fed, and housed, and millions of others suffer in comparison to an affluent few. Yet those figures do not fully reveal the prerogatives of those in commanding social positions. The higher their income, the more likely such individuals are to have resources exceeding their own consumption needs. It becomes more likely that a major portion of their income will be invested in additional income-producing properties. Thus, the cycle of wealth accumulation and unequal apportionment of income is reproduced on an even grander scale.

Unfortunately, it is easier and less dangerous to study the deficiencies of the poor and weak than to investigate the privileges of the wealthy and powerful. Hence, studies of the distribution of wealth are few and far between.

One of the most recent analyses showed that in 1962, the top 1 percent of the population held about 40 percent of the total wealth. The top 2 percent and 5.8 percent held 48.6 and 66.1 percent, respectively.[24] The inequitable distribution described here is even more striking when one considers the actual assets held. For the *lowest 94.2 percent* of the population, nearly 60 percent of the recorded assets were in the form of real property, particularly prime residence and household goods. These are items which meet direct personal needs and as such play no role in the person's claim to control over or benefit from the production process. If these real property items are excluded from the wealth-holding estimates, then the top 1, 2, and 5.8 percent held 54.1, 64, and 79.8 percent of the remaining wealth, respectively.

In Table 2 we detail the disparities in kind and amount of assets held by the lowest and highest wealth groups. There is little in those figures to suggest that the overwhelming number of people have any power over the dominant economic institutions of this society.

---

persons in families below it amounted to 20.8% of that population in 1959 but only 11% of it in 1970. However, if one defines the poverty level as 50.2% of family median income, then roughly the same percentage of families was below the poverty level in 1970 and 1959. See *Statistics of Income, 1972*, pp. 323, 329.

[24] Refer to "The Distribution of Assets Among Individuals of Different Age and Wealth," by John Bossons, Appendix V, *Institutional Investors and Corporate Stock—A Background Study*, Raymond W. Goldsmith, ed. (New York: National Bureau of Economic Research, Columbia University Press, 1973).

TABLE 2

Percent of Assets Held by Top 1% of Individuals		Percent of Assets Held by Lowest 88.6% of Individuals	
All Assets	39.7%	All Assets	16.1%
(in order of decreasing importance)			
Stocks	81.4%	Cash	29.0%
Bonds	47.9%	Miscellaneous Assets[2]	18.8%
Other Financial Assets[1]	44.9%	Other Financial Assets[1]	14.4%
Real Property (other		Bonds	12.4%
than prime residence		Stocks	9.5%
and household goods)	44.8%	Real Property (other	
Miscellaneous Assets[2]	35.3%	than prime residence	
Cash	12.2%	and household goods)	5.0%

[1] "Other Financial Assets" include mortgages and notes, equity in life insurance, annuities, trust assets, and noncorporate business assets.

[2] "Miscellaneous Assets" include assets in profit-sharing plans, retirement plans, and estates in probate.

SOURCE: See note 24.

Perhaps more important, the power of wealthy individuals extends far beyond the limits of their own personal assets. It is often claimed that such power has been weakened because more and more assets are administered by trusts. It is true that there has been a rapid and substantial growth in the assets of private pension funds, banks, life insurance companies, and the trust functions they perform. However, corporate stock still represents the dominant asset held by individuals. In fact, it is precisely because substantial portions of other financial assets are held in trust that the dominance of those who own the bulk of stock is translated into control over those other resources.

Consider for example a recent study of the business and financial empire called the Rockefeller Financial Group.[25] The core of this empire is formed by four enormous commercial banks (the second, third, sixth, and tenth largest in the U.S.) and three giant mutual life insurance companies (the second, third, and fourth largest in total assets). Altogether, these institutions held over $113 billion in assets in 1969. The Group is welded together through direct stock ownership, interlocking directorates, trust connections with corporations, banks, foundations, investment banking firms, and close official and social relationships with law firms and universities. Through them, this group wields tremendous power over a vast array of institutions, a power far in excess of that which would flow from the personal fortunes of the members of the group.

Detailed analyses of that power and the correlated question of the

[25] The Rockefeller Financial Group, by James C. Knowles (Andover, Mass.: Warner Modular Publications, Inc., Module 343, 1973).

relationship between management and ownership in large corporations are very important. They represent essential elements in the process whereby the distributions of income and wealth are maintained.

The abstractions that are corporate shares and bonds and notes represent more than ownership and title to income; they imply command and control. They create a hierarchical system of power in which the mass of workers who produce this society's wealth are excluded from the direction of production. They mean an alienation from work which is mentally and spiritually debilitating and the creation of conditions of work which are physically destructive. They result in a perversion of labor whereby workers as producers and workers as consumers are seen as separate and stand opposed. They establish a situation in which the only apparent answer to the question of "Production for what?" is "Profit." This is the real substance which only rarely pierces through the monetary and financial skin of corporate capitalism. A full analysis of its implications would take us too far afield, but it merits the most serious attention.

GOVERNMENTS AND SOCIAL WELFARE

Rather now we turn our attention to another aspect of "social welfare"—the efforts of governments to enhance it. This phraseology is somewhat misleading because it suggests that governments step in to provide remedies to problems that have arisen out of "normal" social processes and that otherwise those governments are neutral. This notion is false. The behavior of governments is such as to sustain those social processes, to assure the preservation of prevailing property relations and the ideology that secures them in the minds of the populace. Remedial programs are better viewed as attempts to repair rents in the social fabric, a cloth which governments have helped to weave.

We have already referred to the failure of a spate of tax programs to significantly lessen inequities in income. We now turn our attention to the uses of those taxes for specific programs to see whose welfare is benefited and to what extent.

Government spending takes two principal forms: transfer payments and purchases of goods and services. The former refers to income given to persons who have no direct relation to the labor force: the unemployed, the ill, the disabled, the aged, etc. The latter refers to actual government acquisition of goods (such as weapons for wars or bricks for office buildings) or services (of soldiers to fight those wars or bricklayers to construct the buildings). Government consumption of goods and services accounts for the largest portion of expenditures, totaling nearly $2\frac{1}{2}$ times as much as transfer payments (see Chart 5). However, total government transfer payments have been rising more rapidly than any other component of government costs. Hence, we shall look at them first.

CHART 5

Total Government Transfer Payments to Persons
and Purchases of Goods and Services

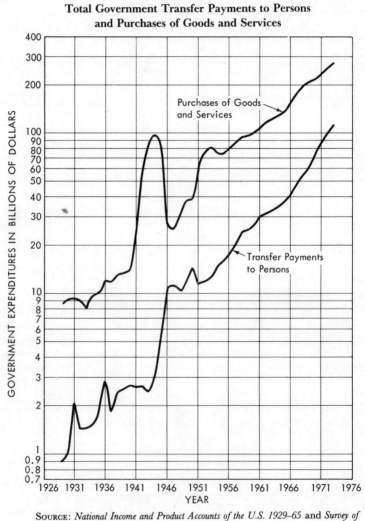

SOURCE: *National Income and Product Accounts of the U.S. 1929–65* and *Survey of Current Business,* July 1973 and May 1973.

TRANSFER PAYMENTS

The most important and rapidly growing component is social security (federal Old Age, Survivors, and Disability Insurance—OASDI). A corollary program, with a similar growth pattern, is the federal medical and insurance program known as Medicare. Transfer payments of a more cyclical character are unemployment benefits. In 1973, all three amounted to 62.9 percent of all such government benefits.[26]

Contrary to common belief, the income a typical recipient gets under virtually all transfer payments programs far exceeds any contributions that person may have made. If it is true for people on "welfare," it is equally the case for the recipients of all the categories of aid listed above.

Consider, for example, social security. The Tax Foundation estimated the total participant payments for the period 1937–65 and compared it with estimated benefits which would be received over a ten-year interval.[27] Even after taking into account inflation and loss of interest income, they found that benefits exceeded payments by no less than a factor of 5 and in a few cases, by as large a factor as 10.

Payments under the other programs cited depend upon the incidence of illness and unemployment among the potential recipients. Thus, no clear conclusion can be drawn about the relation between contributions and benefits. However, the unemployment program is financed by employer payroll taxes. At least half of the Medicare program is supported by employers' taxes and another smaller part out of general federal revenues. Thus, substantial portions of the costs are socialized through increased prices of goods and services or through the personal and corporate tax system.

Consequently, the benefits derived from these programs bear only a limited relation to the costs incurred by recipients. This supplemental income is the result of a social decision that certain groups, because of their past relation to the labor force, shall continue to receive an income, even when that relation no longer exists. That decision presumes responsibility for those who have suffered the vagaries of social as well as physical life.

It is the former over which we have greater control. The programs mentioned are specific responses to problems which emerge naturally out of our social organization. That system requires that millions of people not be allowed to contribute to productive activities either because they are beyond some arbitrary age limit or because those who have the power to employ them see it as unprofitable to do so. The multitude of such decisions confronts those judged as so-called "market forces." The particular programs men-

---

[26] Unless otherwise specified, all subsequent figures refer to 1973 and are drawn from the July 1974 issue of the *Survey of Current Business*.

[27] Refer to *Economic Aspects of the Social Security Tax*, Research Publication No. 5, Tax Foundation, Inc., 1966.

tioned, whether they be social security or "welfare," are all demanded by the nature of American society. Until that nature is fundamentally altered, all those programs must be required.

The next major category of transfer payment refers not to the "civilian" or "private" economy, but rather to those employed by the government itself. It accounted for 23.5 percent of the total. Over half of this, about 12.9 percent of all transfer payments, went to people associated with the military. One group of military-related payments encompasses veterans' pensions and benefits. The other involves pensions of retirees from the military service and their dependents. All of these expenses were supported by the taxpayer; none came from the recipients.

Here, too, a previous relation to the labor force allows individuals to claim an income, a burden borne by the general public. One need not begrudge the benefits to those injured, the survivors of those killed, or those who served for many years, to observe that these payments were in great part made necessary by a conception of the American political and military role in the world that is questionable. Indeed, there are compelling arguments that many military adventures are organically related to the dynamics of American society.[28] If so, then these benefits must be seen as an unnecessary burden arising from it—one which has its human and financial consequences long after the sounds of the battlefield have ebbed away.

The remaining portion of government employee transfer payments, 9 percent of the total, are those for federal, state, and local government workers' pensions. These generally involve matching contributions by individuals and the agencies employing them. No estimates of the relationship between payments received and costs incurred appear available. However it has been suggested that "the [federal] civil servant is paying considerably less than one-half of the real cost of his projected pension." [29]

Curiously enough, the income transfer programs—direct relief—which have caused the greatest stir, rank last in importance. They represented only 10 percent of all government transfer payments. In fact, the estimated $11.3 billion spent on direct relief in 1973 was dwarfed by the $26.3 billion in interest paid for the relief (and comfort) of those holding government debt securities.[30] The more well-known direct relief programs include old age assistance (OAA), aid to the permanently and totally disabled (APTD), and aid to families with dependent children (AFDC).[31] All require income tests to demonstrate need.

---

[28] See *The Tragedy of American Diplomacy*, by William Appleman Williams (New York: Delta Books, Dell Publishing Co., Inc., 1962).

[29] Refer to "The Hidden Costs of Federal Pensions," by Arch Patton, *Business Week*, April 27, 1974, p. 26.

[30] Gross interest on U.S. government debt was $26.3 billion in 1973. See *Survey of Current Business*, July 1974, p. 42.

[31] "On January 1, 1974, the supplemental security income program established under the Social Security Amendments of 1972 replaced the former Federal grants to State for aid to the

The last cited, AFDC, has been the subject of greatest controversy. This is despite the fact that the $7.2 billion allotted to it in 1973 paled in comparison to over $408 billion in total government expenditures that year. Nonetheless, images of sexually hyperactive, Black, and unwed mothers with numerous progeny, living off the fat of the land, continually incite the public imagination. Others have ably disposed of such myths and fantasies.[32] Our concern therefore will be with the financial aspects of AFDC and other direct relief programs.

There is little doubt that AFDC expenditures have risen substantially over the years. However, the large growth in the late 1960s has been evaluated as largely a political response to the condition of that period.[33] People who had been long entitled to benefits finally became aware that the funds were available. They mobilized to secure those benefits which were already established in law. Similarly, the increase in payments per recipient was closely related to an increased application for those which the law allowed. In addition, there were similar, if not quite as large real increases in other, but less controversial direct relief programs.

Moreover, if the bounds of generosity are supposedly strained by public assistance expenditures, then those bounds are rather narrowly defined. The average payments received by an average AFDC family have been and remain substantially below the paltry sum defined by the poverty level (see Chart 6). When compared with the programs for people who have been in the labor force, those which benefit individuals totally excluded from it are small indeed.

This is in a way strange, for there is a well-populated continuum of families with low incomes ranging above as well as below the official poverty level. However, if there is a virtual identity of income there is not the same perception of social status and role. In the eyes of those who labor long and hard at this society's onerous tasks, their meager rewards seem to be justified (if falsely) in terms of their position relative to the "others," in positive terms, as productive contributors to the society, and in negative terms, as the "just" reward for their efforts in a hierarchy of wealth, power, status, and income.[34] The validity of that perception is secured by contrast with the inferiority and poverty of those below. The prior is accomplished through the stigma of not being attached to the labor force and the latter through main-

---

aged, blind, and permanently and totally disabled. The SSI program provides for both Federal payments based upon uniform national standards and State supplementary payments, which vary from State to State." See "Early Experience Under the Supplemental Security Income Program," by James C. Callison, *Social Security Bulletin* (June 1974), pp. 3–12. At that time 1.9 million aged and 1.3 million disabled people received payments under that program.

[32] See *Blaming the Victim*, by William Ryan (New York: Vintage Books, 1971), and *Welfare Mothers Speak Out*, by the Milwaukee County Welfare Rights Organization (New York: W. W. Norton & Co., 1972).

[33] See *Regulating the Poor: The Functions of Public Welfare*, by Frances Fox Piven and Richard A. Cloward (New York: Vintage Books, 1971).

[34] Refer to *The Hidden Injuries of Class*, by Richard Sennett and Jonathan Cobb (New York: Vintage Books, 1973).

CHART 6

Typical Government Transfer Payments Compared to the Poverty Level

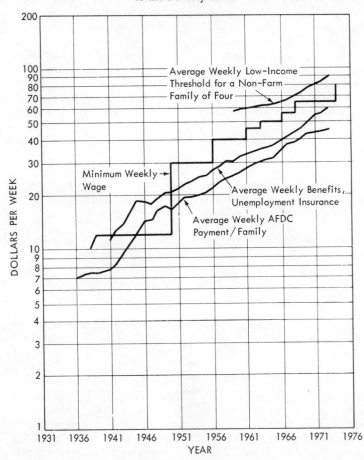

DEFINITIONS AND SOURCE: *Average weekly low-income threshold for a non-farm family of 4:* The yearly figure divided by 52; 1959–71, *Current Population Reports*, Series P-60, No. 86; 1972–73, *Current Population Reports*, Series P-60. No. 94.

Minimum weekly wage: Gross income of a worker working at the prevailing minimum wage for 40 hours per week; 1938–68, *Employment Effects of Minimum Wage Rates*, by John M. Peterson and Charles T. Stewart, Jr. (Washington, D.C.: American Enterprise Institute, August 1969); 1968–74, "The 1974 Amendments to the Federal Minimum Wage Law," by Peyton Elder, *Monthly Labor Review* (July 1974), pp. 33–37.

Average weekly benefits, unemployment insurance: 1941–55, *Historical Statistics, Colonial Times to 1957*: 1956–62, *Historical Statistics, Continuation to 1962*; 1963–64, 1966–67, *Economic Report of the President, 1973*; 1965, 1968–71, *Social Security Bulletin, Statistical Supplement, 1971*; 1972–73, *Social Security Bulletin*, July 1974.

Average weekly AFDC payment/family: The monthly figure multiplied by 12 and divided by 52; 1936–55, *Historical Statistics, Colonial Times to 1957*; 1956–62, *Historical Statistics, Continuation to 1962*; 1965, 1967–71, *Statistical Abstract of the U.S., 1972*; 1972–73, *Social Security Bulletin*, July 1974.

CHART 7

Typical Retirement Benefits Compared to Poverty Level for Retired Couple

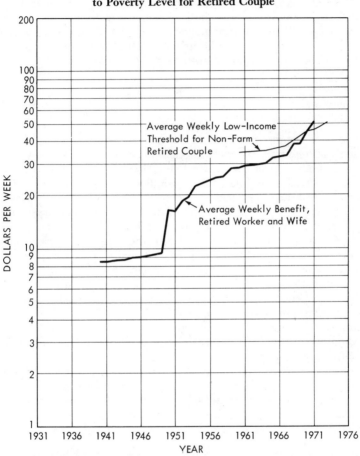

DOLLARS PER WEEK

YEAR

DEFINITIONS AND SOURCE: *Average weekly benefit, retired worker and wife:* Monthly figure multiplied by 12 and divided by 52, 1940–71, *Social Security Bulletin, Statistical Supplement, 1971.*

Average weekly low-income threshold for non-farm retired couple: Yearly figure divided by 52; 1960, 1965, *Social Security Bulletin*, April 1966; 1967, 1969, 1970, 1971, 1972, 1973, *Current Population Reports*, Series P-60, Nos. 54, 76, 81, 86, 95, and 94, respectively.

tenance of welfare levels sufficiently distant from the lower rung of incomes.

All the benefits shown in Chart 6 are below and in some cases, substantially below, the poverty level.[35] Only in recent years have the payments to retired couples edged above the line of poverty (see Chart 7). Recall that the poverty level is falling further and further below a typical worker's wages. This, in conjunction with inflation—which takes a far heavier toll of the poor than the affluent—means that for the former the welfare state is still far removed from paradise.

GOODS AND SERVICES

One might be tempted to say that this is a harsh judgment. Governments consume vast resources themselves, ostensibly to promote social well-being. The goods and services so acquired, the dominant factor in government accounts, involved an estimated $276.3 billion, 21.4 percent of the GNP in 1973. How were these resources allocated?

Although it is often believed that federal expenditures are of greatest importance, Chart 8 shows that state and local payments for goods and services dominate. Since the late 1940s, the latter have experienced a continual rise. They now far exceed those made by the federal government. However, because they draw so much attention, federal activities will be our first subject of analysis.

Military expenditures have been and remain the outstanding item in federal purchases of goods and services, accounting for about 70 percent of the total. At the present time, they represent a hefty $80 + billion. In recent years there has been a slight downtrend in percentage. Whether or not this will continue remains to be seen.

Total federal purchases of goods and services have always shown sharp increases associated with wars; there is little evidence to suggest that this may not occur again. Moreover, in face of the economic difficulties summarized by the phrase "stagflation," a resort to increased military spending is not unlikely. It is interesting to note, however, that compensation of employees

---

[35] We have not included workmen's compensation, the entirely state-run workers' disability compensation program, in Chart 7 because there is very little data available on it. We may note, however, that in 1964, a married man with two dependent children received an average of 51% of his take-home pay in states without a dependents' allowance and 73% in the 16 jurisdictions with them. Because 73% of spendable earnings for a typical worker in 1964 was about $60, this meant that average benefits for *all* such disabled workers were *below* the weekly poverty level of $60.94. Moreover, it has been observed that "despite statutory changes, the proportion of wage loss compensated . . . has fallen sharply since 1939. The deterioration in the relation of benefits was particularly acute during the postwar period, reaching a low point in the early 1950's. Since then improvements in the laws have started to catch up with economic developments. Nevertheless the evidence is that the average worker is still meeting out of his own resources the larger share of the cost of work injuries." See "Twenty-Five Years of Workmen's Compensation Statistics," by Alfred M. Skolnik, *Social Security Bulletin* (October 1966), pp. 3–26.

represents an increasingly important factor in military expenditures in contrast with the purchase of "hardware" (missiles, bombs, electronic equipment, etc.). This is partly because of the monetary incentives used to create a volunteer army. One might call it a perverted form of transfer payment, particularly for poor young people who see no opportunities other than those afforded by the armed forces.

Altogether, the cost of military and allied support services (atomic energy research, veteran's medical and hospital care, space program, etc.) amounted

CHART 8

Government Purchases of Goods and Services

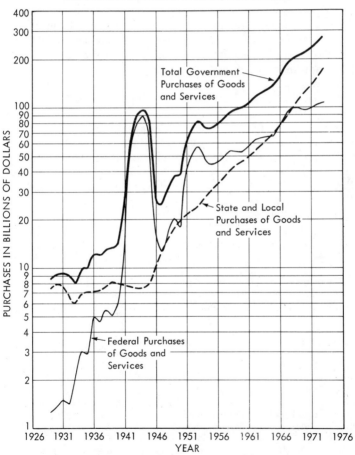

SOURCE: *National Income and Product Accounts, 1929–65* and *Survey of Current Business,* July 1973 and May 1974.

to 74.8 percent of all purchases of goods and services by the federal government. The costs of general governmental functions and the handling of foreign affairs bring the total to 84.2 percent. If to this are added the maintenance of transportation (primarily air), the subsidization of agriculture (or rather, wealthy farmers), and the small effort for conservation and development of natural resources, the total balloons to 89.3 percent.

In other words, less than 11 percent of all federal consumption is applied to what are traditionally thought of as social welfare areas: public housing, education, health, etc. These have grown rapidly in recent years, but in absolute terms are still very small.[36]

Moreover, they are tiny compared to the enormous expenditures by state and local governments, particularly for education. Education represented about 42.2. percent of all state and local purchases of goods and services; a similar fraction has been maintained over the past two decades. By far the largest amount is devoted to elementary and secondary education, nearly three-fourths of the resources. The remainder is shared between higher education (universities, colleges, and community colleges) and vocational, manpower training, rehabilitation, and related programs. The share of the former is by far the larger.[37] The latter have been stimulated in recent years by federal grants.

To the extent that funds for elementary and secondary school education are a function of the local property tax rate, [38] then the quality and character of that education would be closely correlated with family income. In that sense, this extremely important area of social welfare is not nearly as "socialized" as less important ones. With the government as an agent for collection and administration, various income groups "privatize" the benefits from their tax collections. In turn, to the extent that "success" at lower educational levels is correlated with opportunity for and potential success in (public) higher educational institutions, which are primarily supported out of general revenues, then the benefits accrue to families of higher income.[39]

[36] This figure is misleading in the sense that the federal government gives substantial sums to states in the form of grants-in-aid for highway construction, public assistance, etc. However, our analysis is based on a study of final transfers and purchases—that is, by the governments that actually make them.

[37] It has been observed, for example, that "most of the benefits of college, the costs of which come mainly from the public treasury, flow to the sons and daughters of the New Class [owners, professionals, executives, etc.]. In 1966 about $15 billion was spent on higher education. This was about half the expenditure on all elementary and secondary education in which enrollments were about nine times greater than in higher education." See *Blue Collars and Hard Hats*, by Patricia Cayo Sexton and Brendan Sexton (New York: Vintage Books, 1971), p. 176.

[38] In its recent *Rodriguez* decision, the Supreme Court upheld the use of property taxes to finance public schools. This was despite the fact that sharply unequal expenditures for students in different school districts result from that system of taxation. See "The Court of Some Resort," by Norman Dorsen, *The Civil Liberties Review*, 1, No. 2 (Winter/Spring 1974), 90.

[39] For a study showing how the affluent benefit disproportionately from the public higher education system, see "The Distribution of Costs and Direct Benefits of Public Higher Education—the Case of California," by W. L. Hansen and B. A. Weisbrod, *Journal of Human Resources*, 4 (1969), 176.

In contrast, the goods and services received by those of greatest need are smaller. It is true that the "health, education, and welfare" category of purchases has grown steadily over the years, and rather quickly in recent ones. In 1972, its principal subdivisions were: (1) health and hospitals (9.2%); (2) civilian safety—police, firemen, corrections—(8.1%); (3) sanitation (2.4%); and social security and special welfare services (8.0%).

The last group has been the source of the spurt in purchases of recent years. Though some of it may have its source in increased administrative costs, a substantial portion must be attributed to the Medicaid program as an adjunct to public assistance efforts. This does not mean an enormous bonus to AFDC recipients. In 1972, over 60 percent of Medicaid payments went to individuals who were blind, disabled, or over 65. The remainder was equally split between other adults and children under 21.[40] As a subsidy program, however, it might better be viewed as an income support program for doctors, with reports of corruption and price-gouging rife.

Nearly as much is devoted to the maintenance of "law and order" as to social security and welfare services. Police and corrections dominate the costs. Thus it appears that almost as much is devoted to the preservation of the prevailing social relations which produce pathologies as to the slight amelioration of their symptoms by public assistance.

Both of these areas, in fact, are small in comparison to the vast sums allotted to "transportation," which accounts for 13 percent of all purchases of goods and services on a state and local level. The maintenance and construction of highways far outweighs other expenditures for air and water travel. Such enormous costs reflect the long-term consequences of the extensive postwar "suburbanization" which was spurred and fed upon by the automobile, trucking, and construction industries. A corollary of this development was the debilitation of many American cities. It is ironic that substantially less should be spent on the solution of cities' troubles than on the aggravation of the conditions which helped to create them

Even the performance of general bureaucratic governmental functions rivals other expenditures, totaling 10.1 percent in 1973. The preservation of natural resources and recreation (2.5%), the support of various public utilities (2.4%), the "regulation" of commerce (1.1%), aid to agriculture (0.8%), and housing and community development (0.7%) are small by comparison.

CONCLUSION

As we warned earlier, it is easy for author and reader alike to be caught up in numbers. Charts, table, graphs, and other sorts of numerical evidence have been displayed. However, they were merely means to an end; that end was to give a sense of social welfare in the United States today.

[40] See *Programs in Aid of the Poor for the 1970's*, by Sar A. Levitan (Baltimore: The Johns Hopkins University Press, 1973).

More important than that end is what we can learn from it. Each of us can be a force in forming this society and each in turn feels the society as it affects our deepest desires and dreams. Each generation has its opportunity—in greater or lesser ways depending upon its time—to define through its actions the society it wishes to live in. A conception and practice of social welfare is thereby created.

The efforts of previous generations have yielded numerous programs to improve the general condition of our people and to ameliorate the special difficulties of the aged, ill, disabled, poor, etc. We have suggested here that as well-intentioned as those efforts may have been, they have fallen short of providing the measure of well-being and prosperity which we want our citizenry to enjoy. Rather, income is shared as inequitably as it was a quarter of a century ago. The redistributive effects of taxes have changed this picture little, if at all. Those who are excluded from full participation in this society find themselves at the bare subsistence level or below; in recent years, even the average family has found the oft-promised prosperity an elusive one except when the burden of more work is painfully accepted. In the vast area of governmental action, the enormous resources consumed for ostensibly useful purposes are wasted on dubious military ventures, find their way into the pockets of the affluent, or result in projects which do not promote the common good; little in relative terms is devoted to those who need aid the most.

We have asserted that this is a capitalistic society at root. It finds its primary motive in the pursuit of profit. It emerges through the command of a vast army of wage laborers by those who possess productive property. Their power derives from a complex pattern of relationships; but at its core is the vast concentration of wealth in productive property from which emanates control over the primary economic, social, and political institutions of our country.

We suggest that it is the failure to strike at this root that has led previous generations astray in their efforts to fulfill the highest potentials for human experience. It is our opportunity, having an understanding of the past and of the present, to fulfill our own vision of social welfare.

who rules the social services?

—*Betty Reid Mandell* *

Things fall apart; the center cannot hold . . .

William Butler Yeats
The Second Coming

The dominant ideology is the ideology of the dominant class, said Karl Marx. That is as true for the social services as for any other social institutions. People disagree about who belongs to the dominant class, and indeed the membership varies between communities. However, when one examines the background of members of the board of directors of a major hospital, college, or United Fund drive, one finds that most of them own property (business executives), serve those who own property (lawyers and political officials), or earn large salaries in a profession (doctors). Occasionally a union leader sits on a board, but hardly ever an assembly-line worker or a waitress.

One could argue that this should make little difference to the actual work of an agency, which is carried out by professionals. Yet the administrator of an agency carries the board's wishes to the workers. Agency administrators may make some policy contrary to the wishes of some board members, but the board will have to be convinced of the wisdom of it before the policy is funded. Although the focus in this chapter is on the conservatism of boards and fund raisers, I am sure there are some agencies in which the professionals are more conservative than the board. Professionals have their own jobs and agency and professional culture to protect.

The Victorian philanthropists could not envision working with the poor as equals. With precious few exceptions, the twentieth-century human service workers and their boards of directors are no different. Top-down elitism still prevails, rather than bottom-up democracy. Yet during the 1960s, people challenged the hegemony of elitists in the social services, and once the people have tasted power, the battle has been joined.

* The author is grateful to Robert Bourne for his helpful suggestions during the preparation of this chapter.

Philanthropy may be the very glue that keeps capitalism from falling apart at the seams. The economist Kenneth Boulding believes that "nonexchange" transfers of funds, such as foundation grants, are essential to the survival of American capitalism. A "grants economy" mitigates the evils of a "true exchange economy," which would be deficient in public goods and might produce such gross inequalities of income that it

> might destroy its own legitimacy, destroying the minimum sense of community and maintenance of order which is necessary to sustain exchange.[1]

In other words, if there were no charity to mask the gross inequalities of income and wealth, people might catch on to what is happening and get angry enough to change it.

When he speaks of nonexchange transfers of funds, Boulding no doubt includes governmental transfer payments, which make up the vast bulk of philanthropy, even though private giving amounts to the considerable sum of over $22.5 billion a year.[2] Public philanthropy is ruled by the people who rule the government.[3] I shall deal here mainly with private philanthropy. I shall argue that much of private philanthropy is dominated by corporate

[1] Kenneth Boulding, "Toward a Pure Theory of Foundations," unpublished paper prepared for the Kettering Foundation, cited by Waldemar A. Nielsen, *The Big Foundations* (New York: Columbia University Press, 1972), p. 402.

[2] See Larry Beeferman's article in this book for a discussion of governmental transfer payments. The following table shows the amounts and the sources of private philanthropy.

TABLE 1

Private Philanthropy
(in millions of dollars)

	1960	1965	1970	1972
Total	8,912	12,210	19,300	22,680
Individuals	7,150	9,276	14,400	16,910
Foundations	710	1,125	1,900	2,200
Business corporations	482	785	800	840
Charitable bequests	570	1,024	2,200	2,730
By allocation:				
Religion	4,545	5,983	8,300	9,750
Education	1,426	2,076	3,050	3,570
Human resources (welfare)	1,337	885	1,370	1,610
Health	1,070	2,076	3,140	3,680
Civic and cultural activities	{ 534	488	1,180	1,540
Foundations and other	{	732	2,260	2,530

SOURCE: *Giving USA*, American Association of Fund Raising Counsel, Inc., New York, 1972.

[3] For a discussion of political and corporate control of the AFDC (Aid to Families of Dependent Children) program, see Frances Fox Piven and Richard Cloward, *Regulating the Poor* (New York: Random House, 1972).

elites, and that this generally sets conservative limits to the kinds of services that institutions give.[4]

Boulding's theory about the function of philanthropy gets sociological support from Aileen Ross, who has studied philanthropy extensively. She describes philanthropy as the reflection of a class society because it depends on the division between rich givers and poor recipients. Even when the poor themselves give, they make up the largest proportion of recipients.

> The wealthy have not only given because they have more but because, by alleviating distress, they have secured their own positions against those who might displace them and thus have avoided revolt.[5]

Corporations agree that philanthropy helps to create the good will that they need to continue making profits.[6] The stockholders sometimes may prefer to have the money returned to them in dividends, but corporate management is jealous of its right to give without consulting anyone. In 1953 a group of stockholders of the A. P. Smith Manufacturing Company brought a friendly suit against the company because of its gift of $1,500 to Princeton University. The New Jersey Supreme Court, ruling for the corporation, gave an opinion quite similar to Boulding and Ross's:

> Modern conditions require that corporations acknowledge and discharge social as well as private responsibilities as members of the communities in which they operate. . . . Indeed, the matter may be viewed strictly in terms of actual survival of the corporation in a free enterprise system.[7]

Beyond building those assets of good will, some corporation executives have that "frantic fear of 'creeping socialism' that gripped American business leaders in the postwar years." [8] After Truman's upset of Dewey in 1948, corporation philanthropy stepped up.

> The years 1945–1964 witnessed much heated talk on the part of businessmen about the virtues of "free enterprise" and much concern for the "corporate image." [9]

A good deal of corporate giving is to conservative and right-wing institutions that disseminate propaganda supporting the free enterprise system. Harding College in Searcy, Arkansas, which serves as a propaganda machine for ultraconservative causes, has been generously supported by corporations. Alan Westin, professor of law and government at Columbia University,

---

[4] I define social welfare services broadly, including hospitals and colleges as well as agencies staffed primarily by social workers, such as family service and child welfare agencies and settlement houses.

[5] Aileen D. Ross, "Philanthropy," in *International Encyclopedia of the Social Sciences*, David L. Sills, ed., Vol. 12 (New York: The Macmillan Company and The Free Press, 1968), p. 78.

[6] Scott M. Cutlip, *Fund Raising in the United States* (New Brunswick, N.J.: Rutgers University Press, 1965), p. 513.

[7] Ibid., p. 514, citing A. P. Smith Manufacturing Co. v. Barlow et al., 98 Atlantic Reporter, 2d 581 (1953).

[8] Ibid., p. 515.

[9] Ibid.

estimated that the business community contributed nearly $10 million to the Radical Right in 1961.[10]

As the organization of business in America has changed, so has the organization of philanthropy. Religious institutions and wealthy individuals dominated large-scale philanthropy in the nineteenth and early twentieth century, but now corporations dominate private philanthropy. Family name is no longer a crucial requirement, but important business connections are essential.

In terms of actual amounts given, corporate giving makes up a relatively small share of private philanthropy.[11] Most of the money comes from individuals, including the money they put in church collection plates (see Table 1). Furthermore, corporations gave only a fraction of what the law allows them to deduct.[12] And, beginning in the 1950s, an increasingly large share of corporate giving has gone to higher education, with less to community chests and health agencies.[13] The reason for this is that

> the corporation has a strong self-interest in providing a flow of well-trained, highly educated employees to meet its operating needs.[14]

Some businessmen are concerned about the dangers of eroding good will if corporations do not give more generously. The Peterson Commission, headed by the (then) president of Bell and Howell, urged corporations to form consortiums for collective philanthropy, to counteract the "tyranny of the small decision," that psychological process involved when a single individual or corporation refuses to give in the belief that one contribution can make little difference. The commission reminds businessmen that corporations have long known how to band together when their narrow self-interests are concerned.

> In a society in which education, health facilities, and social services generally are beset by precipitously mounting costs, the long-run dangers to the business community may be far greater than the threats against which firms have stood together in the past.[15]

[10] Donald Janson and Bernard Eisman, *The Far Right* (New York: McGraw-Hill, 1963), p. 92.

[11] The corporate share of philanthropy in the mid-60s was estimated to amount to about 4 to 5 percent of private philanthropy. Larger corporations contribute a smaller proportion of their net income than do smaller corporations. Of 46 percent of tax returns reporting annual incomes in excess of $250,000, deductions for contributions were less than 2 percent of income. (Willard L. Thorp, "The Poor Law Revisited," in *Philanthropy and Public Policy*, Frank G. Dickinson, ed. (New York: National Bureau of Economic Research, 1962), p. 133.)

[12] In 1970 corporations, which were allowed to deduct up to 5 percent of corporate profits, gave only a little more than 1 percent of profits. Individuals were more generous; those who itemized deductions contributed as much as 4 percent of adjusted gross income. (Commission on Foundations and Private Philanthropy, *Foundations, Private Giving, and Public Policy* (Chicago: University of Chicago Press, 1970), p. 277).

[13] A survey by the Russell Sage Foundation of corporate giving, covering 326 corporations, showed that 16 percent went to education in 1950, as compared to 39 percent in 1959. In 1950, 70 percent of corporate giving went to health and welfare, as compared to 45 percent in 1959. (Cutlip, *Fund Raising in the United States*, p. 512.) Support of education nearly trebled its share of corporate giving between 1955 and 1965. (*Foundations, Private Giving, and Public Policy*, p. 264.)

[14] Cutlip, *Fund Raising*, p. 519.

[15] *Foundations, Private Giving, and Public Policy*, p. 277.

It is easy for corporations to see their self-interest allied with higher education, because colleges and universities train their personnel. Irving S. Olds, former chairman of United States Steel, envisions a further ideological function for the college beyond turning out trained employees:

> Capitalism and free enterprise owe their survival to our private independent colleges. Just as private industry has given us material weapons with which to repel the armies of foreign aggressors, so we have looked to our privately endowed education for the intellectual weapons to resist invastion by totalitarian ideologies.[16]

As can be seen from Table 1, total philanthropic support for education rose sharply between 1960 and 1970, but increased much less between 1970 and 1972. In the absence of hard data, one can only speculate about the reasons for this. College administrators are fond of blaming it on the radical students. David Packard, chairman of the Hewlitt-Packard Company and a former Deputy Secretary of Defense, advised corporations not to make unrestricted gifts to private education. He said,

> Almost every board of trustees must have its members selected from a wide array of constituents—students, faculty, alumni, various ethnic groups,

and these people cannot be counted on to spend the money in ways the corporation can defend to its stockholders.[17] Because contributions to higher education have increased recently,[18] most corporations apparently do not share Mr. Packard's alarm over the alleged egalitarian thrust. Corporation executives are no doubt aware of the token nature of the participation of a "wide array of constituents" on boards of trustees.

Because of their concern for adverse publicity, corporations and corporate foundations seldom give grants to individuals, but contribute to institutions, projects, and causes. They channel their money "through noncontroversial agencies which would presumably be approved by the overwhelming majority of the stockholders."[19] Apropos of this conservatism, Thorp asks, "Why is so much money going into medical research and so little into racial problems?"[20] A summary of the 1962 conference where Thorp asked the question revealed the low level of thinking about "the Negro problem" among the assembled philanthropists:

> The migration to the city by the Negro poses problems that are, of course, different from those of earlier migrations. For example, the Irish were eager to own property and the Italians and Jews were ambitious to have their children educated. . . . Should a special effort be made to instruct Negroes about the dangers of going into debt?[21]

---

[16] Cutlip, *Fund Raising*, p. 519.

[17] *The New York Times*, October 21, 1973.

[18] Roger Ricklefs, "Selling Business on Giving to Colleges," *Change*, September 1974, pp. 13–15.

[19] Thorp, "Poor Law Revisited," p. 135.

[20] Ibid., p. 143.

[21] Frank G. Dickinson, "Highlights of the Conference," in *Philanthropy and Public Policy*, Frank G. Dickinson, ed. (New York: National Bureau of Economic Research, 1962), p. 123.

It is probably a safe bet that there were no Black people at the conference, since the commission's stereotyped thinking apparently went unchecked.

Although corporations do not contribute as much to philanthropy as do private individuals, corporate executives exert control over philanthropy that is out of proportion to the amount of their financial contributions. The first step in their control comes through their fund raising.

THE FUND RAISERS

Green turtle soup was a predictable feature of Victorian charity dinners in nineteenth-century London. One hundred years later, the New York City charity dinner might be a pasta bash at the 58th Street Spaghetti and Macaroni Factoria, after the opening night concert of the New York Philharmonic, to benefit the Girls' and Boys' Service League. It might also be a vernissage with champagne, or an around-Manhattan cruise with rock music and victuals. Among the over 300 charity events in a full-page *New York Times* listing for the 1973–74 season were

—A benefit at the Plaza that combined a dinner dance for Project Hope with presentation of the second Hope award for international understanding to Dr. Henry A. Kissinger.

—A Day at the Races at Belmont Park to aid the Mental Health Association of Nassau County.

—A Fox Hounds Hunt Race Meeting at Far Hills, N.J., to benefit the Somerville Hospital.

—The twentieth annual art and antique auction preceded by a champagne supper to aid Irvington House, both at Sotheby Parke-Bernet Galleries, Inc.

—Annual Waif Ball to aid the Adoption Division, International Social Service, at the Plaza.

—Big E for Epilepsy luncheon at the Americana.

—Fashion show and bridge party to benefit Little Sisters of the Assumption, Grand Ballroom, Plaza.

But the real money comes from the $1,000 pledge luncheons of the Women's Division of the United Jewish Appeal, from the Diamond Ball, and, yes, from Claude Philippe's April in Paris gala.[22]

A *Boston Globe* columnist comments that

Judging by the number of benefit events, you might think the capitalist system has broken down completely. It looks as if the rich, in Robin Hood fashion, are robbing themselves to help the poor. But, it really doesn't work that way. As one person said: "I dread to think what would happen to us if the income tax laws were amended.[23]

[22] Russell Edwards, "Private Charities Take Up the Slack," *The New York Times*, September 16, 1973, p. 68.

[23] Alison Arnold, "Not all benefits alike," January 25, 1974. Courtesy of *The Boston Globe*.

The columnist goes on to discuss the prestige involved in working for a charity. While many people are genuinely concerned with the less fortunate, there are also many others

> who join the charity circuit to gain prominence for themselves. For them, choosing the "right" charity is a serious problem.[24]

The "right" charities, supported by the "older families" in Boston, include the Symphony Orchestra, the Ellis Memorial Settlement House, Massachusetts General Hospital, and Vincent Memorial Hospital—the project of Boston's exclusive Vincent Club. In New York, the charities supported by the social set include the New York Foundling Hospital and the Lighthouse for the Blind. In Chicago the "social" charity is the Passavant Hospital.

> They are all sought after by newcomers who hope to climb the social ladder.[25]

The leisured wives and daughters of the rich volunteer an enormous amount of time to sponsor charitable benefits and to serve on boards of trustees of charitable agencies. Some women spend so much time on fund raising that they consider it a career. Women subtly initiate their children into their future philanthropic roles, and reinforce the training in such associations as the Junior League, the top social club for young North American women, where practical training is given for leading roles in voluntary agencies.[26] Women on boards and as canvassers comprise a small inner circle that controls decision making. Ross' study of women active in charitable causes showed that few of the women conceived of charity as preventive, but rather as a patch-up service for the destitute, starving, homeless, indigent, and old people.

> They also thought that they had the right to maintain their own controlling position in philanthropy in the city, and that the lower strata must fit into this pattern. One of the important functions of philanthropy in this respect was to keep workers "happy and contented" so they would not question this hierarchy.[27]

They feared that "their way of life" was being threatened by the lower classes, and feared too that their position of authority in philanthropy was being threatened by professional social workers.[28]

The husbands and fathers of these women serve on boards of trustees of social agencies, as founders and trustees of philanthropic foundations, and as fund raisers and directors of United Fund drives. These are time-consuming activities. A *Fortune* article said that most top-echelon business executives spend from five to fifteen hours a week raising money for "worthy causes"—universities, churches and synagogues, hospitals, civic and cultural

---

[24] Ibid.

[25] Ibid.

[26] Ross, "Philanthropy," p. 78.

[27] Aileen Ross, "Control and Leadership in Women's Groups: An Analysis of Philanthropic Money-Raising Activity," *Social Forces*, 37, No. 2 (December 1958), 124–25.

[28] Ibid., p. 125.

organizations, and social welfare organizations. One person estimated that the executive time spent on philanthropic activities was worth up to $5 billion a year.[29]

> Only the chief, and not his Indians, can carry out the critical fund-raising function. But it is not uncommon for the chief executive of a corporation to groom an understudy in the art. And most of today's rising young executives aspire to the apprenticeship.[30]

Philanthropic activity is important to a businessman's career advancement, as Ross pointed out.[31] At the bottom rung of the philanthropic career ladder is the door-to-door canvasser. From there the businessman works up to team captain, divisional captain, a low position on the executive committee, vice-chairman, and finally chairman. Then he is put on the Special Names committee, composed solely of influential businessmen who canvass the largest individual and corporation subscribers. Eventually he may become chairman of that committee, "which is the pinnacle of campaign positions." [32]

The man in charge of a city's United Fund drive is always one of that city's most successful businessmen. His advancement in business parallels his success as a fund raiser. Success in fund raising "will mean that other positions of importance in the community will open out to him . . ." [33]

A fund raiser is chosen by an "inner circle" of important businessmen, and the inner circle perpetuates itself. These men participate in philanthropy partly because it is an important part of public relations for businesses. As one general manager of a bank said,

> We *have* to do it—the competition between banks is so great. So we are all trained to take community responsibility. We expect to see the result of it somewhere in our balance sheet! [34]

In fact, says Ross, "participation in the large citywide campaigns now gives a man and his firm more publicity than many of the usual advertising channels." [35]

Businessmen also participate in philanthropy to make contacts that will be of business or social use. Furthermore, philanthropy serves as important training in salesmanship, and provides a way to test a man's ability. And finally, philanthropy can be written off as a tax deduction.

The United Fund drive was begun by big business, and has been run mainly by big business since. The first United Fund drive was in Detroit in

[29] Robert Sheehan, "Pay to the Order of Those Fund-Raising Businessmen: Eight Billion Dollars," *Fortune*, January, 1966, p. 149.

[30] Ibid., p. 182.

[31] Aileen Ross, "Philanthropic Activity and the Business Career," in Mayer N. Zald, ed., *Social Welfare Institutions* (New York: John Wiley & Sons, 1965), pp. 341–52.

[32] Ibid., p. 342.

[33] Ibid., p. 342.

[34] Ibid., p. 346.

[35] Ibid., p. 352.

1949, organized by Henry Ford II, with the concurrence of Walter Reuther, then president of the United Auto Workers. It was organized in response to the annoyance of businessmen and labor leaders at the number of campaigns they were asked to conduct in their plants. The name was changed from Community Chest to United Fund.[36] Despite the participation of organized labor in the United Fund concept, labor representatives do not get the same prestige from participating in the drive as do businessmen. While a business executive gains status from participating in philanthropy, and is probably given time off for it,

> A labor leader's contribution, however, must often come during his leisure time; organized labor favors government programs instead of private philanthropy in so many of these areas.[37]

Probably one reason that many workers are disenchanted with the United Fund is that they are subjected to so much pressure at their work place to contribute. Many of them regard it as similar to a compulsory tax, since contributions are sometimes exacted through payroll deductions. Recently the United Teachers of New Orleans (American Federation of Teachers) protested pressure being put on teachers to contribute to the United Fund. At one school, the principal sent teachers who did not contribute a letter pointing out that the school had a contribution "quota," and that failure to contribute "could reflect in your overall evaluation as a member of the staff." In another school, the principal sent a letter to teachers urging them to contribute, indicating that a carbon copy would be placed in each teacher's file.[38]

The largest share of money collected by United Fund drives comes from workers. In 1970 in Boston, for example, 50 percent of funds collected came from working people; 27 percent from businesses, and 23 percent from high-income individuals.[39] In private welfare as in public, it seems that the workers carry the lion's share of the burden for their own social services.

THE FUND ALLOCATORS

Funds for social service agencies come from several sources. Public agencies are of course supported entirely by public tax funds. Private agencies have been supported traditionally by voluntary private contributions, including foundation grants and allocations from United Fund drives. Private agencies are, however, increasingly supported by public funds, usually given on a contract basis. A survey of fifty-one Chicago philanthropic organizations

[36] Cutlip, *Fund Raising*, p. 496, citing Position Paper presented by E. V. Graef, Executive Director, Pittsburgh Health and Research Services Foundation, January 29, 1959.

[37] Dickinson, "Highlights of the Conference," p. 120.

[38] *American Teacher*, 58, No. 5, January 1974.

[39] Boston United Black Appeal flyer, undated.

showed that the median proportion of government funds to total budget was 23 percent in 1968, as compared to 7 percent in 1963. Fourteen percent of their funds came from user fees and 63 percent came from private sources. Ninety-four percent of them received some foundation grants, and these comprised a median of 10 percent of their funding.[40] Sectarian child welfare agencies often get over 50 percent of their funds from the public welfare department. Beck points out that as funds for voluntary agencies became scarce, "they redefined their role and became managers of public money." [41]

Another kind of "private" agency is what Alan Pifer called the "quasi-nongovernmental agency" [42]—that is, an agency incorporated on a nonprofit basis but entirely or almost entirely dependent on governmental funds. One example is Mobilization for Youth in New York City's Lower East Side. Other examples, outside the social welfare sphere, are the Rand "think tank" and agencies doing research for the Atomic Energy Commission and National Aeronautics and Space Administration.

Public funds are allocated and administered through a political process that varies according to who holds the public purse strings. The power struggles at the University of Texas provide an interesting example of how the political process shapes a public university. This struggle was between the educational elites and the corporate and political elites. The dominant corporate and political interests wanted the university to emphasize graduate education and research which would serve the corporations. Stephen Spurr, the president of the Austin branch, said that universities are "in every sense big business," [43] and that he intended to make University of Texas "*the* major complex research university in the southern half of the United States." [44] The cast of characters who agreed with this philosophy included Frank Erwin, chairman of the Board of Regents, who was also state chairman of the Democratic Party during the reign of President Lyndon Johnson, and John Connally, governor of Texas.

Representing the educational elites were Harry Ransom, chancellor of the University of Texas, and John Silber, then dean of the College of Arts and Sciences at the Austin campus.

> Ransom and Silber arrive on the scene with the usual commitment to notions of "excellence" and the "great university," and pursue their program through the usual means—purges of the departments, foundation grants, and control of the budget. The inevitable tragic flaw is manifested in their commitment to general education. Silber goes so far as to encourage faculty promotions on the basis of good teaching. The result is a foregone conclusion: the dean of the graduate faculty teams up with Erwin, and Silber is fired; Ransom retires.[45]

[40] *Foundations, Private Giving, and Public Policy*, p. 231.

[41] Bertram Beck, "The Voluntary Social Welfare Agency: A Reassessment," *Social Service Review*, 44, No. 2 (June 1970), 147.

[42] *Annual Report*, Carnegie Corporation of New York, 1967.

[43] Michael W. Miles, "Texas Wranglers," a review of Ronnie Dugger, *Our Invaded Universities: Form, Reform, and New Starts* (New York: W. W. Norton, 1974), in *Change* (April 1974), p. 60.

[44] Ibid.

[45] Ibid.

The Silber-Erwin struggle was a fight between two elites. It did not involve a grass-roots challenge from the students, or from the ordinary citizens of the state regarding how *they* would choose to define the university's function. In his function as president of Boston University, John Silber showed little interest in soliciting the opinions of students or faculty when he brought back Marine recruiters whom students had ousted at the height of their anti-war activity, or when he raised tuition, or when he cut back on faculty and faculty tenure. Neither does he show any concern about the citizens of the state getting a low-cost tax-supported college education, since he is an outspoken advocate of raising tuition at public colleges.

The grass-roots challenges are probably the most threatening of all to those who hold power, because such challenges question the very legitimacy of top-down authority. They make the statement that institutions should be governed by the people whom those institutions are designed to serve. Some institutions are more responsive to those challenges than others. The values and goals of an institution help to shape the actions of its board and administrators. Bryn Mawr, for example, has a long tradition of Quaker pacifism and social concern. One of Bryn Mawr's trustees served as counsel to a Black student who was investigated by the FBI after attending a conference of Black students.[46] Despite a good amount of institutional racism ("benign bigotry," as one alumna described it), it has responded to pressure from civil rights, feminist, and anti-war activists. The trustees of Bryn Mawr supported the school's refusal in 1970 to sign the Pennsylvania Higher Education Assistance Act. Later declared unconstitutional, this act made the reporting of disruptive students mandatory if schools were to receive state aid for scholarships and loans. Furthermore, alumnae have attended corporate meetings to vote against the college holding stock in corporations in South Africa, war-related industries, and corporations that discriminate against minorities and women.[47]

The source of an agency's funding profoundly influences the nature of that agency's work. "Those who control the purse control the program." [48] The more autonomous an agency is in its funding sources, the freer it is to take militant action, as Simmons showed in his comparison of the NAACP and the Urban League. The NAACP gets its funds from membership fees, gifts, and various fund-raising devices. The six Urban League affiliates studied receive 80 percent or more of their total budgets from the local United Appeal or Community Chest. Board members of the NAACP showed no discrepancy between their personal preferences in strategy and their choices as board members. When asked to respond to a hypothetical situation involving an unresponsive landlord of slum property, NAACP respondents favored organizing rent strikes, both as private citizens and as board members. Urban League board members, on the other hand, said that as

[46] Catharine R. Stimson, "Women at Bryn Mawr," *Change* (April 1974), p. 28.
[47] Ibid.
[48] Beck, "The Voluntary Social Welfare Agency," p. 150.

private citizens they would choose coercive courses that would involve confrontation, but as board members they would choose courses directed at attitude change and not likely to draw retaliatory action.[49] As an example of the constraints on United Fund agencies, when the Urban League in Fort Wayne, Indiana supported an eight-day school boycott, a group called Truth About Civil Turmoil conducted a door-to-door campaign to discourage United Fund contributions because 2.5 percent of them went to the Urban League.[50]

"Traditionally United Funds and Community Chests have concentrated the great bulk of their resources in the hands of old-line service agencies." [51] Their executive directors, most of whom are men, prefer conciliation to confrontation. A study of 268 United Fund executives showed them to be against becoming politically involved or even revealing their political affiliation. "They might have indulged in çontest or conflict tactics on occasion, but generally a United Fund must unite the community behind the one big annual campaign effort." [52] They did not want their agencies to make major program shifts that would entail added ongoing expenditures or new supplementary fund-raising campaigns without prior clearance. More executives were Republican than Democrat (32 percent to 26 percent, with 32 percent independents). Adams hypothesized that because most United Fund lay leaders, who hire and fire the directors, are business leaders and most business leaders are Republicans, the executives identify with the business leaders in politics as in other things. Some executives proclaimed themselves fund raisers, not social workers, even when they had been trained as social workers.[53]

Because of the broad-based nature of a United Fund, an agency that does something not broadly acceptable is likely to be in trouble with someone.

In Philadelphia, for example, policemen threatened not to contribute to the United Fund because part of the money was allocated to supporting Legal Aid Society activities they considered inimical to police interests.[54]

The Boston Florence Crittendon Home, formerly only a prenatal residence, opened a clinic to perform abortions in 1972. In the process of making the shift, it encountered a good deal of resistance from some board members and some sectors of the community. United Community Services, the centralized funding agency, withheld funds from the Crittendon Home when it announced plans to perform abortions. The Massachusetts Civil Liberties

[49] Leonard C. Simmons, "Agency Financing and Social Change," *Social Work*, 17, No. 1 (January 1972), 65.

[50] Ibid., citing "Indiana Rights Group Opposes United Fund," *Washington Post*, September 26, 1969, p. A18.

[51] Dexter Eure, "United Fund vs. the Blacks," *Boston Globe*, November 17, 1970.

[52] Dwight S. Adams, "Fund Executives and Social Change: a Study," *Social Work*, 17, No. 1 (January 1972), 72.

[53] Ibid., pp. 69–70.

[54] Simmons, "Agency Financing," p. 64, citing "Institutional Charity Is Meeting Unrest in Nation Over Middle-Class Goals," *The New York Times*, November 3, 1969, p. 50.

Union fought the UCS action by urging people to earmark their contributions to the Crittendon Home. As a result, the Crittendon Home received more money than it would have with UCS funding.

United Funds in many cities were faced with a major challenge from Black communities in the late 1960s and early 70s. Leaders in these communities charged the United Fund with being unresponsive to the poor in the inner cities, especially non-Whites. These challenges were made in Boston, Tampa, Kansas City, Cleveland, San Francisco, Detroit, and St. Louis. In Boston the New Urban League led a demonstration at the United Fund's annual awards luncheon, collecting scraps from the meal and then dumping them on the head table to dramatize the Blacks' contention that they were only receiving "crumbs." In every case, an analysis of how funds were allocated showed the challengers to be correct.

> Of the $14.2 million collected in 1969, only about $1.3 million found its way to agencies serving the inner city. Even that figure is misleading, since $800,000 of it represents the activity of area-wide groups like the Salvation Army. Only about $500,000 found its way to indigenous organizations in Boston's non-white community, a figure that is totally out of proportion to demonstrated needs.[55]

The Blacks argued that because the inner city ranks first on the priority list, at least 20 percent of the United Fund money should go directly to it. They argued, further, that the money should funnel through those who live in the community. If the United Fund can give money directly to such groups as Combined Jewish Philanthropies, the Salvation Army, and the Red Cross, it can make the same arrangement with the Black community. The Boston United Black Appeal said, in a flyer to the public:

> Who needs your United Fund $ more? Boy Scouts of America or low-income housing in Roxbury? A YMCA, a community center, a hospital in Newton or a community health clinic in the South End? Campfire Girls of the Greater Boston Area or organizers of underpaid hospital workers? . . . The United Fund gives over $550,000 to high-income communities like Newton, while denying requests from agencies in low-income areas.[56]

Because the United Fund authorities were unresponsive to this challenge, eight Black community groups initiated their own United Black Appeal with a goal of $4 million.

A few months after the New Urban League challenge in Boston, one hardy soul rose at the annual meeting of the Combined Jewish Philanthropies to ask why the perfunctory nominations for officers were not the subject of open debate at a separate meeting.

> He wanted to know why the agency's leaders had to steamroll through their election choices. He was ignored, of course. The general audience was hardly with him, and one man, engaging in an extraordinary bit of black humor considering

[55] Eure, "United Fund vs. The Blacks."
[56] Boston United Black Appeal flyer, undated.

the times, suggested loudly to his tablemates that the man raising the ruckus about democratic process "must be an Arab." [57]

The speaker of the evening, Brandeis professor Leonard Fein, asked the audience to consider whether "ritual elections and government by the well-to-do is still appropriate." Levey points out that

> charities designed to help the poor can become cloistered clubs for the rich. In fact, there has been considerable self-delusion across the board based on the thinking that most institutions in the high-powered American democracy took their lead from the Constitution and the Bill of Rights.[58]

An outstanding Boston example of someone described both as a "great philanthropist" and a "slumlord" was the late Maurice Gordon. Mr. Gordon gave a men's dormitory and a $100,000 music scholarship to Brandeis and a building wing to Emmanuel College. In 1968, reacting to student charges that he was a slumlord, Mr. Gordon withdrew a gift of $500,000 for a new building for the Boston University School of Nursing.

> His real estate holdings, which once included 14,000 apartment rental units in Boston and another $15 million in property in Miami, were best known for building code violations and two serious fires, which claimed three lives in 1963 and eight in March 1971. . . .

> Mr. Gordon's affiliations with schools, hospitals, and religious and philanthropic organizations were legion.[59]

THE FOUNDATIONS

Guess who the Ford Foundation gave its first grant to?

The poor? Guess again.

Working people? No. Try again.

Middle-class people? Wrong again.

They gave it to millionaires—themselves. When the Ford Foundation was first founded, the Ford lawyers arranged to have the inheritance taxes on the Ford shares paid out of the Foundation shares as its first philanthropy! [60]

Horowitz and Kolodney document that charitable foundations were begun as a result of threats of antitrust actions and heavy income and inheritance taxes to family fortunes. They argue that the bulk of the foundations' overseas efforts have been to protect the interests of American corporations, and that foundations have initiated and financed research institutes to shape legislation protective of business.[61]

---

[57] Robert L. Levey, "What Price Philanthropy?" *Boston Globe*, September 19, 1970.

[58] Ibid.

[59] "Maurice Gordon, 68, major Boston landlord," obituary section, *Boston Globe*, November 6, 1973.

[60] David Horowitz with David Kolodney, "The Foundations: Charity Begins at Home," in *The Poverty Establishment*, Pamela Roby, ed. (Englewood Cliffs, N.J.: Prentice-Hall, Inc., 1974), p. 48.

[61] Ibid., pp. 43–59.

The income of the 596 largest tax-exempt foundations is more than twice the net earnings of the nation's 50 largest commercial banks.[62] The Ford Foundation, largest of all the foundations, has assets exceeding $3 billion, four times the assets of the Rockefeller Foundation (next largest), and more than the gross national product of Cuba. Is annual income from securities is $150 million.[63]

Foundations proliferate in the United States as in no other country in the world. The mushrooming growth of foundations since the 30s, and especially since World War II, is a uniquely American phenomenon, spurred by federal tax policy. Most European governments oppose tax exempt foundations and

> large industrial corporations are likely to have committees of workers sitting with management, and these labor representatives are zealous about seeing that company workers, instead of society at large, are the main beneficiaries of any generous impulses.[64]

In 1971, foundations had $25 billion in assets, and over $1.5 billion annual expenditures.[65] In 1971, there were 5,454 foundations with assets over $500,000 and about 21,000 with assets under $500,000. [66] Nearly half of all corporations with 1,000 or more employees have operating foundations or trusts to handle their philanthropies.[67] The boards of foundations are made up of the American business elite. They consist

> largely of businessmen, lawyers, or bankers, educated in eastern Ivy League schools, white, and Protestant. There is scant representation of the young, women, Blacks, Catholics, and Jews and none from organized labor.[68]

Of the liberal boards, "none goes so far as to include a known Socialist." [69]

Much of the writing on foundations done by businessmen or their representatives lauds the foundation as an instrument for reform and innovation and a bulwark against further state intrusion into the welfare sector. When they express unease about whether or not foundations are fulfilling their expressed functions, their proposals for reform are generally for greater professionalism and managerial expertise among foundation executives instead of the present system of relying on the corporation's public relations department. One author argues for new departures in the direction of foundation giving, and one of his "radical" suggestions is to study ways to contain labor's "outmoded and socially intolerable policy of strikes and confrontations. . . ." [70] He does not, of course, argue for a radical redistribu-

[62] Ibid., p. 43.

[63] Ibid., p. 47.

[64] *Foundations, Private Giving, and Public Policy*, p. 53.

[65] Arnold J. Zurcher, *The Management of American Foundations: Administration, Policies, and Social Role* (New York: New York University Press, 1972), p. 163.

[66] *The Foundation Directory, Edition 4* (New York: The Foundation Center, 1971).

[67] Cutlip, *Fund Raising*, pp. 510–11.

[68] *Foundations, Private Giving, and Public Policy*, pp. 137–38.

[69] Waldemar A. Nielsen, *The Big Foundations* (New York: Columbia University Press, 1972), p. 408.

[70] Zurcher, *Management of American Foundations*, p. 170.

tion of wealth and power, and he opposes the government taking over the functions of foundations because foundations are more "impartial" than the government.

One lone—and, I suspect, embattled—labor voice speaks out in the many books on foundations to challenge the businessmen's claims that foundations are a major instrument of reform and innovation. At a conference of the Peterson Commission on Foundations and Private Philanthropy, Commission Member Lane Kirkland, secretary-treasurer of the AFL-CIO, said that the commission had presented no conclusive evidence that foundations

> can be one of our preeminent institutions of reform. . . . Depending on their orientation, it is equally true that foundations could be one of our preeminent institutions of reaction. What has either necessarily to do with "charity" per se, in the general understanding of that term? [71]

A majority of the Commission recommended "new and better tax incentives." Mr. Kirkland opposed this, saying,

> While I believe the "democratization" of philanthropic giving is an appropriate goal, I would be suspicious of new tax incentives as a means to that end. [72]

Mr. Kirkland wondered whether all the tax-deducted corporation money given to higher education would have been better used in the public interest by charging corporations higher taxes to support elementary and secondary education.

Mr. Kirkland was hitting a raw corporate nerve when he opposed tax incentives. The year before the conference at which he delivered his dissenting opinion, the Tax Reform Act of 1969 exacted more taxes from foundations—a 4 percent tax on net investment income—and set limits on foundation ownership of a controlling interest in the business. Usually stock holdings in excess of 20 percent were prohibited. Foundations were also required to make a minimum annual payout for charitable purposes, either equal to net income or 6 percent of the market value of assets, whichever is higher. Further, they were prohibited from attempting to influence legislation or influence an election, which included most voter registration. [73] This Act was passed partly as a result of the investigations of Representative Wright Patman's House Banking Committee, begun in 1962. Prior to the 1969 Tax Reform Act, grants paid out by the fifteen largest foundations averaged only 57 percent of gross receipts. Forty-three percent of their income was used either for administrative expense or added to the corpus. [74]

On the basis of his study of foundation giving, Nielsen concluded that foundations not only do not produce social change, but "are in fact overwhelmingly passive, conservative, and anchored to the status quo. They are agents of continuity, not change." [75] Most foundation giving seems to be

[71] *Foundations, Private Giving, and Public Policy*, p. 178.
[72] Ibid., p. 179.
[73] *Foundations, Private Giving, and Public Policy*, p. 53.
[74] Nielsen, *The Big Foundations*, pp. 403–404.
[75] Ibid., p. 406.

an extension of the individual giving patterns of the directors. "The dominant qualities of foundation grant-making are prudence, civility, and discretion rather than an eagerness to expose themselves to controversy." [76]

TABLE 2

Foundation Grants 1971

Education	32%
Welfare	16%
Health	15%
Sciences	10%
International activities	10%
Humanities	10%
Religion	7%

SOURCE: *Giving USA*, American Association of Fund Raising Counsel, Inc., New York, 1972. Reprinted from Commission on Foundations and Private Philanthropy, *Foundations, Giving, and Public Policy* (Chicago: The University of Chicago Press, 1970), p. 83.

Over 90 percent of foundation grants go to governmentally certified charitable organizations.[77] The largest proportion goes to higher education, as can be seen in Table 2.

When asked what percentage of their grants could be "considered controversial by some" between 1966 and 1968, foundation executives responded as follows to a survey:

Voter registration	0.1
Studies of subjects directly related to public policy issues, dissemination of information	0.3
Community or neighborhood organizing of an ethnic ghetto, or impoverished group	1.5
Birth control	0.9
Sex education	less than 0.05
Urban youth groups (including gangs)	1.3
Student organizations	0.8

"Foundation involvement in this realm amounted only to a 'hail and farewell.' " [78] Even the Ford Foundation, a leader in "socially relevant" projects, had spent a total of only $440,000 for grants for voter registration

[76] Ibid., p. 414.
[77] Ibid., p. 400.
[78] *Foundations, Private Giving, and Public Policy*, p. 83.

between 1966 and 1968. Only 1 percent of the foundations viewed any of their grants as controversial, and the amount involved was only 0.1 percent of the total grants made. The Ford Foundation judged only 4 out of 1,500 grants to be potentially experimental and activist. Their grant to La Raza, a Mexican-American organization, was criticized by Congressman Henry Gonzales of Texas as "left-wing," but as Nielsen says, it was "well removed from anything that could seriously be termed revolutionary or even radical." [79]

McGeorge Bundy, president of the Ford Foundation, announced on March 16, 1970, that Ford had funded the Southeast Council of La Raza $1.3 million for another two years. This move, according to a *Ramparts* article, was made in order to defuse the more militant demands of Reies Tijerina and his followers in a group called Alianza, who were fighting to reclaim the Tierra Amarilla land grant. The Ford program set up an alternate, and less militant, group in an attempt to draw off Tijerina's following. On the day Tijerina was sent to prison, Ford announced a $1.5 million grant for a feed-lot in LaJara, Colorado. The ownership of the feed-lot passed into the hands of Claude Lowry, a brother-in-law of Boudinot P. Atterbury, a Ford Foundation official. There is no longer any talk of local Mexican-American ownership of the feed-lot.[80]

The Danforth Foundation once gave a scholarship to a Black militant, but were so frightened by the controversy this stirred up that they changed their entire grant-giving policy to a more conservative direction. The late Richard King Mellon, financier of Pittsburgh, under criticism because of his indifference to the welfare of the deteriorating city, responded through the Mellon Foundation by organizing the corporations to revitalize the down-town section—at the expense of the poor, who were moved out. However, when he attempted to revitalize housing for a profit, this failed because there is no profit in low-income housing.[81]

THE AGENCIES

Executive positions on boards of social agencies, including universities and hospitals, "have traditionally been the prerogative of the top social classes." [82] Executive positions on boards of social agencies are an important adjunct to a business career. In the community Ross studied, the most prestigious positions were on boards of universities and hospitals. Agencies that serve predominantly middle-class clients, such as hospitals, universities, and adoption agencies, may have some recipients of service on the board. Agencies that serve predominantly poor people generally did not have recipients of the agency's service on their boards until the 60s, when the Office of Economic

[79] Nielsen, *The Big Foundations*, p. 425.

[80] Rees Lloyd and Peter Montague, "Ford and La Raza: They stole our land and gave us powdered milk," *Ramparts*, September 1970.

[81] Nielsen, *The Big Foundations*, pp. 417–421.

[82] Ross, "Philanthropic Activity and the Business Career," p. 350.

Opportunity challenged the entire social service delivery system. The "War on Poverty" bypassed established social service agencies on the grounds of their excessive fragmentation and rigidity. Both public and private social agencies were considered too middle-class, too White, too paternalistic, and too alien to be acceptable to the very poor.[83]

Such accusations shocked social workers

> who at best saw themselves as altruistic and, at worst as harmless. The social reformer asleep in the heart of every social worker was deeply offended at being termed "establishment." [84]

The Community Action Program of the OEO required "maximum feasible participation" of the recipients of service in policy-making positions, including boards of directors. This loose guideline was later made more explicit in a requirement that one-third of the positions should be held by "representatives of the poor." The traditional guardians of the poor, including local officials and social workers in established agencies, were so accustomed to deciding what was best for the poor that most of them could not conceive of the poor deciding *for themselves* what was best. So in anti-poverty agencies across the country, those guardians of the poor resisted the poor as equal partners in decision making. Calling themselves "representatives of the poor," some of them took their seats on boards of directors, thus keeping the poor from direct participation in agencies set up to help them. Welfare colonialism is as hard to combat as any other kind of colonialism. Neil Gilbert documents this process in the Pittsburgh anti-poverty agency. The early decisions concerning Pittsburgh's antipoverty structure were

> weighted heavily in favor of preserving the status quo; funds were allocated primarily for the expansion of services utilizing existing agencies; and community organization staff, who had the greatest and perhaps only potential for creating strong pressures for change, were held to a bare minimum.[85]

Citizens did not gain representation on the board until sixteen months after the program was funded, by which time its course was fairly well charted. And when the citizens were allowed to participate, they came as representatives of geographic areas, not as representatives of the poor. Many poor people who served on boards were hired by OEO agencies in nonprofessional service jobs, and were no longer eligible to serve on the board.

> Through these jobs, the most responsible, articulate, and enterprising individuals were skimmed off the pool of talent available in the low-income groups,[86]

a process commonly referred to as "creaming" in the vernacular of community action. They were skimmed off to expedite services rather than to

---

[83] Beck, "The Voluntary Social Welfare Agency," citing Alan Pifer, *Annual Report* (New York: Carnegie Corporation of New York, 1967), p. 4.

[84] Ibid., p. 148.

[85] *Clients or Constituents, Community Action on the War on Poverty* (San Francisco: Jossey-Bass, Inc., 1970), p. 67.

[86] Ibid., p. 161.

organize a movement. Thus was the potential radicalism and militancy of the "War on Poverty" defused.

Yet social agencies were given a sharp slap in the face by the OEO, and some of them began to reassess their ways of operating. Agencies that had never before thought about the relationship of their board to the kinds of services they gave at least were forced to think about the consequences of their elite structure, although few of them made any drastic changes. Most of the "quasi-nongovernmental" agencies that had begun as private voluntary agencies and gradually come to the point of getting most of their funds from the state still acted as private agencies accountable to no one but themselves. Beck points out that such agencies should be forced to reexamine their board function, since a board formed to get funds is not the best board to administer.

> Mr. and Mrs. Midtown lack direct knowledge of neighborhood needs. Professional workers of all types are strongly biased in favor of perpetuation of the professional culture.[87]

The private agency is essentially a closed system, without any corrective devices built in to guard against organizational maintenance as its primary goal.[88]

One private agency which did change its decision-making structure was the Henry Street Settlement in New York City. It set up a neighborhood council parallel to the existing board of directors, which was given a major role in directing operations. Although the neighborhood council was allowed to seek representation on the board, the existing board structure was unchanged because of the agency's belief that the major function of a board is fund raising.

The traditional argument for having rich people on boards of directors has been that the rich can raise the money. Conflict arises when the rich also demand to shape the policies. This same conflict arises in universities, where trustees complain that the faculty has too much power relative to the trustees. Robert Nielsen, director of American Federation of Teachers Colleges and Universities Department, argues that trustees should confine themselves to looking after the finances of their institutions and leave policy making to the faculty. Nielsen urges that faculties organize to protect themselves from trustees, who are threatening faculty jobs in various ways.[89]

After the passage of the 1935 Social Security Act, most private social agencies got out of the business of dealing with the financial distress of the poor in any substantial way. They redefined their roles, and

> comforted themselves with the notion that they would be innovative and experimental while public agencies would give routine, day-to-day services. It soon

[87] Beck, "The Volunteer Social Welfare Agency," p. 151.

[88] Ibid., p. 154.

[89] Robert Nielsen, "Changing Roles of the College Trustee," *American Teacher* (April 1974), p. 13.

became apparent, however, that public agencies had no monopoly on hardening of bureaucracies.[90]

Despite their view of themselves as innovative and experimental, the private agencies have not come up with anything very new in the social services. In fact, as Alvin Schorr points out, the pioneering venture of the 1960s were largely inspired and set in motion by government: the juvenile delinquency programs, community action, amendments to the Social Security Act, community care of the mentally ill, and the Model Cities Program.[91]

Despite their willingness to accept government funds, most private agency administrators hang on tenaciously to their concept of themselves as "private," and resist the idea of the government taking over their functions. In a survey of fifty-one Chicago philanthropic organizations, 55 percent of the agencies said they faced a real budget crisis, and 54 percent experienced a deficit in 1968. Yet 53 percent said that preponderant government support would be "quite unfortunate," and 31 percent considered it "a very bad thing." Only 7 percent would prefer it, and 9 percent didn't care. Ninety percent felt private philanthropy should have greater tax incentives.[92] They agreed with the Peterson Commission, which conducted the survey, in their desire for more generous tax incentives for corporate philanthropy, a recommendation that was opposed only by Mr. Kirkland, the labor leader. This conflict between labor and private agencies is not new in the charity field. While organized labor fought for social insurance, private agencies since the nineteenth-century Charity Organization Society have opposed government intrusion into their self-defined province. Roy Lubove documents how, during 1900 to 1930, private voluntary agencies, insurance companies, and organized medicine collaborated to oppose any attempt at social insurance or compensation for disability or illness which they could not turn to their own advantage.[93] Since the 60s, however, social workers, through their professional body—the National Association of Social Workers —have been more outspoken in favor of governmental legislation that helps the poor. NASW has lobbied for various health and welfare measures in Washington. This does not mean that the social work profession as a whole has become more willing to take major social risks on behalf of oppressed clients. Lobbying, while important, is an elitist activity as compared to organizing clients to press for change in their own behalf. Although a majority of social workers describe themselves as liberals, most are deeply entrenched in their professional and agency cultures, and are more inclined

[90] Beck, "The Volunteer Social Welfare Agency," p. 147.

[91] "The Tasks for Voluntarism in the Next Decade," presented at the Centenary Conference on Voluntary Organization in the 1970s, sponsored by the Family Welfare Association, University of Sussex, Brighton, England, June 1969. Cited by Neil Gilbert and Harry Specht, *Perspectives on Social Welfare* (Englewood Cliffs, N.J.: Prentice-Hall, 1974), p. 160.

[92] *Foundations, Private Giving, and Public Policy*, p. 231.

[93] *The Struggle for Social Security, 1900–1930* (Cambridge, Mass.: Harvard University Press, 1968).

to act *for* their clients than to organize *with* them for changes in society. There are outstanding exceptions to this generalization, particularly since the civil rights struggles of the 50s and 60s, when activist social workers joined those struggles; many social workers helped to organize welfare recipients during the 60s.

The greatest threat to a businessman is militancy from workers, which threatens to increase his expenses. When all the liberal rhetoric has been stripped away, there is a basic conflict of interests between labor and management, and labor militancy is very likely to bring on management repression. This is as true when it occurs in the social services as when it occurs in business. When Local 1199 of the National Union of Hospital and Nursing Home Workers began organizing the lowest-paid workers in the hospitals in 1958, they encountered fierce and unqualified resistance from hospital administrators and boards of trustees across the country. When they organized in Pittsburgh, they canvassed the boards of the two largest hospitals in hopes of finding some sympathy, but quickly gave up in despair.

> Six members of Presbyterian Hospital's board are also directors of the Mellon National Bank; two are leading officers of the Aluminum Company of America; the Presbytery's representative is an attachment of the Mellon family. Mercy Hospital has on its board four pillars of Mellon properties, an exact balance with four nuns who represent the order the Church has charged with its administration. Negroes have been noticed, with one person on the board of each hospital. Yet the unions, whose health and welfare funds provide both institutions with their largest single revenue source, cannot show a solitary trustee. The management of Pittsburgh's social property rests as entirely as it ever did in the hands that own its social property.[94]

In 1972 when Local 1199 struck the Massachusetts Rehabilitation Hospital, a profit enterprise run by a partnership of Boston businessmen, members of the Boston Police Department were hired by the hospital as a special security force to break the strike.

> The cops have employed dogs, clubs and arrests against the picketers with a ferocity that is surprising even to veteran observers. Sixty strikers have been arrested, dozens beaten badly, and several more bitten by departmental mastiffs.[95]

When Beth Israel Hospital in Boston was faced with a union representation election, it was served a subpoena by the state Labor Relations Commission, which charged the hospital with unfair labor practices because of its refusal to allow workers to circulate job descriptions and salary information.[96]

When Local 1199 began to organize day-care workers in Boston, members led a demonstration outside Wesley Methodist Church, site of a day-care

[94] Murray Kempton, "Sticking to the Union," *New York Review of Books*, 14, No. 7 (April 9, 1970).

[95] Chuck Fager, "Hospital Workers: 1199's Sick of Being Busted," *The Real Paper*, November 29, 1972, p. 1.

[96] *Boston Globe*, October 16, 1973, p. 8.

center where the average teacher's salary was a little more than $100 a week. The church's advisory council refused to enter into serious negotiations with the union.[97]

Charitable institutions have always been notorious for paying workers low wages and for using free volunteer labor to keep labor costs down. The most exploited laborers are clients, when they are served by agencies that employ them. For example, Morgan Memorial Foundation, which operates the Good Will sheltered workshops, pays a pittance to its handicapped workers and resists any attempt at unionization by its clientele. Prisons also pay a pittance, if anything, to prisoners who work, and they fiercely resist unionization or any kind of collective action. Prisoners do a great deal of valuable work for the state, such as making license plates. Mental hospitals often use patients to do much of the work of maintaining the hospital—laundry, grass cutting, farming. This is called "occupational therapy," but patients are seldom paid for it. Often when patients do creative work such as furniture and rug making, they are not allowed to sell it on the open market because it would compete with established industry.

Agencies in the nineteenth century set up to deal with the poor, such as the Charity Organization Society, Children's Aid Societies, and settlement houses, relied at first mainly on volunteer staffs. Most of the staffs consisted of women, and it was fairly easy to convince them that they were mercenary and irreligious to expect wages for "doing good." Women were made to feel uneasy about working outside the home in any capacity, but working for nothing was not considered the same as paid work. This ethos about human-service workers doing free work "for the love of it" still persists. Hospitals rely extensively on volunteer help, and sometimes use the volunteers as strike-breakers. Schools have recently begun to use many volunteers, and the American Federation of Teachers is questioning the effect of this on the overall wage structure and stability of the school's curriculum.[98] *Giving USA* estimates that 55 to 60 million people (about one-fourth of the population) do volunteer work for philanthropies. If this labor were paid for, it would cost $5 or $6 billion.[99]

All of the fifty Chicago agencies surveyed by the Peterson Commission relied heavily on volunteer labor to carry out their programs. For 71 percent, the number of volunteers exceeded paid employers in 1968. If a value of $3 were placed on each volunteer hour, for one of five agencies this exceeded total payroll expenses. For one of four it amounted to from 20 to 100 percent of costs.[100]

Most of these volunteers are people considered to be marginal to the labor force—women, students, and old people. Many of them, perhaps most of

[97] *Boston Globe*, June 8, 1974.
[98] Robert Bhaerman, "The School Volunteer—Lifeblood of Education," *American Teacher*, 58, No. 9 (May 1974), 13.
[99] Cited by Nielsen, *The Big Foundations*, p. 403.
[100] *Foundations, Private Giving, and Public Policy*, p. 231.

them, would prefer pay but do not have the credentials that agencies want. Many of them harbor a quiet hope that the agency will like their work and hire them as paid staff. The Nixon Administration established a highly publicized volunteer program for human-service workers, the Action program. At the same time, it tried, and to some degree succeeded, to kill the poverty program. Thus free labor has replaced paid labor, as the unemployment rate continues to climb.

As we investigate who rules the social services, it becomes clear that the poor certainly do not. Elite boards of trustees have a great deal of power. Professionals have varying degrees of power, determined according to a hierarchy of status and pay (doctors at the top, nurses and social workers considerably lower). The lowest-paid service workers such as hospital and nursing home attendants, day-care workers, and teacher's aides, have much less power but have made progress in organizing. Middle-class and rich clients have the power of their status and money to choose more desirable services. Poor clients, and especially the poorest of the poor, are usually excluded from any significant voice in the kinds of services they want. Children are also excluded from power and control over their services.

The egalitarian stirrings of the 60s, continuing more weakly into the 70s, witnessed some significant protests against this state of affairs: student organizing; community control demands of hospitals and mental health facilities; tenant organizing; mental health liberation groups; welfare rights groups; counterinstitutions set up by youth themselves such as drug and crisis centers; hostels for street youth; peer-group counseling. These challenges to the social service establishment have forced some changes in some established institutions, but the changes are small and slow and won at the expense of tireless struggle. Progress is easily wiped out, as has happened to many of the victories of the welfare rights groups, because the money and power is still in the hands of the elite. Yet I sense—perhaps too optimistically—that the new egalitarian ethos is establishing roots slowly and deeply, and that the social services can no longer casually ignore the wishes of those they serve.

chapter five

social insecurity:
welfare policy
and
the structure of poor families

—*Carol B. Stack and Herbert Semmel*

In this chapter, Carol Stack and Herbert Semmel show the discrepancy between what legislators claim to want and what they actually do. They claim to want family stability while they make laws that break up the family. This gap between rhetoric and reality occurs because of contradictory demands of the socioeconomic system. Men—and increasingly, women—must be kept at least potentially in the labor market to do the menial work. Families must also be kept intact to preserve social stability. Yet the punitive measures necessary to keep people working act to break up the family. And, ironically, the jobs are not available for all the people who are supposed to be working, and those jobs that are available often do not pay enough to support a family.

Although the family is a less important economic unit than it was in formerly rural America, it is still the major social welfare institution because family members assume the primary responsibility of caring for each other. One might think that poor families would be least able to care for each other, yet Stack and Semmel show that the poor devise powerful bonds of reciprocity within their groups in order to survive. Larry Beeferman's chapter shows that federal spending on AFDC in 1973 represents 1.75 percent of the total $408 billion the government spent. No economist would be so naive as to suggest that the money that absent AFDC fathers might return to the state would make a dent in the national economy. Yet the president, some legislators, and some welfare officials urge further cutbacks in welfare spending to combat inflation and recession, and congressional committees consider ways to extract more money from poor fathers. By a curious logic, the government tries to blame the poor for the troubled state of the economy.

Despite the dubious economic usefulness of hounding poor fathers for money, and the even more dubious social usefulness of breaking up poor families still further, the idea appeals to many congressmen and to much of the general public. Perhaps it has special appeal to those working people who are grinding out a minimal living for their families at joyless and thankless jobs. Status and power and joy in work are in such short supply that working people take some pride in being a little better off than others. Thus working people turn on each other and, while they are thus diverted, the rich continue to shape our institutions.

THE ABSENT FATHER

What is one to conclude when Congress passes legislation that purports to be concerned with the welfare of children but actually deprives them of whatever support payments are available from the father and threatens to deprive them of additional material and affective resources from the father's kin? In December 1974, after this chapter was completed, Congress adopted amendments to the Social Security Act concerning child support and establishment of paternity.[1] In general, the law takes an aggressive stance toward recoupment of welfare payments from fathers, with almost no benefits for the children. In some states, it will result in a reduction of income to AFDC families.

The statute requires each state to establish a separate organizational unit to establish paternity of fathers of AFDC children and to pursue the father for "support." At the top of this nationwide bureaucracy is a separate organizational unit in the Department of Health, Education and Welfare which coordinates, assists, and regulates the work of the state units. Any money recovered from AFDC fathers must be paid directly to the state, not the family. After September 30, 1976, the statute appears to *require* that the entire amount of paternal support be applied first to reimburse the state and federal governments for current AFDC payments. Thus, in states which now permit AFDC families to retain all or a portion of support payments by the father, the new statute appears to result in a reduction of income for AFDC families receiving some paternal support.

Mothers are required to identify the father of AFDC children and to cooperate fully with the state in securing payments from the father and to assign to the state any rights to support from the father. A mother who refuses to cooperate is removed from the AFDC budget. Payments for the children may continue but they must be made as "protective payments" through a person other than the non-cooperating mother. This chapter[2] is based on our knowledge of the family structure of poor people, and specifically on the study of an urban Black ghetto conducted by Carol Stack.[3] We shall show how public policy that concentrates with tunnel vision only on saving money for the State destroys the security that society claims to want for its children while, ironically, saving little or no money for the State.

---

[1] Public Law 93-647, 93d Cong., 2d Sess. (1974).

[2] This article is adapted from "The Concept of Family in the Poor Black Community," by Carol B. Stack and Herbert Semmel, in *Studies in Public Welfare*, Paper No. 12 (Part II). Printed for the Joint Economic Committee (Washington, D.C.: U.S. Government Printing Office, 1973).

[3] *All Our Kin: Strategies for Survival in a Black Community* (New York: Harper & Row, 1974).

The absent father has troubled legislators since the AFDC program began in 1935 during the Depression.[4] The father was excluded at the start of the program because legislators thought he should go to work. The general theory was that the government, as employer of last resort, would provide work for every able-bodied male; public assistance would be necessary only in families lacking a male breadwinner. Legislators therefore provided federally supported public assistance only to adults who were disabled, blind, or aged and to children with one parent either dead, disabled, or absent from the home. The needs of mothers were not included in AFDC grants until 1950. Despite their assumption that men should be working, the legislators did not see to it that jobs would be available for everyone who needed them, as Henry Allen points out in his article in this book. The "absent father" requirement provided strong encouragement for unemployed or underemployed fathers to leave their homes so that their families might receive AFDC benefits.[5] Rather than passing a law that would require all states to make fathers eligible for AFDC benefits, federal legislators are instead proposing to force support payments from absent fathers.

THE MEAGER AFDC BENEFITS

Public aid recipients receive exceedingly low benefits by any definition. The Social Security Act leaves to the states the determination of the actual dollar grant paid to AFDC recipients.[6] Each state prepares what is supposed to be a budget of minimum needs, but these have little meaning because the state is not compelled to pay the amount budgeted and because the budgets themselves are artificially low. Only fourteen states pay 100 percent of "budgeted need";[7] some states pay reduced percentages of

[4] The program was titled Aid to Dependent Children (ADC) when it was first enacted because benefits were paid only to children. The title was later changed to Aid to Families of Dependent Children. The 1962 amendments to the Social Security Act permitted, but did not require, states to pay AFDC benefits to families where an unemployed father with a recent history of employment remains in the home (42 U.S.C. §607). Only 23 states and the District of Columbia now pay such benefits, known as AFDC-U. In the rest of the states, the presence of the father in the home renders his children and their mother ineligible for AFDC.

The 1967 amendments to the Social Security Act limited federal AFDC-U payments to cases in which fathers had employment for over a year in the three-year period before assistance was granted. The same amendments prohibited families that received benefits through unemployment insurance from receiving supplementary help through AFDC-U.

Prior to 1968, many states had "man-in-the-house" rules which declared that a man who cohabited with an AFDC mother was *ipso facto* a "substitute father" for any and all of her children, rendering the children ineligible for AFDC. The Supreme Court ruled that an Alabama "man-in-the-house" rule violated the Social Security Act. (*King v. Smith*, 392 U.S. 309 [1968]).

[5] See *King v. Smith* (see previous note).

[6] *Rosado v. Wyman*, 397 U.S. 397 (1970).

[7] Department of Health, Education, and Welfare, *State's Method for Determination of Amount of Grant for an AFDC Family Size of Four* (as of March 31, 1972). Unpublished. Hereafter cited as HEW Survey.

budgeted need, others impose flat dollar maximums per family or recipient.[8]

In March 1972, only one state, Connecticut, paid an AFDC family an amount sufficient to meet the barest survival needs measured by the official poverty level of $4,000 per annum for a family of four.[9] And this $4,000 figure contemplates a diet likely to result in long-run malnutrition, allowing only 91 cents a day per person for food. Eleven of the states paid maximum AFDC benefits of less than 50 percent of the minimum poverty level (less than $167 monthly). Seven other states, for a total of eighteen, paid $200 monthly or less. Mississippi computed the minimum needs of a family of four at $277 monthly and paid that family $60 a month. Maine computed need at $349 monthly and paid $168; in Delaware, the maximum was $158.[10] Some states have not raised benefits since 1969, although the cost of living has risen by 30 percent since that time. Families that try to raise their total income through earnings face the frustration of seeing most of their earnings go to the state and federal governments in the form of reduced AFDC payments. Income from sources other than employment, including support payments, often result in dollar-for-dollar reduction in AFDC benefits, even though the benefits otherwise payable are less than budgeted need.[11]

FAMILY STABILITY: WELFARE POLICY AND BLACK RESPONSES

The rhetoric of official welfare policy gives fulsome praise to the virtues of family stability. The Social Security Act provisions on AFDC stress the provision of "financial assistance and rehabilitation and other services" to dependent children and the importance of providing them with "continuing parental care or protection" and of maintaining and strengthening family life.[12] State welfare laws often speak in terms of providing sufficient income to protect the health and well-being of children. Judicial decisions abound with expressions such as ". . . protection of such [dependent] children is the paramount goal of AFDC." [13] Welfare regulations and administration, on the

---

[8] HEW Survey. See also *Jefferson v. Hackney*, 406 U.S. 535 (1972); and *Dandridge v. Williams*, 397 U.S. 471 (1970).

[9] HEW Survey. Compare the poverty line of $4,000, drawn by the Office of Economic Opportunity, Instruction No. 60044c (November 19, 1971), with the U.S. Department of Labor minimum adequate budget in April 1972 which required net income of $6,200 ($7,214 less $1,010 payroll and income taxes), USDL 72-240 (April 27, 1972). The 1974 official OEO poverty line is $4,500. The Department of Labor survey of 38 metropolitan areas showed that a family of four needed an average of $12,626 to maintain an "intermediate" level of living in autumn, 1973. The OEO poverty index is computed by government officials as an estimate of what is needed for subsistence living; the Department of Labor surveys actual expenses.

[10] HEW Survey.

[11] The Social Security Act requires the states to take into consideration in determining need any income or resources of any AFDC recipient, 42 U.S.C. §602 (7), except for limited income from employment. See text of 42 U.S.C. §602 (a) (8).

[12] 42 U.S.C. §601.

[13] *King v. Smith*, fn. 4, *supra*.

other hand, make it difficult to achieve the stability considered so desirable by welfare officials. When a father cannot find a job and AFDC is needed to support his family, he may have to leave the family so that it will be eligible for AFDC benefits. The majority of states do not allow benefits if the father resides in the family home, even if he is unemployed; if the absent father provides any support, the AFDC grant may be reduced.

The odds were against AFDC families before they applied for welfare. Less educated and less skilled than the general working population, and disproportionately of a minority race, they have a hard time finding jobs. If they do find work, it is often temporary or sporadic and pays too little to support a family. Poor families have virtually no financial reserves to meet emergencies. Lack of regular employment deprives the poor of many of the social and private insurance benefits available to those with steady employment. Because of their uncertain economic future, many poor men and women are reluctant to assume the responsibilities of a legal marriage.[14]

In the face of such massive economic insecurity, how do poor people survive? They help each other out, as shown by Stack's study. Contrary to the assertions of many academic sociologists about the "breakdown of the nuclear family" in the poor Black community, Stack found that poor Black people have developed an extensive network of kin and friends to help themselves survive in a hostile environment. Although they do not enter into legal marriages as frequently as more affluent people, the majority of fathers care for their children to the extent that they are able. Even when a father is absent, many of his kin typically continue to care for his children. Poor Blacks define their family network in broader and more complex ways than many middle-class sociologists have recognized.

The findings contained in this paper are based on a participant-observation study of the domestic strategies of urban-born Black Americans whose parents had migrated from the South to a single community in the urban North. Carol Stack, an anthropologist, conducted this study between 1968 and 1971 in the Midwestern city of Jackson Harbor,[15] a city in the 50,000–100,000 population range, 10 percent Black. The families studied lived in the Flats, the poorest section of the Black community of Jackson Harbor.

---

[14] Elliot Liebow, *Tally's Corner: A Study of Negro Streetcorner Men* (Boston: Little, Brown, 1967).

[15] The name of the actual city and individuals' names have been changed to protect the privacy of those involved in the study. Although it cannot be said that Jackson Harbor is typical of every urban Black community, it appears to be representative at least of Midwestern Black communities, and possibly those in many other urban areas. Blacks composed 10 percent of the population of Jackson Harbor, roughly comparable to the percentage of Blacks in the state in which Jackson Harbor was located, and in the nation. The county in which Jackson Harbor was located was among the 20 highest of income in the United States, according to the 1970 census, but 60 percent of the Black families had incomes of under $4,000 per annum. In 1968, a year of record low unemployment nationally, in Jackson Harbor there was virtually no White unemployment, but Black unemployment consistently exceeded 20 percent, and two-thirds of employed Blacks were in unskilled jobs. Nonetheless, Jackson Harbor also had a substantial Black middle class.

The study concentrated on family life among second-generation urban dwellers whose families had received public assistance during their childhood. Now adults in their twenties to forties, they were raising their own children and receiving public assistance under the AFDC program. The main purpose of the study was to analyze the nucleus of social and economic cooperation which best characterizes the poor urban Black family.[16] The study reveals that Black families have strengths and stability previously unrecognized by most academic studies. The family structure developed by poor urban Blacks appears to represent a flexible adaptation to the daily social and economic demands of life on the poor urban family. Individuals who are members of different households align in domestic networks to provide the basic functions often attributed to nuclear families. These domestic networks are broad enough so that while some participants may move in and out, a hard core usually remains constant, particularly adult female kin and siblings. From the standpoint of the child, the economic and psychological effects of the death, temporary absence, or desertion of a parent may be less than in the nuclear family because the child has come to rely on a variety of adults to provide the multiple functions of a parent. Equally important, adults readily assume responsibilities for the child without regarding them as unfair or

[16] A further note on methodology. Prior to the participant-observation study, Stack conducted a statistical study from data in the files of the welfare department in Jackson Harbor. A total of 188 AFDC case history records were examined. These included data on 951 children who were AFDC recipients—half the total number of AFDC children in Jackson Harbor in 1969—and 373 adults, of whom 188 were "grantees" responsible for AFDC children. Confidentiality was insured by coding all data before removal from the welfare office.

Early in the study, Stack became immersed in the daily lives of one domestic family unit—the household of Magnolia and Leo Johnson—and their network of kinship which proved to number over 100 persons. Their home became her home base, a place where she was welcome to spend the day, week after week, and where she and her year-old son could sleep, usually sharing a bed with children in the household. Stack's presence in the home of Magnolia and Leo and their eight children enabled her to meet all of their relatives who resided in the Flats and those kin and non-kin who actively participated in their daily domestic lives. The network of people involved in this study expanded as she visited and shared experiences with individuals who were participants in the personal networks of those families who provided her with her first home base. Stack's personal network of informants expanded naturally in this process, coinciding with the social networks of participants in the study. Her home base changed as she became personally accepted by families, and ultimately she acquired a place to sleep whenever she wished at several unrelated households. Each of these households were participants in cooperative networks which radiated out to include over 300 individuals who Stack eventually visited, although the locus of her intensive observations was limited to 10 unrelated coalitions of kinsmen. It was in these homes that Stack's presence ultimately affected daily social relations the least.

Stack eventually spent almost 3 years in the Flats, attempting to comprehend the strategies people evolved for coping with the everyday human demands of ghetto life. Early in the study, she became aware of coalitions of individuals trading and exchanging goods, resources, and the care of children. The intensity of their acts of domestic cooperation, and the exchange of goods and services among these kin and non-kin, was striking. Stack began to learn how participants in exchanges were defined by one another, who was eligible to become a part of the cooperative networks, how they were recruited, and what kept participants actively involved in the series of exchanges.

unwanted burdens. In short, the domestic networks provide the assurance that all children will be cared for.

When economic resources are greatly limited, people need help from as many others as possible. This requires expanding their kin networks—increasing the number of people they hope to be able to count on. Mothers expect little from fathers, but hope they will help out. Something is expected from the father's kin, especially from his mother and sisters. Mothers continually activate these kin lines, bringing kin into the network of exchanging and obligating. Often the biological father's female relatives are also poor and also try to expand and increase the number of people on whom they can depend. The expansion and integration of networks thus is accomplished through the nexus of a newborn child.

Middle-class families, which are largely economically self-sufficient, rely on insurance, savings, pensions, and social insurance benefits to survive emergencies. They do not necessarily depend on the extended family to help care for children, because they can afford to pay for baby-sitters and nurseries. They rely less on adult relatives for domestic support than they used to. Housing for senior citizens is only one reflection of the growing separation of the grandparent from the home of his children and grandchildren. Public policy increasingly reflects these changing attitudes. Support obligations in some states are being terminated except for spouse and children. In others, the nuclear family must provide parents and collaterals only limited amounts of support and only if the nuclear family's income exceeds the level deemed necessary for its own support.

Poor families, on the other hand, need an extended kinship network in order to survive. Domestic networks develop rights and obligations in much the same fashion that jural relations evolve in broader societal groupings. Indeed, the trading of goods and services pervades the whole social-economic life of the participants in the network. Trading refers to the offering of goods or services with the intent to obligate. It is, in one sense, a contractual relationship, based on offer and acceptance, with enforcement of the obligation left to kinship or community pressure and the risk of being excluded from the network. Failure to satisfy an obligation may result in someone else's child not eating that day.

Trading is the insurance and savings institution of the poor urban Black, allowing him to call on others for assistance because he has paid his premium by having offered or supplied goods or services at a previous time. Poor Blacks say, "You have to have help from everybody and anybody" and "The poorer you are, the more likely you are to pay back."

We believe that the poor Black urban family has not developed along the nuclear pattern partly because of the need to provide an alternate system of economic security. We find that various domestic networks of cooperative support sustain and socialize the family members. The membership in domestic networks is based largely on kinship, including that of the father of children.

When an unmarried woman in the Flats becomes pregnant or gives birth to a child, she often tells her friends and kin who the father is. The man has a number of alternatives open to him. Sometimes he publicly denies paternity by implying to his friends and kin that the father could be any number of other men, and that he has "information that she is no good and has been creeping on him all along." The community generally accepts the man's denial of paternity because it is doubtful that under these conditions he and his kin would assume any parental duties anyway. The man's failure to assent to being the father leaves the child without kinship ties reckoned through a male. Subsequent "boyfriends" of the mother may assume the duties of discipline and support and receive the child's affection, but all rights in the child belong to the mother and her kinsmen.

The second alternative open to a man involved in a sexual relationship with a mother is to acknowledge openly that he is the genitor. The father may indicate "he owns it" by telling his people and his friends that he is the father, by paying part of the hospital bill, or by bringing milk and diapers to the mother after the birth of the child. The parents may not have ever shared a household and the affective and sexual relationship between them may have ended prior to the birth of the child. By validating his claim as a parent the father offers the child his blood relatives and their husbands and wives as the child's kin—an inheritance, so to speak. As long as the father validates his parental entitlement, his relatives, especially his mother and sisters, consider themselves kin to the child and responsible. Even when the mother "takes up with another man" her child retains the original set of kin gained through the father who sponsored him. The frequency with which Black children derive their kin through females has been stereotyped and exaggerated in the literature on Black families. In contrast, according to information supplied by AFDC mothers as reflected in their case records, fathers in the Flats recognized 484 (69 percent) of the 700 children included in Stack's AFDC survey.

The more a father and his kin help a mother and her child, the more completely they validate their parental rights. But a common situation in the Flats occurs when a man assents to being the father, and offers his kinship affiliations to the child, but rarely performs a parental duty or claims any rights in relation to the child. Many American Black males have little or no access to steady employment at adequate pay levels. Poor employment opportunities contribute to their difficulties in assuming stable roles as jural parents. People in the Flats believe a father should help his child, but they know that mothers cannot count on his help.

A significant indication of the importance of the father and the father's kin to the child is revealed in the statistical survey of AFDC cases. Asked to rank in order who they would expect to raise each of their children if they died, one-third of the women listed the father or the father's mother as first choice even though the father was not residing with the children in almost all cases. The expectations and reliance which the mothers place on the father and his kin demonstrate the importance of the support available and expected from the father's kin—support dependent on the father's recognition of paternity.

Members of poor Black communities adopt a variety of tactics to expand the number of people who share reciprocal obligations with them. These strategies include the activation of kin ties, and the creation of kinlike ties among non-kin. For example, despite the comparatively smaller number of marriages that may occur between childbearing parents, if a father openly acknowledges his paternity, he and his kin may actively provide affection and economic aid to his children. Friends may also be incorporated in one's domestic circle; and if they satisfy one another's expectations, they may be called kin—"cousin," "sister," "brother," "daddy," and so forth. The expansion of the domestic network increases the security of the individual by expanding the circle of persons who may be called upon in case of need—risk spreading, in the insurance analogy.

Cooperative networks range in size as large as fifty or more individuals and include up to seven or more households. Participants in these networks are drawn from kin and friends, but of the two, the kin network is more enduring. An individual's kin are recognized as having some duties toward him and some claims on him. On the other hand, fictive kin relations are maintained by consensus between individuals, lasting months in some cases and a lifetime in others. Children very often establish close and affectionate ties with their "aunts" and "uncles"—for example, their mother's sister's "old man" and their mother's brother's "old lady." These aunts and uncles, on the basis of their original consensual relationship, can remain in a child's person network for a long time. Long-term ties between adults are frequently formed on the basis of the birth of a child. A woman and the sister of the father of her child often maintain long-term friendships, and these relationships are continued by children and their aunts and uncles long into adulthood.

Household composition—that is, where people sleep—does not reveal the scope of the domestic network, which may be diffused over several kin-based households. Fluctuations in household composition, defined in terms of where people sleep, rarely affect the network of daily exchanges within the domestic network. A person may sleep in one household, eat in another, contribute to a third, and consider himself a member of all three households.

CHILD SUPPORT IN PERSPECTIVE

Because AFDC benefits will probably continue to be low and unemployment will probably continue to rise, the family patterns described above are not likely to change in the foreseeable future. How is the new federal policy of vigorous pursuit of fathers likely to affect AFDC children? We believe that it will be counterproductive; large-scale efforts to seek contributions from nonsupporting fathers would do little or nothing to help most dependent AFDC children. As explained below, some poor children may even lose previous financial and psychological resources as a result of a policy of vigorous pursuit. We also know of no evidence to support the government's contention that this policy would save the taxpayer money. It has never been satisfactorily demonstrated that a broad scale of legal proceedings against AFDC fathers will produce any substantial savings for the taxpayer. Certainly no program should be undertaken that threatens the resources of poor children until there is proof that the program will achieve some benefit for someone.

Most people in the United States share three major premises regarding child support: that children should have adequate financial, social, and affective resources; that the parents, not the state, should be primarily responsible for the support of their children;[17] and that children should be cared for at the least possible cost to the taxpayer. It follows from these premises that the government should attempt a large-scale effort to obtain child support contributions only if the benefits in terms of taxpayer savings outweigh the enforcement costs, and if there is no substantial adverse effect on the resources available to the children involved. We shall consider the effects on children and the effects on taxpayers separately.

1. Effects on Children of Vigorous Pursuit Policy

Nearly all the support payments that states now collect from AFDC fathers goes not to the children but to the state in the form of reduced welfare payments. An HEW survey in 1972 showed that in thirty-five of the fifty states, any payment recovered from the father of a welfare child goes solely to the state, the child receiving nothing.[18] In twenty of these thirty-five states, the child receives nothing even though the state is paying public assistance benefits that are less than the state's own version of minimum needs. In West Virginia, for example, the standard of need for a family of four is $265 monthly, but the state only pays $138. If the father were to contribute $100 either voluntarily or by court order, the state payment is reduced to $38, leaving the family with only $138, still $127 short of the budgeted figure for minimum subsistence needs. In nine other states, a portion of the father's payment goes to his children and a portion to the state, but the state receives the greater portion in most of these cases. In only seven states would a father's payment go entirely to the child, and these states all pay assistance benefits less than budgeted need. Even in these seven states, as with the nine in which the child receives a portion of the support payment, the child benefits only to the extent that the public assistance payment plus his share of the father's payment brings the family up to the state's budget of minimum need. Thus, in the seven-state group (assuming a budgeted need of $300 and a maximum public assistance payment of $250), if the father pays $100 support, the children receive only $50, the other $50 going to the state. The current

---

[17] Every state requires parents to support their children. A state that requires a biological father to support his legitimate children must also require support of illegitimate children. *Gomez v. Perez*, 93 S. Ct. 872 (1973).

[18] HEW Survey.

situation on payments by AFDC fathers should more accurately be called "state reimbursement payments" rather than the commonly used expression "support payments."

Not only would AFDC children gain little or nothing from a vigorous pursuit of their fathers, but the net effect may be a reduction in the total resources available to the children. The findings of Stack's study indicate that many children could lose the precious financial and psychological resources that absent fathers and their families now provide on an informal and voluntary basis. The crucial issue in terms of the resources available to a child is whether the father openly acknowledges the child to be his, thereby bringing the father's kin into the child's domestic network. The actual financial support from the father may be small or nonexistent. The significant element is the variety of material and psychological resources the child obtains from the father's kin if the father openly accepts the child. These resources cannot be measured in terms of dollars; they include providing child care, feeding the child, providing furniture, sharing clothing which circulates among children in the network, and including the child in social and recreational activities. On occasion the father's kin assume complete care of the child. Moreover, a substantial number of AFDC fathers maintain close relationships with their children and play an important parental role in affection and discipline, even though offering no financial support.

The importance of the supportive role of the father's kin must be evaluated in terms of the inadequacy of AFDC payments. The strengthening and expansion of domestic networks is vital to the survival of poor families. A child's network can be doubled in size by inclusion of its father's kin, but this is dependent on the father's acknowledgment of paternity.

A program that actively seeks legal sanctions against low-income Black fathers who are not voluntarily contributing to the support of their children is likely to deprive some poor children of sorely needed material, psychological, and social support which would otherwise be forthcoming from the father and his kin. It is reasonable to assume that some fathers will refuse to acknowledge paternity to reduce the legal harassment that may follow. Although we have found no reliable data on this, it seems reasonable to expect that people in poor Black communities will soon learn that open acknowledgment of paternity increases the speed and certainty of judicial decrees of support. *But whatever a court may decree, the father's determination will prevail as to whether the child receives support from his kin.* A court may order support, but if the father loses his job, neither the child nor the state will receive funds. Even where a father has first accepted a child, his later disaffirmation usually results in a withdrawal of his kin from the child's domestic network (except that where close, long-term relationships have developed between the child and certain of the father's kin, those kin may remain in the network).

In some cases, the pursuit of low-income fathers to reimburse the state for public assistance payments may result in a loss of additional financial benefits available to a child. A father may not offer regular support but may make occasional gifts of money, or pay some rent in a crisis, or buy the child clothing. Such cash outlays may occur on occasions when the father is able to obtain a job after a period of unemployment. The amounts may appear small to the more affluent, but a gift of $30 is more than is generally budgeted by welfare authorities for food for a child for an entire month. In many states, small gifts not regularly received are not considered as resources or income and do not reduce the amount of public assistance payment; if technically a resource, they are unlikely to be reported.[19] If a father is saddled with a reimbursement order, he is less likely to have the funds or desire to make an additional payment to his children. Public policy should encourage, not discourage, AFDC fathers to give assistance, however small, to their children living on below-subsistence incomes.

Vigorous support programs can have additional negative effects on poor families. Increasing the contributions of a low-income father can hurt the father's current family while not helping his children from a prior union, because the amount taken from the father will generally go to the state. Some low-income AFDC fathers are supporting or contributing to the support of children other than their AFDC child, and often living with those non-AFDC children within a marital family. A division of the father's income to reimburse the state for its AFDC payments to a child by a prior union may result in adding his present family to the welfare roll, or driving that second family deeper into poverty. Or it may be the last straw which leads the already overburdened father, struggling at a thankless job at low pay, to give up and disappear. Gelhorn suggested that the financial return on support actions are achieved at the cost of

> later social expenses for institutionalization of the parties, for lawlessness by men whose latent grudges against society are aroused, and for the economic and emotional wounds that may be suffered by the defendant's other family. In short, there are hidden as well as direct costs in collecting these moneys.[20]

The policy of legal proceedings against large numbers of low-income fathers of AFDC children is potentially harmful to children. The decision as to whether a nonsupport proceeding should be instituted against the father should turn on whether the action will increase or diminish the totality of resources available to the child. The person best able to make this determination is the mother, not the district attorney or the social worker. Only the mother can measure the value of support available from the father's

---

[19] The prospect of small sums of money received by an AFDC family going unreported to the welfare authorities raises for some the spectre of "welfare cheating," for others the issue of inequalities of administration. We are not referring to families with adequate income of their own committing fraud in its true sense to obtain welfare payments. We are speaking of eligible families living on below-subsistence welfare payments who must utilize every available resource to survive. It is the system that pays a family less than its minimum need and then attempts to deprive the family of a father's occasional gift that causes such "irregularities." If the family were permitted to retain a father's contribution up to a standard of minimum adequate needs, the "nonreporting" issue would virtually disappear.

[20] Ernest Gelhorn, *Children and Families in the Courts of New York City*, 196 (1954).

kin network and the potentiality of its loss if legal action is brought against the father. The mother too is more likely to know or be able to learn whether the father is earning enough on a regular basis to make a legal proceeding worthwhile.

Mothers, of course, must obtain financial benefits for their children if they are to pursue legal remedies voluntarily. As noted above, in most states there is an effective 100 percent tax on support payments from the AFDC father because they go entirely to the government.

There are of course some cases in which the father's income is more than adequate for his own needs and those of relatives he already is supporting voluntarily, and where a refusal of a mother to press for support of children fathered by such a man would be unreasonable. There is no reason why a simple system cannot be developed to collect support from AFDC fathers who are fully employed and perfectly capable of supporting their children. A model already exists for such a program in requirements for support of indigent adult relatives, usually aged parents. Federal regulations require that support can be required only if relatives whose income exceeds "a minimum level of adequacy that takes account of the needs and other obligations of the relatives."

2. Savings for Taxpayers—Myth or Reality?

Available information from this and other studies on reimbursement payments from AFDC fathers indicates that an enforcement program against the broad population of AFDC fathers will lead to low per capita returns. Although Stack did not undertake a study of employment or income of AFDC fathers in the Flats, her observation there permits an attempt to draw a composite picture of AFDC fathers in the Flats. The father would be a young man between 18 and 35, a high school dropout, unskilled or semiskilled worker, unemployed or sporadically employed in low-paying positions. This profile conforms with the statistical information available concerning AFDC fathers and Black males living in low-income urban areas. A national survey of AFDC families in 1971[21] found that among those fathers whose educational status could be determined, only 27 percent had finished high school.[22] This rate of graduation is only one-half the already low graduation rate for all Black males in the labor force, age 22 to 34, living in low-income urban areas.[23]

Additional evidence on the economic opportunities of Black males in low-income areas shows much the same picture. In an analysis of 1970 census

[21] National Center for Social Statistics, "Findings of the 1971 AFDC Survey" (hereafter National AFDC Survey), Pt. I—"Demographic and Program Characteristics," DHEW Publ. No. (SRS) 72-03756. Pt. II—"Financial Circumstances," DHEW Publ. 72-03757.

[22] National AFDC Survey, Pt. I, table 20.

[23] U.S. Bureau of the Census, *Census Population: 1970 Employment Profiles of Selected Low Income Areas.* PHC (8) 1, January 1972 (hereafter Low Income Census), table 2 (a).

statistics for low-income urban areas, the National Urban League found the "real" unemployment rate among all Blacks to be 23.8 percent.[24] This rate undoubtedly increased in the recession/depression of 1974–75. This real rate includes those officially counted as unemployed and those "discouraged" workers who would accept employment if available but who no longer seek work actively because of repeated inability to find work. Earnings and occupations are other indicators of economic status. Of all Black males living in low-income areas, 42 percent earned less than $6,000. Only 25 percent worked in white-collar occupations and only 12 percent worked as craftsmen or foremen.[25]

The second piece of evidence against the belief that a vigorous pursuit policy would yield taxpayer savings is based on actual experience. The national survey of AFDC families by HEW's National Center for Social Statistics revealed that only 13.3 percent of the absent fathers of AFDC children were making "support" payments in 1971[26] and that the total of these payments comprised only 17.6 percent of the total income (including public aid) of the families to which they were contributing.[27] The average payment from contributing fathers was $85 per month, but more than half of these fathers contributed less than $75 monthly.[28] These figures of actual payments are probably much higher than collections from an enforcement program against the entire population of AFDC fathers would be. In view of the limited and sporadic nature of enforcement proceedings against AFDC fathers, those actually making reimbursement payments are a select group, likely to represent a more highly paid, regularly employed group than would be found in the overall AFDC absent-father population.

There is little data available on whether more widespread support enforcement programs against AFDC fathers would produce substantial income in excess of the costs of the program. The national AFDC survey for 1971 found that the whereabouts of 53 percent of absent AFDC fathers was unknown.[29] Whether this reflects actual difficulties in locating fathers or the lack of enforcement procedures is speculative.

Many state officials share the view of Arkansas welfare officials that an intensive program for securing payments "would not be worthwhile because most absent parents did not have the means to support their families."[30] In

[24] National Urban League, Inc., *Black Unemployment: A Crisis Situation* (1972), table 3.

[25] Low Income Census, table 5 (a).

[26] National AFDC Survey, Pt. II, table 62.

[27] National AFDC Survey, Pt. II, table 54A.

[28] National AFDC Survey, Pt. II, tables 56 and 62.

[29] National AFDC Survey, Pt. I, table 16.

[30] Comptroller General of the United States, *Collection of Child Support Under the Program of Aid to Families With Dependent Children*, 22 (1972) (hereafter cited as Comptroller General's report). See also Kaplan, *Support From Absent Fathers of Children Receiving ADC*, U.S. Bureau of Public Assistance Report No. 41 (1960). The author of a field survey of support enforcement in Kentucky doubted whether any substantial cost savings would result from a state enforcement program against AFDC fathers, 57 *Ky. L.J.* 228, 255 (1969), but favored such a program if the funds collected were primarily retained by the children, not the state. Under Kentucky practice

Jackson Harbor, support proceedings against AFDC fathers are rare. On the other hand, the Comptroller General claimed that the state of Washington received reimbursement payments from AFDC fathers five times greater than what it cost the state to collect them. His data, however, is ambiguous and suspect,[31] and the findings of the 1971 national AFDC survey sharply challenge his conclusion that Washington was more successful than three other states in collecting child support.[32]

In short, no case has as yet been made that the taxpayer would benefit from devoting substantial amounts of public funds to finance a vigorous program of enforcement of current state support laws.

---

at the time, 85 percent of AFDC support payments went to the state. Further, if a support order was in effect, the state reduced the AFDC payment on the assumption that the required payment would actually be made, so that the children suffered the loss of nonpayment while the state reaped the benefit even if the payment was never made. Gardner, *Maintaining Welfare Families' Income in Kentucky: A Study of the Relationship Between AFDC Grants and Support Payments From Absent Parents*, 57 Kentucky Law Journal, 228 (1969).

[31] It appears that the Comptroller General uncritically accepted the cost estimates of state officials. For example, the cost figures used by the Comptroller General cover only the statewide central collections section of the state welfare agency. This section does not appear to employ any attorneys, enforcement proceedings being referred by the collection section to law enforcement officials. (Comptroller General's report at p. 14.) Costs of law enforcement agencies and judicial agencies in proceedings against AFDC fathers were not computed, even though it appears that approximately 40 percent of the cases involved judicial proceedings. (Comptroller General's report at p. 17.) These costs will be substantial in any broad experiment.

[32] The Comptroller General concludes that Washington was more successful in collecting child support for AFDC children than were Arkansas, Iowa, and Pennsylvania. Washington differed from the national average in percent of contributing fathers by only 5.5 percent (18.8 percent to 13.3 percent) and in average contribution by only $3.63 monthly ($88.52 to $84.89). Pennsylvania, which appears to follow the usual pattern of limited pursuit of AFDC fathers (and which was criticized by the Comptroller General), does almost as well as Washington, Pennsylvania fathers contributing in 16 percent of the cases an average amount of $92.88.

The Comptroller General based his conclusions about Washington on a sample of only 50 cases out of a total AFDC caseload of 37,840, hardly a statistically valid sample. The national AFDC survey is based on a sample of 1 percent of caseload, seven times as great as that used in the Comptroller General's report. The difference in sampling alone requires a rejection of the impression given by the Comptroller General's report that 43 percent of absent AFDC fathers are making support payments in the light of the finding of only 18.8 percent by the national AFDC survey.

the children
of the "dangerous
and perishing classes"*

—Betty Reid Mandell

Some academics and policy makers feel that when a family cannot care for its children or is considered unfit to do so, the state can provide better substitute care. Many so-called "experts" make recommendations without any knowledge of how this type of care has actually worked. The fact is that state-subsidized substitute care has not done the job well up to now, and perhaps cannot do the job well under the present economic system because poor people receive fewer public resources than affluent people, due to their having less political clout. Again the "experts" appear to be blaming the poor rather than helping them gain a larger share of society's resources.

Substitute care is often the end of the road for families who have inadequate jobs, health care, housing, and income maintenance. The children that I discuss in this chapter are also some of the children that the other authors are talking about in this book. When AFDC payments do not support a family; when government work programs do not provide jobs or a decent salary; when the health-care system discriminates against the poor; when the criminal justice system fails to rehabilitate; when an overburdened mother cannot pay for an abortion and Medicaid will not pay for it; when a father leaves his family because he cannot support it, the children may end up in foster care. It is surely perverse logic to consider that any sort of "solution."

Victorian philanthropists didn't mince words when they talked about poor kids—those kids were dangerous or perishing—that is, in danger of becoming criminals or already sunk in crime. The philanthropists formed charity schools, "Ragged Schools," and Sunday Schools to teach these children some morals and a little reading—not enough to give them big ideas about their station in life, but enough to get them to work a little more efficiently and obediently. Boys got a little math; girls didn't because they were headed for domestic work. The Sunday Schools, held on the only day when the children

---

* This chapter is adapted from the author's book, *Where Are the Children?* (Lexington, Mass.: Lexington Books, 1973).

did not work, had a further purpose—to keep the "city Arabs" off the streets so that the respectable citizens could have a quiet Sabbath.

In the streets of New York City, poor children were as much of a threat to the bourgeoisie as the London kids were. Charles Loring Brace, founder of the New York City Children's Aid Society, conceived the idea of shipping "the children of the dangerous classes"—mostly children of poor immigrants —to farms in the West, Midwest, and South. The farmers needed farm hands and their wives needed domestic help. Thus foster care began in the United States, and between 1854 and 1929 the Children's Aid Society shipped about 100,000 children out of New York City. Some were orphans, but many had parents who were too poor to care for them. Some people called the program "the wolf of indentured labor in the sheep's clothing of Christian charity." Westward expansion ended, the Catholic church protested placements of Catholic children in Protestant homes; child labor was no longer as profitable, so the "free" foster home changed into the agency-supervised foster home. Social agencies then gave small board payments—but not wages—to foster parents. Since its beginning, state- and agency-sponsored foster care has been mainly a program for the children of the poor.

Echoes of the Victorian age return to haunt us now. The children of the "Other America" are once more high on the social agenda. It may be too old-fashioned to call them children of the dangerous classes, but it has become fashionable to speak of their inferior genes. Some social planners are now preoccupied with both the children of the poor and the reproductive habits of the poor. Government money has been used to sterilize adolescent girls and AFDC mothers. Roger Freeman, former assistant to President Nixon, urged us to do away with euphemisms such as "family planning" and proposed a "birth prevention" program for the poor. (I prefer the euphemisms. When officials bare their teeth and claws, we're in worse trouble than when they worry about what we might think.) Freeman proposed a cash bonus for welfare parents who volunteer for sterilization. He also proposed that Congress consider taking children away from some welfare mothers and raising them in "well-run" government institutions. The electrical engineer William Shockley proposed as "a thinking exercise" that the government offer bonuses to those citizens who, paying no income tax, submit to voluntary sterilization.[1] In *The Unheavenly City*, the sociologist Edward Banfield considered the advisability of sterilizing members of the "lower class," and proposed strictly supervised housing compounds for some "lower class" families.[2] The Republican Ripon Society journal carried an article proposing day care for children of the poor as a relatively cheap and politically safe anti-poverty program.[3] Bruno Bettelheim believes that group care similar to that in Israeli kibbutzim should be instituted for disadvantaged children.[4] Child welfare specialist Martin Wolins, dismayed by the

[1] *Boston Globe*, January 28, 1972.
[2] *The Unheavenly City* (Boston: Little, Brown, 1970).
[3] B. Mooney, "Day Care: A Proposal," *Ripon Forum* (April 1970), pp. 18–19.
[4] Bruno Bettelheim, *The Children of the Dream* (New York: Macmillan, 1969).

failure of the foster care system and impressed by Israeli and European forms of group care, also recommends group care for the children of the poor.[5] The child development specialist H. Skeels, encouraged by the positive results of the effects of adoption on children from institutions, proposed a large-scale adoption program to counteract poverty and both sociocultural and maternal deprivation.[6]

Affluent people are often most uneasy about their affluence when they see poor children suffering. They may tell themselves that poor adults could have pulled themselves up by their own bootstraps if they had the same "get up and go" as those affluent observers. But how can you blame children for being born to poor parents? If one assumes that the parents are to blame for their poverty, then what can be done for the children? Cesar Chavez has an answer that seems simple and obvious: "This generation of children will get the food and the education it needs when the parents have enough money to take care of them." [7] Yet this answer is not obvious to the affluent people who blame parents for their poverty. They reason that if the parents were so inadequate as to stay poor, if they had more money they would probably waste it and neglect the children. The specter of the mother in the bar and the child without shoes has a perennial fascination for the victim-blamer. It is woven in the same mental tapestry with hordes of unmarried mothers wantonly getting pregnant year after year so they can get more welfare money.

The alternate explanation of poverty—that an unjust distribution of wealth and power is to blame—would mean that wealthy people would have to give up some of their wealth. It is safer to blame the poor. Those who do can even feel somewhat justified in their belief that the poor neglect their children, because poor people can't give their children material advantages, and if one measures parental competence by material advantages, then the affluent are *ipso facto* better parents. The logic is tautological, but, from the point of view of the victim-blamer, irrefutable. The next step in this logic is to assume that middle-class child welfare professionals could make better arrangements for poor children than the children's own parents can. Following this mandate, the professionals file neglect complaints against poor parents and a judge orders a state or private child welfare agency to take the children from their parents and place them in a foster home or institution. People seldom bring neglect charges against affluent people, despite the fact that some affluent people do neglect and abuse their children.

[5] Martin Wolins, "Political Orientation, Social Reality, and Child Welfare," *Social Service Review*, 38 (December 1964), 429–42; "Group Care: Friend or Foe?" *Social Work*, 14, No. 1 (January 1969), 35–53; "Another View of Group Care," *Child Welfare*, 44, No. 1 (January 1965), 15–16.

[6] H. Skeels, "Effects of Adoption on Children From Institutions," *Children*, 12, No. 1 (1965), 33–34; M. Skodak and H. Skeels, "A Final Follow-up Study of One Hundred Adopted Children," *Journal of Genetic Psychology*, 75 (1949), 85–125.

[7] "La Causa and La Huelga," *Community Organizers and Social Planners*, Joan Ecklein and Armand Lauffer, eds. (New York: John Wiley & Sons, 1972), p. 47.

Malcolm X, describing in his autobiography how the state put his mother in a mental hospital and placed him in a foster home, called foster care legalized slavery:

> We were "state children," court wards: [The judge] had the full say over us. A white man in charge of a black man's children! Nothing but legal, modern slavery—however kindly intentioned. . . . I truly believe that if ever a state social agency destroyed a family, it destroyed ours. We wanted and tried to stay together. Our home didn't have to be destroyed. But the Welfare, the courts, and their doctor, gave us the one-two-three punch.[8]

In a 1966 survey of 624 children in foster care in New York City, Shirley Jenkins and Elaine Norman reported that some Puerto Rican and Black parents expressed the same feeling that Malcolm X had; they felt that their children had been "taken by the Whites." [9] These parents obviously did not accept the need for foster placement, nor did they trust the agency and its social workers. Indeed, they regarded foster care for their children as a symbol of White oppression. Many of the parents in this study were alienated, distrustful, and angry. Puerto Rican parents were the most alienated of all. About 15 percent of the parents studied—those on the lowest socioeconomic level—thought agencies were usurpers and believed that "agencies act like parents have no rights at all—they think they own the children." When asked what they would want if they had three wishes, about half answered, "to have my child back" and "to have a home with my family all living together." Many of them wished for "happiness"—in terms of mental or physical health, or a good spouse to get "off welfare." After studying the families of children in foster care, Jenkins urged that philanthropic funding organizations give high priority to changing radically the foster care system. She said that if parents whose children were taken into foster care against their wishes to organize to regain their parental rights, they might improve the entire field. Jenkins also advocated neighborhood lay guardians to help parents deal with bureaucratic agencies.

The options for placement of children outside their natural homes are (1) care by foster parents in the foster parents' home; (2) foster care in a small group home[10] owned either by an agency or by the foster parents; (3) care in an institution for emotionally disturbed children or for children who have been adjudged either neglected and dependent or delinquent; and (4) adoption by other parents. Only adoptive parents have legal rights to the child; foster parents generally do not. The parents of foster children retain some legal rights to the children unless the state or an agency has taken over full custody of the child. When the state becomes a child's guardian, the

---

[8] *The Autobiography of Malcolm X* (New York: Grove Press, 1965), pp. 20–21.

[9] "Families in Foster Care," *Children*, 16, No. 4 (July–August 1969).

[10] A small group home differs from individual foster family care in that a group (usually between five to twelve) of foster children live in one large house or apartment. Small group care is most often used for adolescents and the foster parents are usually paid a salary, rather than just board payments.

child's legal and social status is ambiguous and marginal. His or her status is somewhat akin to the status of an illegitimate child in medieval England—*filius nullius* (nobody's child) or *filius populi* (everybody's child). It amounts to the same thing; everybody's child stands a good chance of being nobody's child. The majority of foster children are moved about from home to home until they grow up. If they do not return to their own home within the first year of placement, their chances of ever returning home are slim. A recent Seattle study[11] showed that six of ten foster children had undergone four or more moves. Half had been moved from four to seven times, and 12 percent had had between eight and seventeen different placements. Only 5 percent remained in one home. Such dismal statistics clearly put the burden of proof upon the state to demonstrate that the state is, in fact, the better parent. A large number of children in foster care have been as severely neglected by the state as they allegedly were by their parents—from whom the state had removed them. A study in the 60s found that children in 43 percent of public placements and 17 percent of private agency placements were suffering from neglect and abuse.[12]

The number of children who are in such a serious plight is not small: in 1970 there were over a quarter of a million foster children. Their numbers increase by about 9,000 a year, so that by 1975 there will probably be over 300,000. There are about 75,000 children in institutions for the dependent, neglected, and emotionally disturbed.[13] The obvious question that arises is, since foster children are wandering in limbo as "nobody's children," why not make them somebody's children and place them in adoptive homes? Why not simply sever their ties with their parents once and for all and give the children "better" homes?

It is not so simple. In the first place, if the state forcibly severed parents' legal ties to their children on a large scale, it would in effect be declaring war on poor parents. In these days of heightened consciousness among the poor, if large numbers of parents lost their children, the already smoldering resentment the poor feel toward the government might flare up. Class antagonisms—already deep—would become exacerbated. From the government's point of view, it simply might not be safe to initiate a large-scale child-snatching program. From the point of view of parents who lose their children, their suffering would be intense.

In the second place, a large-scale adoption program would be practically impossible to carry out because it would probably be impossible to find homes for all of the children. Most of the middle-class people who apply to adopt want perfectly healthy babies, and have a slight preference for girl babies (by

[11] Benson Jaffee and Draza Kline, *New Payment Patterns and the Foster Parent Role*, Child Welfare League of America, New York (1970), p. 46.

[12] Abraham S. Levine, "Substitute Child Care: Recent Research and Its Implications," *Welfare in Review*, 10, No. 1 (January–February 1972), 3.

[13] United States Department of Health, Education, and Welfare, National Center for Social Statistics, "Children Served by Public Welfare Agencies and Voluntary Child Welfare Agencies and Institutions—March 1970," March 10, 1972.

about 54 percent). Most children taken from their parents on neglect charges are beyond the infant stage, and there are more boys than girls in foster care. Many of the foster children have physical handicaps or emotional problems. Working-class people are somewhat more accepting than are middle-class people of these "different" children, but adoption agencies have generally preferred middle-class to working-class applicants. Agencies controlled and mainly staffed by White people have discriminated against Black adoptive applicants, and children of minority groups and interracial parentage are less likely than White children either to be placed in adoptive homes or, if they have been taken from their parents, to return home. Despite the fact that the proportion of Black children who come into foster care and temporary shelters is higher than the proportion of White children, a far higher proportion of White children are adopted. The number of White homes accepted for children generally exceeds the number of White children accepted for adoption, but there were only 64 non-White homes approved per 100 non-White children accepted in the last half of 1973.[14] As Andrew Billingsley and Jeanne Giovanonni documented in their book *Children of the Storm*,[15] whenever Black-controlled agencies have handled adoption placements, they have placed a much higher percentage of children in homes than have White-controlled agencies.

A similar problem exists for Puerto Rican and Mexican-American children. Henry Maas and Richard Engler, in their classic study of foster care and adoption in nine communities, *Children in Need of Parents*, described the situation in one Southwestern community where 60 percent of the population had Spanish surnames:

> La Paz always presented a picture of a "we" group caring for a "they" group in its health and welfare programs. It was Anglo money, Anglo medicine, and Anglo welfare programs that took care of the "Spanish needy," and the gulf between the givers and the recipients seemed quite wide.[16]

In all nine communities, the child of minority ethnicity (Negro, Spanish-speaking, American Indian, Portugese, French-Canadian) "was more likely to remain in foster care than to be adopted." [17] Interestingly, however, these children less frequently exhibited psychological disturbance and experienced fewer moves than did the majority child. (The two facts are probably related because psychological problems of children in foster care increased with the number of different moves they made.) Mothers of these children had less cooperative relationships with agencies.

In the New England coastal town of Brighton (town names are fictitious), a highly stratified community, no Black children were adopted. In the segregated Southwestern metropolis of King City, Black people went to out-of-town agencies to adopt in order to avoid the stigma associated with

[14] Barbara Haring, "Adoption Statistics," *Child Welfare*, 53, No. 5 (May 1974), 329.
[15] New York: Harcourt Brace Jovanovich, 1972.
[16] New York: Columbia University Press, 1959, p. 87.
[17] Ibid., p. 354.

welfare agencies in the community. In the "liberal" city of Westport, a progressive metropolis on the West Coast, 91 percent of the adopted children were White, although only 65 percent of children in foster care were White. Not one Black child in Westport returned home, and few Black children were adopted. Forty percent of the children who attained their majority in foster care in Westport were Black, although only 18 percent of the foster care population was Black. On the other hand, in the more blatantly racist Southern community of Jamestown, proportionately as many Black children were adopted as came into foster care—because agencies were segregated and Black agencies handled Black adoptions. Jamestown was more reluctant to take Black children into foster care than was Westport, even though they had a much higher Black population and the Black people were much poorer than Blacks in Westport. One can only speculate about which situation proved to be better for Black children in the long run—staying in the limbo of foster care in Westport or growing up with parents in poverty in Jamestown.

Most agencies were reluctant to arrange transracial adoptions until the late 50s and early 60s, when this policy began to change and some minority children were placed with White couples. However, as the number of transracial adoptions increased—to an estimated total of 2,600 in 1971[18]— some Black Liberation groups decided that their need for cultural solidarity was an overriding value and they took a stand against placing Black children in White homes. At its conference in April 1972, the National Association of Black Social Workers announced its official position against transracial adoptions.

Alvin Schorr points out that interracial adoption took hold only after the declining birthrate and the increased availability of abortions led to a severe shortage of adoptable babies.

> It is difficult to test cause and effect; still, the supply provided by the poor was made to respond to the demand for children among the nonpoor (and, in the process, a small sector of discrimination fell away). Though they were wrong in principle, one understands the rage of militant Black social workers who took a stand against interracial adoption.[19]

Although they are now willing to place Black children in White homes, adoption agencies have never placed White children in Black homes.

In Shakespeare's *Henry IV*, Part I, Glendower boasted that he could call spirits from the vasty deep. Hotspur replied laconically, "Why, so can I, or so can any man; but will they come when you do call for them?" In the same spirit, some social policy makers may boast that placing poor children in middle-class homes would solve the problems of large numbers of poor children. But can those policy makers find the adopters? And even if they could, what then? Is adoption *really* a panacea for poor children?

[18] Ursula M. Gallagher, "Adoption in a Changing Society," *Children Today*, 2, No. 1 (September–October 1972), 2–6.
[19] "Poor Care for Poor Children—What Way Out?" in *Children and Decent People*, Alvin Schorr, ed. (New York: Basic Books, 1974), p. 188.

I won't go into the question of whether adopted children are better or worse off, or the same as "natural" children, because no one really knows. The question is hard to research because of the problem of deciding whom to compare adopted children with and what criteria to use. Comparative studies have been done, but the body of research so far is unconvincing. In one respect, however, adopted children are clearly different from natural children—they have two sets of parents. One set, the biological parents, are kept hidden. The adoption agency makes certain that the adopted child does not know their identity, and often does not tell the adoptive parents much about them. This constitutes a problem that keeps recurring in the research and literature on adoption with almost obsessive regularity—the problem of telling the child that he or she is adopted, and of dealing with the questions that then come up. The fact that an adopted child was born to another set of parents seems to pose an insoluble problem to many adoptive parents. In addition, the fact that most adopted children were born out of wedlock poses a further problem to many adoptive parents. They often don't want to discuss either fact with their adopted children. The "other parents" and their illicit sexuality embarrass them. Of the 100 adoptive couples studied by Benson Jaffee and David Fanshel,[20] most of them had not told the children anything about their biological parents' marital status or why their parents had given up their children. A few parents had given false information. On the basis of their interviews with the parents, the researchers concluded that giving such information was not crucial to the children's adjustment. However, when they interviewed the grown children of the same adopters, the story was quite different. The adoptees perceived more problems in their current adjustment than did their parents. More than half of the children said they had pressed their adoptive parents for more information about their biological parents, while only one-fifth of the adoptive parents said this. About one-fourth of the adopters, but only about one-tenth of the adoptees, reported they had been given full and truthful information about their biological parents' marital status and social-personal traits.[21]

A study in the 1950s by Jean Paton[22] concluded that when adoptive parents are not threatened by the child's search for natural parents and sometimes even help in the search, the child resolves his or her anxieties about adoption more easily than does the child whose parents are threatened by the search. Paton believes that many children want to conduct the search but refrain for fear of hurting their adoptive parents' feelings. A few adopted children in Paton's study had "noteworthy success" in incorporating two sets of parents. Paton believes that until biology becomes unimportant culturally, adopted children will inevitably have some curiosity about the natural parents.

[20] *How They Fared in Adoption: A Follow-up Study* (New York: Columbia University Press, 1970).
[21] Benson Jaffee, "Adoption Outcome: A Two-Generation View," *Child Welfare*, 53, No. 4 (April 1974), 211–24.
[22] J. M. Paton, *The Adopted Break Silence* (Acton, Calif.: Life History Study Center, 1954).

The British National Council for Civil Liberties says that a child's new parents should be required by the court legalizing the adoption to tell the child that he is adopted. Their report, *Children Have Rights*,[23] emphasizes that this puts the relationship between the child and parents on an honest basis and indicates that the parents are being honest with themselves about the adoption. They say, "At this moment it is virtually impossible for an adopted child to find out who his natural parents were, unless his adopted parents are prepared to disclose the child's original name." In the United States, a great many adopted adults have recently begun to search for their natural parents. A New York City detective agency reports that adoptees searching for their natural parents constituted a large new clientele for the agency. In 1972, they received 1,514 such requests, most of them from women. Some were worried about the possibility of passing on hereditary illnesses to their own offspring. Many had waited until after their adoptive parents had died for fear of hurting their feelings. All reported feelings of insecurity and of going through an "identity crisis." [24] Some adoptees have formed groups to discuss their identity problems and to search for their natural parents.

Many people are searching for their historical origins these days, including Blacks, Jews, women, and adopted children. The historian Christopher Lasch speaks of the superficiality of the progressive political ideology in America which caused a radical discontinuity in American culture and resulted in a ceaseless search for new beginnings, a flight from complexity and from the past, and the belief that the past "is an encumbrance that can painlessly be discarded in the restless search for a better future.[25] The ideology of adoption agencies which encourages discontinuity in genealogy and prefers adoptive parents who are geared to achievement and upward mobility seems particularly in keeping with the American character structure. Some adult adopted children do not believe that the past "is an encumbrance that can painlessly be discarded." An adult adoptee told Jean Paton:

> Couldn't an adopted child know he had two sets of parents, equally indispensable, the natural and circumstantial, without the latter going into a tailspin at the mention of the former?[26]

People are so accustomed to thinking of children as their private property that the idea of having two sets of parents simultaneously often seems weird. Yet there have been, and still are, societies where adoption does not entail a radical break with the natural parents. Noteworthy among these are the societies of Eastern Oceania, which includes Hawaii and Tahiti. Several anthropologists studied these societies and published their findings in *Adoption in Eastern Oceania*.[27] As I read these studies, it occurred to me that the

---

[23] "A Child's Rights," *Boston Sunday Globe*, Parade sec., June 13, 1971, p. 7.

[24] John Culhane, "The Case of the Runaway Wives," *The New York Times Magazine*, June 10, 1973, p. 90.

[25] Christopher Lasch, "On Richard Hofstadter," *New York Review of Books*, March 8, 1973, p. 8.

[26] *The Adopted Break Silence*, p. 162.

[27] Vern Carroll, ed. (Honolulu: University of Hawaii Press, 1970).

historical forms that substitute child care take provide a rough index of a society's economic and political system. One could conceive of children as a form of property (which, indeed, they were legally until relatively recently in some states of the United States), and trace the shifts in child care from primitive communism to the present highly stratified industrialized societies. In the Eastern Oceanic societies where adoption has been common, land was originally owned communally by the clan, and children were also in a sense communal property. Adoption cemented ties between families, usually in the same clan, and kept a stable population so that natural resources would roughly provide for the population. Frequently grandparents adopted grandchildren so they would have someone to care for them in their old age.

All of these societies have been changed to one degree or another by occupying colonial powers—France, Germany, Japan, Spain, England, the United States. In the process, clan ties loosened and in some societies gave way to the Western-style nuclear family. Colonial administrators changed communal ownership of property to private ownership; wage-labor and a money economy replaced a subsistence agricultural economy; missionaries introduced moral prohibitions against permissive sexuality and against adoption, which made permissive sexuality easier. When land was owned communally, adopted children kept their ties to their natal family and clan. As communal land tenure gave way to private property, however, the norm of communal ownership of children began to give way to the norm we know in the United States—children as private property.

As this process developed, fosterage and adoption seemed to become two separate systems of child care, with foster care the lower-status system because foster children had an ambiguous legal status in terms of who owned them. In some societies, foster children are used as slave labor; indeed, in the developing stage of capitalism in Western societies, foster children were first indentured as apprentices to work homes and later placed in "free" boarding homes, particularly in rural areas, to provide labor for farmers, tradesmen, and housewives. Some foster children are still used for labor, especially in rural areas.

In Euro-Asian societies, adoption has historically been very closely tied to the inheritance of property. In classical Greece, ancient Rome, Hindu India, prerevolutionary China, and Japan, sons were adopted by propertied childless couples to continue the family line. The Russian Bolsheviks abolished adoption in 1918 as part of their attempt to abolish private property and inheritance. Russia reinstated adoption in 1926, apparently to provide homes for the thousands of children left homeless by the war. In most European and Latin American countries today, adoption is still hedged about with many laws to protect the inheritance of blood relatives. Even in the United States and Canada, the adoption laws of states and provinces pay careful attention to inheritance. In general, however, adopted children in the United States have about the same inheritance rights as do natural children, and are under the exclusive legal jurisdiction of the adoptive parents. Natural parents are excluded so completely that adoption agencies take pains to place children far away from them so that they will not meet. Beginning about the middle of the nineteenth century, when states began to pass adoption laws, the function of adoption shifted from an aristocratic privilege to secure orderly inheritance of property to a way for middle- and upper-class childless couples to obtain children from poor, usually unmarried, women. Around the turn of the century, adoption agencies formed by upper-class women took on the function of arranging adoptions, first using volunteer staff and then paid professionals. In order to insure exclusive possession of their adopted children unencumbered by claims of the natural parents, the agencies gradually erected almost impenetrable barriers against natural parents continuing any contact with the adopted children.

After World War II, states became more active in regulating adoptions, so that now in most states it is illegal to adopt a nonrelated child independently of some social agency approval. Because there is no hard proof that agency-supervised adoptions work out better than independently arranged adoptions, I suspect that one of the most important functions of agency intervention in adoptions is to erect a state-sponsored barrier against the natural parents. This system, however, contained the built-in contradictions that are beginning to manifest themselves on a large scale by adoptees searching for their natural parents.

Adoption, then, is problematic in the United States because of two deeply held norms: (1) children are the exclusive possession of their parents, and (2) extramarital pregnancy is not sanctioned by the majority of people. Adoption violates both these norms. Until relatively recently in England, adoption agencies were somewhat on the defensive in "respectable" society because they were accused of encouraging immorality by helping the pregnant woman get rid of "the fruits of her sin." Adoption was originally a women's liberation program when it first began in England in 1912, sponsored by the Adoption Committee of the Cambridge Branch of the Church League for Women's Suffrage. Its aim was to "rehabilitate" unmarried mothers and to turn unwanted into wanted children. However, as the demand for adoptable babies increased, the criticism against adoption decreased. The main public criticism against adoption agencies in the United States for the past few decades has been that they make it hard for couples to get babies.

Ironically, although adoption began as a women's liberation program, it is now being proposed by some people as a conservative alternative to the current women's liberation program of abortion. Some opponents of abortion carry bumper stickers on their cars urging "Adoption, not Abortion." The sexual revolution and women's liberation have softened the stigma against out-of-wedlock pregnancy to such an extent that many women are keeping their out-of-wedlock babies rather than releasing them for adoption. This, combined with availability of contraception and legalization of abortion, has drastically decreased the number of adoptable babies. Some adoption agencies stopped taking applications for new babies from couples in 1971. Some of these applicants are adopting Third World babies from Korea, Viet Nam, Bangladesh, Colombia; and Eskimos and American Indians in the

United States. Most of the adoptable children in the United States now are either older than infants, handicapped, non-White, or racially mixed—the children who have been taken from their parents or released by their parents and left in limbo in foster care or shelters. Until recently, most child welfare agencies have not made much effort to find adoptive homes for these children. Now that babies are not as available, some agencies are putting more resources into finding homes for these children or providing resources such as day-care centers to mothers who want to keep their babies. Before the onset of legalized abortion, the main resource that agencies provided—aside from arranging for adoptions—was a prenatal residence home where unmarried mothers could live during the last stage of pregnancy. The mothers received good prenatal and obstetrical care, and frequent contacts with a social worker, who often put subtle pressure on them to give up their babies for adoption. In 1972 the Florence Crittendon Home for unwed mothers in Boston became the first such agency in the country to add an abortion clinic to its services.

Even though some agencies are paying more attention to finding homes for older children, the couples who want babies are not necessarily interested in adopting older children. Many of the older children are adopted by families who have children of their own and could have more. By 1973, twenty-two states had passed laws to allow adoptions to be subsidized for people otherwise too poor to adopt, or for people who could afford the care of a healthy child but could not afford to take a handicapped child who will need extensive medical care. These subsidies are not generous. Some agencies are becoming more flexible about allowing single women and men to adopt, and are relaxing their previously rigid rules against working mothers. All of these reforms are desirable, but they still do not get to the heart of the issue: why were the children taken from their parents in the first place?

The problems in both foster care and adoption lead us back to the problems of a polarized class society, and especially to the people on the bottom rung of that class society—poor women. About three-fourths of the parents of foster children are women trying to raise a family alone, living either on substandard welfare payments or substandard wages. Most are poor, ill-fed, ill-housed, and simply ill. The foster mothers who care for their children are somewhat better off, but not much. They are mostly wives of working-class men, and they received in 1970 median board payments of between $64 and $80 monthly. The state is cheap when it comes to paying foster parents to care for poor kids. As with most service agencies for the poor, state child welfare agencies are understaffed, overworked, underfinanced, and overbureaucratized. The federal government is even cheaper. It contributes about 10 percent of child care money, less than for any other service program with federal matching funds. Private sectarian agencies get a large share of their funds from the state, and despite their sectarian control, they are more public than private in their financing. Some New York City child care agencies are being sued for misusing public funds by discriminating against Black and minority children in their admissions policies.

Despite the low board payments to foster parents, the total cost of raising a child from infancy to the age of 18 is staggering: according to a 1972 New York City study, it costs the state $122,500 to raise a foster child to the age of 18! This, compared to $34,464 for raising a child in a natural home to the age of 18! The money spent on keeping one child in foster care would provide an annual income to that child's parents of about $7,000.[28] The chances are good that if the parents had that income, the child would not be placed. Although middle-income families sometimes neglect their children, they seldom take each other to court. The middle and upper classes may admit that their children's behavior constitutes a "social problem," but they seldom admit that they are neglectful parents.

FOSTER CARE REFORMS

There is simply no way to bring about the radical changes that are needed in the foster care system without a significant redistribution of wealth and power. Yet such redistribution is not at the moment a high social priority. In the meantime, there are ways to prevent many foster placements, and to improve the foster care system after children are placed. Many reform proposals have been urged by child welfare specialists for over two decades but few have been implemented on any large scale because foster care is not a political issue and therefore there has been little pressure for change. I shall list some of these reform proposals.

1. The first line of defense against breaking up a family is to provide social supports to families, especially single-parent families. These supports include adequate income maintenance, health care, adequate housing, day care and after-school child care, and homemaker service when a parent is physically or emotionally ill. Such family supports would prevent much neglect. Communities need to be educated to the importance of helping families rather than punishing them. For some families, supports would need to be continued until the children grow up. This would still be cheaper to the taxpayer than foster care, and usually healthier for the children than placement away from home.

2. If foster care is essential, the possibility of relatives or family friends caring for the children should be investigated. They should be paid as foster parents, because most relatives and friends of poor children are themselves poor. If no such people can be found, children should be placed close to their families. Studies show that children placed close to their families are more likely to return home eventually than are children placed far away. Even those children who remain in foster care until adulthood are likely to have a better self-image when their parents continue to be interested in them.

3. Agencies should give high priority to working with families toward the child's return, especially during the first year of placement, the critical time for decisions about returning to the family.

[28] David Fanshel and Eugene B. Shinn, "Dollars and Sense in the Foster Care of Children: A Look at Cost Factors," cited by *The New York Times*, February 13, 1972.

4. Agencies should act on their knowledge that foster care in a strange family is very risky, especially for children above the age of 5 or 6. Small group homes generally have a higher success record than individual families. Despite their dismal record of foster home failures, most agencies doggedly keep placing children in a succession of private homes rather than investing in group homes.

5. Foster parents—or child care workers, as I prefer to call them—should be treated and paid as skilled child care workers. They should be co-professionals and should help to shape the policies of agencies they work for. They are too often treated as clients in need of treatment rather than given decent pay and prestige. Many foster parents are able and should be encouraged to work supportively with natural parents. Foster parents have recently formed their own organizations, and this should put some much-needed pressure on the system.

6. Aggrieved parents of children in foster care should organize to protect their interests in the system. Their children have been taken from them by a legal system that does not allow them full due process and often does not provide them with counsel, or indeed often does not even recognize their right to counsel. Parents often do not participate in placement decisions, nor are they often provided with alternatives to placement. Advocates or ombudsmen could help parents negotiate with complex child welfare bureaucracies to protect their interests. Massachusetts has an Office for Children which is empowered to act in an ombudsman capacity.

7. Foster children who are old enough to participate in decision-making should also be fully consulted in decisions about their lives. One of the most insidious abuses the foster care system imposes on the children is the failure of agencies to involve children in critical decisions, thus leaving children in an almost constant state of anxiety about their future. Foster children gain mutual support and reassurance from sharing in the decisions affecting their lives. They can also get support from each other and develop some political leverage through group discussion and action.

ADOPTION REFORMS

Historical circumstances have forced some long overdue reforms on the adoption system. Adoption agencies are now doing more of what they should have been doing all along—finding adoption homes for children in foster care who have been relinquished by their parents. A few agencies are turning foster homes into quasi-adoption homes. Foster parents were formerly forbidden to adopt their foster children or to initiate contact with the foster child's parents. This is still true in many agencies.

Other needed reforms in adoption would require agencies to rethink the entire issue of kinship and possession of children. The radical breaking off of ties between a child and its natural parents has posed serious identity problems for children. The sociologist H. David Kirk concludes from his study of adoption[29] that it is healthier for adoptive parents to acknowledge that their status is different from natural parenthood. Kirk advises encouraging open communication between adoptive parents and natural parents before the child is placed, to help the child cope with questions about his or her background. I know of no agency, however, that has followed this advice. Kirk also recommends group discussion among adoptive parents as a means of resolving anxieties that stem from the adoption experience. Some agencies and adoptive couples have, in fact, formed such groups. The same suggestion would benefit adopted children, to give them reassurance about their status.

I should like to make an even more heretical suggestion to some courageous adoption agencies and adoptive parents: Why not try an experimental demonstration project in which adoptive parents and natural parents share responsibility for a child, as long as the child wants two sets of parents? There are some mature and stable natural parents who could handle this responsibly; there must be a few adoptive parents who would see it as a challenge in parenting. Is there an agency that would dare to make such a break with tradition?

I suspect that many unmarried women are keeping their babies because the thought of forever giving them up is repugnant to them. By keeping the child, however, they may be severely limiting their life options. It is not easy to prepare for and pursue a career when one has full-time responsibility for a child. Perhaps some of these mothers would be receptive to allowing another parent or couple major responsibility for the child. While the child could be legally adopted by the substitute parents, the natural parent(s) could retain visitation privileges. The people who would dare to try such an experiment would be pioneers in redefining parenthood from an act of possession to a shared social trust.

---

[29] *Shared Fate* (New York: The Free Press, 1964).

reproduction and capitalist development: uses of birth control and abortion

—Mie Watanabe

Welfare and population issues must be considered together, and on a worldwide scale. In this chapter, Mie Watanabe argues that the current alarm about food shortages and the growing population in underdeveloped countries is linked to the needs of American economic domination.

Few United States legislators and policy makers are giving the Biblical advice to "be fruitful and multiply" to the poor. Ever since the gloomy predictions of Malthus and his prescriptions for reducing the numbers of the poor, welfare and population policy makers have kept a careful watch over the reproductive habits of the poor. Both population and welfare policies are shaped in accordance with corporate and state needs for workers and warriors. Henry Allen shows in this book how the government initiated work and training programs in the 1960s to quell unrest. So were sterilization and family planning services for low-income persons begun in response to the struggles of the unemployed and working poor. Rationalized as a generous response to the wishes of the poor, government programs often engaged in coercive sterilization programs. Such programs seek to cure poverty by reducing the numbers of the poor rather than by spreading the wealth.

Governments of all political persuasions are concerned more with their own political and economic goals than with women's right to control their own reproductive functions. Therefore, women may find their feminist demands coopted and misused by the state. This raises profound political questions which are implicit in all the articles in this book. Whose interests does the State represent? If it does not work to enhance the welfare of most of its citizens, is it not a misnomer to call it a "welfare" state?

In the past decade there have been significant advances in the technology of fertility control as governments have begun to incorporate rational population planning in their programs for economic development.[1] As North

---

[1] At a recent conference on menstrual regulation, a doctor from the Philippines said of menstrual extraction as a form of abortion: "It is something we will be able to bring practically into the rice paddy." *The New York Times*, December 20, 1973.

American women have won a number of reforms regarding the availability of birth control and abortion services, we have seen that at this particular historical moment our desire to limit family size and to control reproduction coincides with a government interest in fertility control. What is the common issue at stake? From the viewpoint of women, making birth control and abortion more available is a means of giving us *control over our own reproductive capacity* and therefore over our own collective social power. The work of motherhood would no longer be imposed on women as a biological necessity and a social limitation. From the government's viewpoint, it is also a matter of control. Providing "family planning" services gives the government new and more powerful ways of *controlling the flow of workers* in and out of the labor market and therefore of influencing the size and the composition of the labor force.

In the midst of a world food crisis, population experts are arguing that there are basically too many people for too little food and that most countries should limit their rate of population growth. In practice, however, several governments have initiated programs for changing population growth which appear to be contradictory: some developing countries like Brazil and Argentina are encouraging growth, while others like India are attempting to limit it; several countries in Eastern Europe are attempting to increase population despite a low standard of living, while the United States, with a relatively high standard of living and a declining birth rate, has initiated sterilization programs. In this chapter, I will examine how the different forms of government and corporate involvement in population control (through contraception, sterilization, and abortion services) are in fact consistent with a need to maintain social stability and to fulfill the demands of the labor market under different forms of economic development.

ECONOMIC DEVELOPMENT AND POPULATION CONTROL

United States corporations and the United States government have funded a number of advisory councils and agencies for population control in developing countries. The programs of these organizations involve large-scale efforts to reduce fertility and tend to be based on Malthusian assumptions concerning "overpopulation." For advocates of Zero Population Growth, mass levels of starvation in developing countries are interpreted as the necessary outcome of a basic historical conflict between an ever-increasing population and diminishing world resources. Thus a country very often will be defined as overpopulated if its people are underfed. In actuality, the problem facing the developed world is not a problem of too little food for too many people but of how to deal with a surplus of food on the world market. The Great Plains of North America already provide 60 percent of all wheat in world trade even though large amounts of productive land are kept idle.

Some population experts contend that the land that has been taken out of cultivation alone could supply enough food to make up the minimum caloric deficits of the non-socialist developing world.[2]

To further understand the politics of the food-population problem, we must look at the trends in the world food market. Since United States-based multinational corporations have a virtual monopoly on existing food supplies, it becomes possible for them to manipulate the availability and price of food on a world scale, and thus to determine which classes in which countries will eat what kind and quantity of food. In 1972, a well-timed wheat sale of 20 million tons to the USSR combined with a crop failure in India (not an unforeseeable event) induced an international "shortage" and ultimately set the stage for a worldwide food price inflation in 1973 and 1974. This one act of international diplomacy hastened the détente between the United States and the Soviet Union and raised both the domestic and foreign profits of the United States food industry.

In addition to regulating their food exports, the developed countries have attempted to reduce their fertilizer exports as a way of limiting the production of food supplies *within* developing countries. The United States government, for example, discouraged new export contracts of fertilizer to developing nations during most of the 1974 crop season, and shipments of fertilizer under its aid programs "virtually dried up." [3] The resultant world fertilizer shortage was largely responsible for a 7 million ton short-fall in India's 1974 spring wheat harvest and hence for its large import needs. By raising the food import needs of developing countries like India, the fertilizer shortage has already stimulated a rise in prices on the world market. In addition, by raising food relief needs it has required the United States government to enter the wheat market as a buyer in order to continue its foreign aid program. This of course will further inflate prices domestically. Food experts have begun to suggest that the structure of the world economy has entered an "era of chronically tight supplies." [4]

In the fall of 1974, when India faced a grain deficit of 7 million tons, the United States continued to maintain its political priorities. Only a few days after President Ford approved a 2.2 million ton wheat sale to the Soviet Union, Kissinger told Indian officials that the United States could supply only about 500,000 tons of grain at reduced prices in the next few months.[5] Thus underdevelopment in the Indian subcontinent continues to raise the possibility that a "*demographic* explosion will sooner or later become the *revolutionary* explosion." [6] As the president of Planned Parenthood Alan Guttmacher wrote, "Reckless population growth without parallel economic

[2] Heady and Mayer (1967), *Food Needs and U.S. Agriculture in 1980*, cited in Population Action Group of Philadelphia, "Population Growth—Problems and Solutions" (unpublished).

[3] *The New York Times*, August 28, 1974.

[4] Ibid., May 12, 1974.

[5] Ibid., November 5, 1974.

[6] Bonnie Mass, *The Political Economy of Population Control in Latin America* (Montreal: Editions Latin America, 1972), p. 33.

. . . growth makes for a constant lowering of the standard of living. Such a decline, with its concomitant mounting poverty and hunger, leads to political unrest." [7] In the face of a revolutionary explosion, population control in the Indian subcontinent has begun to assume the form of genocide. The most apparent case is Bangladesh where the government has set up 4,500 "gruel camps" that are not unlike concentration camps. Refugees from the villages are herded off the city streets into these camps which ostensibly provide emergency relief. They actually serve as "internment camps whose inmates are slowly dying." [8] Armed policemen guard the entrances for the sole purpose of keeping the refugees from getting out and sparking food riots in the city.

Thus we can see that the cost and distribution of food as well as the rate of growth of the agricultural industries in several developing countries like India are not determined by the rate of population increase but by the needs of American economic domination. In fact, the greatest drain on world resources is the requirement of capitalist production in developed nations: United States capitalism, for example, needs at least 34 percent of the world's energy and 30 percent of the steel, to a large extent because it must produce the means for its international military domination.

In opposition to the traditional United States approach to "overpopulation" in the developing world, governments of several developing nations recommend rapid population growth as a basis for political stability because they are planning for a period of economic development.[9] In Brazil, for example, where a recent period of economic growth without a parallel growth in the labor force has strengthened the bargaining position of the working class, thereby raising wages, the government has chosen to double the country's population over the next twenty years as one means of curing a "troubled economy." According to Brazilian economist Paul Singer, "Workers didn't fight for their rights while they were competing for jobs, but now the jobs are competing for them. . . . The Government will have to provoke a recession to take the heat out of the economy because we are *running out of manpower* and raw materials." [10] The government's program entails a two-stage strategy. On the short term, the government must induce enough unemployment through the traditional monetary tools to restrain the workers' wage offensive while on the long term it must give a free reign to the rate of population growth.

In Argentina, the Peronist government is actively trying to pressure women back into the work of reproduction and child care. The government has promised to double Argentina's population to 50 million by the end of this century for the purpose of stimulating economic growth. In March of 1974, it issued a decree restricting the sale of contraceptive pills; oral

[7] Quoted in Mass, p. 23.
[8] *Boston Globe*, October 21, 1974.
[9] Ibid., June 9, 1974.
[10] Ibid., April 2, 1974 (italics mine).

contraceptives are available now only with a prescription signed by three medical authorities. The dissemination of birth control information has also been prohibited because, according to the Health Ministry, giving women the knowledge and techniques of birth control undermines their "fundamental maternal function." With the threat of an economically, powerful Brazil, Argentina also wants to establish sovereignty over its large areas of undeveloped land. The Peronist magazine *Las Bases* has warned that, without a larger population, "we will not have the arms to work this immense and rich territory, and if we do not do it, there will be others who will." [11] The magazine goes on to suggest that rapid population growth will serve to improve economic conditions: "We will never have these ideal conditions if we do not have the men who can contribute to production . . . First we must have active men and for that it is necessary that this generation discard its egotisms and be generous in procreating . . . We must start from the basis that the principal work of a woman is to have children." [12]

Several critics have pointed out that while the Peronist campaign attacked the former army dictatorship for its one million unemployed, in the period since Peron assumed power there has been no dramatic increase in employment. In view of this persistent unemployment, policies which attempt to make women reproduce a larger work force can only mean greater profits for Argentinian corporations by allowing them to increase their rate of economic development without incurring the kind of labor shortage experienced by Brazil with its consequent labor militancy.

SOCIAL UNREST AND FAMILY PLANNING

In the United States, a developed country with a declining birth rate, the government has also been prompted by social unrest to assume an active role in population limitation.[13] This country is experiencing the problem of a "labor surplus" which has become increasingly militant in demanding more money in the form of unemployment and welfare benefits and in refusing to take available low paying jobs. The large-scale government involvement in sterilization and family planning services for low-income persons which began in 1967 was initiated in response to the struggles of the unemployed and working poor during the 1960s. Since 1968, HEW programs alone have sterilized an estimated 100,000 to 150,000 low-income persons per year.[14] During the 1960s, social scientists spent much time and energy trying to demonstrate that such family planning services were consistent with the needs

[11] Ibid., March 17, 1974.

[12] Ibid.

[13] Nathan Keyfitz, quoted in Robin Elliot, Lynn C. Landman, and Richard Tsuruoka, "U.S. Population Growth and Family Planning: a Review of the Literature," in *The American Population Debate*, David Callahan, ed. (Garden City: Doubleday, 1971), pp. 185–225.

[14] *Boston Globe*, April 26, 1974.

of the poor. Most of the studies of attitudes toward contraception revealed that Black people and the poor wanted as few children as anyone else, yet their fertility rates were higher.[15] Related studies indicated that when family planning services were actually made available to Black women, they used contraception as effectively as White women.[16] Taking these results as proof of "excess fertility," sociologists then concluded that government subsidy of family planning clinics provided a progressive social service strongly desired by Black women themselves.

Once the government did extend a "helping hand" through family planning services, it became clear that the forms of birth control promoted and the methods of encouraging their use were not in the interest of women. Poor and non-White women who had to rely on government health-care services found themselves in a contradictory relationship to birth control. Although birth control can allow a woman to determine when she will have children if she wants them, the actual practice of family planning clinics in many cases functioned to control her reproductive capacity permanently through sterilization.

The case of the Relf sisters is an example of the kind of population control poor and non-White women encounter under the guise of family planning. Twelve-year-old Mary Alice Relf and her fourteen-year-old sister Minnie Lee had been receiving Depo-provera injections from a family planning clinic in Montgomery, Alabama. In the summer of 1973, after the FDA had banned this experimental birth control drug for its dangerous side effects, a nurse from the clinic came to the Relf home and convinced Ms. Relf to sign her "X" on a parental consent form authorizing the sterilization of her daughters. She was told that the two girls were going to "get some shots" at the hospital. She did not know that they were to be permanently sterilized, nor did she know that they had already been human guinea pigs for an experimental birth control drug. The clinic decided to initiate these measures because the two sisters were "found not to have the mental talents to take birth control pills." [17] Upon later investigation, however, the clinic could offer no proof that they needed birth control assistance in the first place.

The case of the Relf sisters was not an isolated incident. By the time it made national headlines, many other young women defined as retarded and incompetent had been sterilized. The federally funded clinic in Montgomery had arranged for eleven sterilizations, all involving minors, ten of whom were Black. In all instances, it appeared that the parents had not been adequately informed. Several of the 3,260 federally funded clinics serving low-income families had sterilized eighty other minors in the country over a fifteen month period.[18] Finally, in March 1974, the Washington, D.C. District Court permanently enjoined HEW from funding the sterilization of minors and

[15] Betty Sarvis and Hyman Rodman, *The Abortion Controversy* (New York: Columbia University Press, 1973), p. 165.

[16] Ibid., p. 165.

[17] *Liberation News Service*, June 30, 1973, and *The New York Times*, July 1, 1973.

[18] *The New York Times*, July 8, 1973.

"incompetents" and ordered that sterilization candidates under Medicaid and family planning programs must be informed orally from the beginning that they cannot lose their benefits if they refuse an operation.[19]

Despite these legislative changes prohibiting coerced sterilization through government agencies, poor and non-White women have no protection from the men who control the rest of the medical profession. Doctors who work in hospitals, as well as those in private practice, often employ coercive methods to induce welfare women to undergo sterilization operations. In August 1973, in Aiken, South Carolina, Marietta Williams was sterilized by the only doctor in town willing to deliver babies to welfare women. According to the *International Herald Tribune*, Dr. Clovis H. Pierce makes deliveries on the condition that women who have three children and receive Medicaid agree to be sterilized. It was later found that eighteen out of thirty-four deliveries paid for by Medicaid at the Aiken County Hospital had included sterilization. Sixteen of the women involved were Black. All the deliveries had been performed by Dr. Pierce who, over an eighteen-month period, had received Medicaid payments of $60,000 for his services.[20]

In November 1973, a Nader-affiliated Health Research Group (HRG) completed a study documenting coercive sterilization practices in several big-city hospitals: Boston City Hospital, 1971; Baltimore City Hospital, 1972; and Los Angeles County Hospital, 1972 to 1973. According to an HRG lawyer:

> A typical case involves a welfare mother, twenty years old on the average. She has one child, maybe two, and she has never expressed any interest in sterilization. She comes to the hospital to have another baby, this time by Caesarian section. While she is in labor, she is approached by an intern and she is pressured to accept sterilization.[21]

HRG found further that these women were subjected to sterilization methods that posed a higher risk than other methods in use. In Baltimore City Hospital, many women were given sterilization permits to sign literally minutes before a Caesarian section and sterilization were to be carried out. In most cases the woman was in labor when asked for her consent. In not one case was there evidence that the woman had expressed an interest in sterilization, even though it is routine procedure to ask a woman if she wants such an operation when she registers at the clinic prior to delivery. In the twelve cases mentioned in the report, seven women were under twenty years of age, most of the women were Black and poor, and in all cases the subject of sterilization was raised by the doctor and not by the woman herself.[22] In the Los Angeles hospital, HRG quoted one doctor instructing interns to "ask every one of those girls if they want their tubes tied, regardless of how old they are." [23] In many cases women were threatened with the loss of their welfare benefits.

[19] *Boston Globe*, April 26, 1974.
[20] *International Herald Tribune*, August 18, 1973.
[21] *Boston Globe*, April 26, 1974.
[22] *The New York Times*, October 30, 1973.
[23] *Boston Globe*, April, 26, 1974.

What is the purpose of these coerced sterilizations? Government agencies tend to rationalize them as a means of reducing the extent of poverty by reducing the potential number of children in poor families. Nowhere, however, has population control succeeded in eliminating poverty. If we consider that the U.S. economy now requires a 9 percent rate of unemployment to keep up its rate of profit, we can see that poverty is not caused by the "excess fertility" of the poor, but by the needs of the economy. Take the case of unemployment. Why is the unemployment rate today in the United States increasing? One of the primary reasons for this increase is that lower levels of unemployment have failed to place a check on the employed workers' wage gains. In spite of a peak unemployment rate of 5.8 percent in 1970, wage rates kept rising through the 1969–70 recession. To the extent that wage demands are absorbed through a rise in prices, the trade-off between unemployment and inflation has become progressively worse (in the 1960s a 6 percent unemployment rate would have bought a 1 percent rate of inflation; in 1971 it bought 5 percent; in 1974 it is no longer enough to buy a one digit inflation).

Far from reducing the number of the poor, government-funded family planning functions as one means of controlling the poor. The sterilization programs have directed their efforts primarily to mothers and daughters in the families of the chronically poor. These problem poor include people who cannot work or will not work and thus cease to function as a reserve labor force. They include single women with children who refuse to take a wage job in addition to child care: women who have demanded a guaranteed income for themselves and for others who want the right to refuse low paid work. As Moynihan pointed out in his book *A Guaranteed Income*, the difficulty the government faces when it provides welfare payments to the poor, and, in particular, to women who are heads of households, is the political response of the poor. "The issue of welfare is the issue of dependency. It is different from poverty. To be poor is an objective condition; to be dependent, a subjective one as well." [24]

Piven and Cloward's social history, *Regulating the Poor*, documents the rise of the welfare rights movement led by Black women in the 1960s, the concurrent rise of female-headed families on the welfare rolls, and a growing revolt of inner-city youth in the schools.[25] From the viewpoint of the government, this rising militancy (along with an increasing number of "broken homes" and an increase in "juvenile delinquency") was a threatening indication that the family as a form of social control and a means of maintaining stability was rapidly losing its grip on women and youth. "Broken families" means that parents no longer control children. "Broken

[24] Daniel Moynihan, *The Politics of a Guaranteed Income* (New York: Vintage Books, 1971), p. 235.

[25] One indication of the degree of this revolt is the sudden increase in attacks on school property: e.g., in New York City 161,000 windows were broken during 1959 but ten years later the number had risen to 275,000. Frances Piven and Richard Cloward, *Regulating the Poor* (New York: Vintage Books, 1971), p. 235.

families" means that women who work in the home as mothers must begin to demand their income directly from the State. "Broken families" also implies that greater numbers of the unemployed who are outside the discipline of wage work are also outside the institutional control of "family ties."

Historically, the government's response to the demands of the wageless sectors of the work force is welfare. For the poor, welfare provides a "guaranteed" income regardless of an individual's relation to wage work. For the government, it provides a new channel for social control. Through welfare practices like home searches for "immoral" behavior, interrogations regarding children and lifestyle, and through residency requirements and work training programs, welfare agencies try to reinstitutionalize forms of social control that the family structure has ceased to enforce. By dictating to a woman the terms of her sexual life, her place of residence, and by imposing on her the discipline of wage work, welfare agencies try to take away her capacity for self-determination. Through government day-care programs like Head Start or federally funded corporate programs like KLH Day Care, the government hopes to rediscipline youth. A KLH day-care proposal written in 1967 reads:

> In times of high unemployment, it is important for the government to encourage programs for developing human resources to prevent children from being transformed into unproductive citizens by the deadening effects of poverty. In times of manpower shortages, it is valuable to government that employment be offered to a wider group of workers, including some mothers on welfare. This could help prevent competition for workers that pushes up wage rates, promotes inflation and causes production bottlenecks.[26]

Thus it was in the context of a rising militancy among the poor that the government sought to reduce the fertility of low-income families. It was in the late 60s that a growing number of bills were introduced on the state legislatures to sterilize welfare women; in 1967, large-scale funding of sterilization programs was initiated; and by mid-1969, forty bills had been introduced to create a commission on "Population and the American Future" which would establish the criteria for a national policy on population.[27]

The present resurgence of interest in selective population control in the U.S. is a symptom of reform that failed. Because compensatory education and poverty programs have neither altered employment and income discrepancies between Blacks and Whites nor alleviated the rebellion of youth in the schools, several social scientists have begun to argue that the basis for poverty and "antisocial" behavior must be *inherited.* In their analysis, the poor must be poor because they are born with subnormal IQs. Thus they fail in school and eventually enter the bottom levels of the job market, if they get jobs at all.

---

[26] KLH Child Development Center, "A Proposal to Establish a Work-related Child Development Center" (1967), quoted in Katherine Ellis and Rosalind Petchesky, "Children of the Corporate Dream," *Socialist Revolution,* 2, No. 6 (November–December, 1972), 8–29.

[27] Mass, *The Political Economy of Population Control,* p. 7.

Physiologist Dwight Ingle, for example, has called for selective breeding as the only realistic solution to the fact that Blacks score lower than Whites on White IQ tests: "While a difference that has developed over hundreds of years cannot be solved quickly, a start could be made if the reproductive load were shifted to upper and middle class Blacks." [28] Stanford professor William Shockley has recently suggested a bonus program for those willing to be sterilized. The amount of the bonus would depend on "best scientific estimates of hereditary factors" ranging from IQ and heroin addiction to arthritis. "At a bonus rate of $1,000 for each point below 100 IQ, $30,000 put in trust for a 70 IQ, moron potentially capable of producing 20 children might return $250,000 to taxpayers in reduced costs of mental retardation care." [29]

These racist theories for dealing with poverty simply deny the facts. If, in the past decade, the education gap between Blacks and Whites has narrowed but the income gap has remained the same, if the more education a Black person achieves, the greater does the income discrepancy become between herself/himself and a White with a comparable education, and if IQ can vary as much as thirty points in response to teachers' attitudes, what remains to be said for individual responsibility for achievement and the heritability of IQ?

Most of the methods for controlling the birth rate in developed countries like the United States devised by population experts involve economic disincentives that have a selective impact on the poor. One proposal for limiting or eliminating education, medical services, and housing for families with more than two children is perhaps redundant. In the United States, disincentives to childbirth have always been operative in the class nature of social services like medical care and child care and in the shortages and high cost of housing.

A number of methods for fertility control attempt to regulate women *directly* through their biological capacity for motherhood. Social scientists have proposed compulsory abortion of out-of-wedlock pregnancies or the sterilization of women with more than two children. While vasectomy has been widely used in countries like India where health services are limited, the Ehrlichs have suggested that for women in developed countries,

> A program of sterilizing women after their second or third child, despite the greater difficulty of the female operation, might be easier than trying to sterilize the fathers. At least this would be the case in countries where the majority of babies are born in maternity hospitals and clinics, and where the medical corps is adequate. The problem of finding and identifying eligibles [sic!] for sterilization would be simplified in this way.[30]

Professor John Postgate of Sussex University has made an even more formidable proposal for controlling fertility through women's reproductive

[28] *New York Post,* June 19, 1973.

[29] *Financial Times* (Great Britain), March 23, 1973.

[30] Anne and Paul Ehrlich, *Population, Resources, Environment* (San Francisco; W. H. Freeman and Co., 1972), p. 338.

capacity: "Since overall fertility depends largely on the proportion of females, a rapid transition to a female minority would be the fastest route to reducing population growth." [31] The recent breakthroughs in methods for determining the sex of the fetus could place this proposal on a future agenda for population control.

Population experts have also suggested using methods of fertility control which regulate women's participation in housework and child care and hence their relation to reproduction. In developed countries like the U.S. and England, which have an extensive network of social services, the government has an institutional access to the means of regulating the kind of work women do. Because women have primary responsibility for child care and housework and, at the same time, face discrimination in jobs outside the home, legislation regarding equal employment opportunities, the availability of child care services, and the amount of welfare payments for households headed by women, all have a direct effect on the reproductive rate. Thus, suspending a woman's welfare payments after the first two children and/or forcing her to be sterilized could be a means of reducing the fertility rate of poor women. For all women the government could decide to decrease or eliminate family allowances (as in England in 1973); it could offer pensions for women over 45 who have less than three children; or it could require women to work outside the home while providing few day-care services and no maternity leaves.[32] The President's Commission on Population and the American Future has even suggested incorporating feminist demands which might reduce women's desire to have children. Thus, in the U.S., where a lowered birth rate and an increased employment of women at discriminatory wages is functional to the growth of the economy, capitalism might attempt to use one major feminist demand, such as the demand for "equal employment opportunity," as a force for its own development.

ABORTION REFORM

The history of abortion laws in the developed countries shares some aspects with the history of birth control. The present abortion laws are the outcome of women's struggle to control reproduction. The history of this struggle, however, has not been one of continual liberalization. Governments have often tried to regulate abortion laws in relation to the needs of economic development and the demand for a specific rate of population growth.

In the Greek city-states and in ancient Rome, liberal abortion laws were the basis for rational population limitation. For the early Christians, abortion was not considered murder if performed before the fetus was infused with a "rational soul" (which, incidentally, was forty days for a male and ninety

[31] John Postgate, quoted in a London women's group unpublished article on population control.
[32] Elliot et al., in "U.S. Population Growth and Family Planning," p. 206.

days for a female).[33] Strict laws forbidding abortion are only a century old and coincide with industrialization, advances in contraceptive techniques, and a growing birth control movement. Lawrence Lader argues that, although Malthus had written in favor of population limitation as early as 1800,

> It is doubtful, however, that England's rulers shared the same concern. The nation's meteoric industrialization, which would soon make it manufacturer to the world, demanded an increasing flow of workers. And if children of 10 were expendable at the mills and mines, and often eliminated before adulthood by the ravages of disease which medicine had not yet learned to control, the labor supply obviously had to be accelerated beyond the recent increase in births.[34]

In England and much of Europe, pronatalist policies prohibiting abortion continued throughout the world wars (contraceptives were outlawed in Germany, France and Italy in the 1930s). The first laws against abortion in the U.S. also date from the mid-1800s, a period in which the demands of industrialization and Western expansion made rapid population growth an economic asset.[35] Thus, while restrictive abortion laws were implemented ostensibly to protect women from poor medical practice, the court decisions often contained pronatalist rationalizations.

Once the United States adopted restrictive abortion laws, the availability of abortion depended primarily on a woman's economic situation. A woman with money could obtain an abortion by flying to Puerto Rico, Japan, Sweden, or England. Of legal abortions performed in the U.S., four out of five involved private patients and not clinic patients. Nine out of ten legal abortions involved White women and not Black women.[36] In a study of New York City in 1963, it was found that 91 percent of women getting therapeutic abortions were White and 93 percent of those receiving them could afford a private room.[37] The abortion reforms passed between 1967 and 1970 in which mental health factors were included as justification for abortion increased this economic difference. In a study of hospitals in Buffalo, N.Y. during the 1940s when the majority of abortions were performed for medical reasons, the incidence of abortion for ward and private patients was about the same. In the 50s, medical reasons accounted for fewer abortions and the incidence for private patients was two times that for ward patients. By the 60s, the incidence of abortion for private patients had become twenty times greater.[38] Thus, in some hospitals, "reform" legislation deepened the abortion crisis for poor women.

Restrictive abortion laws have their most destructive impact on poor and

[33] Lawrence Lader, *Abortion* (Boston: Beacon Press, 1966), pp. 76–77.

[34] Ibid., p. 83.

[35] Ibid., p. 86.

[36] Arts and Science Undergraduate Society of McGill University, *Birth Control Handbook* (Montreal: Journal Offset, 1970), p. 42.

[37] Diane Schulder and Florynce Kennedy, *Abortion Rap* (New York: McGraw Hill, 1971), p. 143.

[38] Sarvis and Rodman, *The Abortion Controversy*, pp. 171–73.

non-White women. A woman who cannot afford to pay three psychiatrists to tell her she is mentally unfit to sustain a pregnancy must resort to illegal abortionists or to self-abortion. Before the abortion reforms of 1971, there were at least 1 million illegal abortions a year.[39] In a study by Harriet Pilpel (1967), 42 percent of pregnancy-related deaths in New York in the 1960s resulted from illegal abortions and only 6 percent of these women were White.[40] In another study of New York City between 1951 and 1962, it was estimated that the maternal mortality rate for Black women was four times greater than for Whites and the Black maternal mortality rate due to abortion was nine times greater.[41]

The difficulties non-White women face in seeking an abortion have even graver implications because their alternatives to abortion are also less available. In a recent study of teenage pregnancy, Melvin Zelnik and John Kentner (1974) found that about two-thirds of premarital first pregnancies to Black teens resulted in "illegitimate" births, whereas only one-fifth of such pregnancies resulted in "illegitimate" births for Whites.[42] This implies that more White women than Black women have the alternative of "shotgun" marriages owing to the more favorable economic situation of White men. A White woman who does not marry and decides not to keep her child is also more likely to receive help with adoption and her child is more likely to be adopted.

Since the 1970 reform laws in New York, there has been a reversal of some of the racial and economic trends in abortion. Given women's past experiences with abortion, however, it is important to look at the early progress of these reforms and make a concrete evaluation of their shortcomings. It seems, for example, that in the struggle for free abortion, the women's movement has encountered several allies whose reasons for supporting its demand are not in the interests of women. Thus sociologists who favor population control for the poor are citing as a positive trend since the liberalized abortion laws the fact that those women who had the highest rates of "excess fertility" now have the highest rates for abortion. We should also note that while the number of maternal deaths resulting from illegal abortion have declined significantly, ward patients continue to have higher complication rates than private patients.[43]

The direction of recent legislation shows that abortion has become one of the battlegrounds in the doctors' fight to retain their monopoly on skilled health-care delivery. Through the medical schools and the American Medical Association, doctors have successfully limited the supply of medical professionals. By isolating those doctors who become involved in group practice (e.g., by persuading hospitals to deny such doctors staff privileges or

[39] Arts and Science Undergraduate Society, *The Birth Control Handbook*, p. 42.

[40] Sarvis and Rodman, *The Abortion Controversy*, pp. 171–73.

[41] Ibid.

[42] *The New York Times*, June 28, 1974.

[43] Christopher Teitze and Sara Lewit, *Family Planning Perspectives*, cited in Ellen Frankfort, *Vaginal Politics* (New York: Bantam Books, 1973), p. 75.

discouraging referrals of patients), they have also resisted the trend of engaging more health workers as salaried employees of large hospitals. These combined efforts have produced exceptionally high incomes for doctors and a general shortage of health-care services.

The legalization of abortion presented a challenge to the doctors' monopoly of medicine. Because the constituency for abortion is over half the population, existing health services could not meet the new demand without necessitating changes in the availability of medical professionals. Although a reform law restricting abortion procedures to licensed physicians might insure better health care than the black market, it would also further reinforce the high cost and low availability of these services. In New York City, this restriction proved to be a doctors' victory. One immediate result was a flourishing business of private referral agencies. Before they were banned, these agencies managed to profit from the desperation of out-of-state women who were trying to avoid a dangerous waiting period for an abortion. For example, the Abortion Information Agency grossed about $70,000 a week for Director John Settle by charging $285 in cash in advance for an early abortion in a hospital that charged the agency $175.[44] One doctor set up his own referral service and literally referred women to himself.[45] In 1970 in New York City, the going rate for abortion was $300 to $1,500, providing individual doctors with an annual average profit of $150,000 for abortions alone. One doctor reportedly earned $350,000 the first year he performed salines.[46]

Considering that childbirth is eight or ten times riskier than abortion, the existence of programs training nurses as midwives seems to contradict reform laws which rule that abortions must be performed by a doctor. It may actually be safer to go to a paramedic specially trained in the vacuum aspirator procedure than to go to an inexperienced doctor.[47] When abortion was illegal, a doctor was preferable to a butcher abortionist at black market prices. However, medical practice since the New York reform law has further confirmed our experience that male doctors are not particularly concerned about women's health. Nonprofessional women counselors were responsible for reporting cases in which doctors were reluctant to send a woman with serious complications to the hospital. And it was such women who were also responsible for stopping more dangerous saline abortions from being done in doctors' offices.[48]

In an article on abortion counseling, Rika Alper, Pris Hoffnung, and Barbara Solomon discussed their work in New York clinics since the reform law went into effect. They were involved in counseling sessions in which they explained the medical procedure to other women and encouraged them to

[44] Ibid., p. 54.
[45] Ibid., p. 60.
[46] Ibid., pp. 53–54.
[47] Lucinda Cisler, "Abortion Reform: The New Tokenism," *Ramparts* (August 1970), pp. 19–25.
[48] Frankfort, *Vaginal Politics*, p. 66.

express their feelings about abortion, sex, and motherhood before the operation. In the course of this work, they realized that many clinics were using nonprofessional women to create the illusion of good, comprehensive health care that had special concern for women's needs. Several abortion clinics tried to capitalize on the women's movement by changing their names to include "women" in the title when it proved to be more lucrative. For many women, four hours of counseling seemed to justify the high cost of a ten-minute medical procedure. Counseling sessions tended to reinforce a woman's feeling that something was wrong with her because they often focused on her feelings and not on what caused them. These sessions could provide a situation for pushing sterilization or IUDs on women at a time when they were feeling most vulnerable, while they never functioned directly to encourage men to be more responsible for birth control. Finally, counseling further legitimized a male-dominated medical hierarchy: doctors continued to be insensitive medical technicians with decision-making power and substantial incomes while nonprofessional women counselors assumed the emotive role of mediating the relationship between women clients and male doctors.

Feminist counselors found themselves in a difficult position. They felt that it was better that they, as women and feminists, did the counseling, but saw that their role functioned more to channel women's discontent by making them responsive to the medical system rather than to change health care to meet the needs of women.

> In fact we've seen the job of abortion counsellor as a good job because it is tied in with our work in the women's movement, and it offers good hours and high pay. But every time we visited a clinic we felt weird about what the counsellors were doing—their ideas and sympathies which came out of the women's movement had become a formal, marketable part of the abortion industry.[49]

As we have seen with sterilization and contraception, making birth control services available to women can be a form of government control over women's reproductive capacity. Now that abortion laws have been liberalized, an evaluation of possible government and corporate uses of abortion from the viewpoint of women is especially urgent.

> When abortion laws are repealed, . . . we have to make sure above all that abortions are voluntary as well as free and safe. . . . We do not know from our own experiences—since we are white and middle class—but we suspect that other women are forcibly made to abort or to be sterilized.[50]

This position statement from a book on women's health issues, written before abortion reforms were won, expresses an attitude that was typical of the women's movement in its relationship to non-White women on the issue of

---

[49] Rika Alper, Pris Hoffnung, and Barbara Solomon, unpublished article on abortion counseling in New York City.

[50] Boston Women's Health Collective, *Our Bodies, Ourselves* (New York: Simon and Schuster, 1973), p. 139.

population control: it is apologetic, indecisive, individualistic. The history of *White* women alone contains many examples of nonvoluntary abortion: women who have aborted because they labored in factories and sweatshops, because they lacked adequate nutrition and prenatal care, or because they were victims of a medical system which distributes dangerous drugs and contraceptives (on August 21, 1974, the FDA reported that 11 deaths and 209 septic abortions had been associated with the use of an IUD called the Dalkon Shield).[51] We know what a forcible abortion is, but what is a voluntary abortion? It seems that sometimes we put so much energy into legalizing abortions that we lose touch with why we wanted them in the first place. In most cases, the right to abortion is a necessary but limited right: it is not the right to adequate birth control, child care services, or the economic means to have children when we want them. How voluntary is it when a single mother with a dependent child decides to abort because she faces the loss of her job? For many women the fight to legalize abortion is a necessary but *defensive* reaction against a system which forbids abortion but forces women to abort.

THE SOCIALIST "ALTERNATIVE"

In looking for progressive models of abortion and contraception reform, many of us have turned to the experiences of women in socialist countries. For example, Bonnie Mass writes,

> In socialist society, *birth control is always put into the context of the whole economic system. Threats of economic deprivation* were not used as fear tactics to force the masses to limit their numbers; instead the masses understood through extensive self-education that all facets of daily life must be revolutionized in order for a socialist future to become a permanent reality. It was realized that population redistribution would be accomplished, not by temporary monetary bribes or deception for the benefit of a few, as we have seen in Latin America, but by wide acceptance of a far-reaching political purpose.[52]

It is true that in existing socialist societies birth control is "put into the context of the whole economic system." But as we have seen, it is also integral to the rational economic planning of capitalism. To the extent that each economic system must plan the investment of capital (in relation to the same world economy), whether through the State or through the multinational corporation, the consequent need to regulate the labor force requires population policies that directly control women. Given the low standard of living in many socialist countries, we find that "threats of economic deprivation" are not unknown.

One of the most commonly cited examples of involvement by a socialist

---

[51] *Valley Advocate*, October 2, 1974.
[52] Mass, *The Political Economy of Population Control*, p. 46 (italics mine).

state in population control is Russia. In response to feminist demands, Russia passed very progressive legislation in the 1920s aimed at liberating women from the burden of child care. Divorce was made freer and was automatic for each partner, the legal concept of illegitimacy was abolished and abortion was legalized. The government's decision to legalize abortion was to a large degree a recogition of the poor living conditions faced by many families which forced women to seek illegal abortions despite the high mortality risks involved. Although there was little effort to spread the use of contraception, the People's Commissar of Health felt that abortions should be made available "as long as the moral survivals of the past and the hard economic conditions of the present force women to decide on this operation." [53]

In 1936, in the context of a general social and economic repression of the working class, Stalin reintroduced the traditional and more restrictive legal status of women as a means of stepping up the growth of the labor force for a period of rapid industrialization and a buildup of the armed forces. In 1956, on the wave of labor insurrections in Eastern Europe, abortion was again made available on request up to twelve weeks, and the current policy continues to maintain that the basis for abortion should be removed through noncoercive incentives like better housing, nursery schools, etc. Several studies show, however, that *economic* pressures on women to have abortions still exist. In one analysis of the U.S.S.R., it was found that the abortion rate among women who must work during their reproductive years is over three times as large as for nonworking wives, and in another study it was found that, in a sample of 26,000 married urban women, one-third requested abortion because of inadequate housing and child care facilities.[54] This past year in the city of Alma Ata, 25,000 families were on waiting lists for preschool kindergartens and nurseries. Even in Moscow and Leningrad, day-care centers were unable to meet the demand.[55]

In Czechoslovakia, women could virtually obtain abortion on demand. By 1970 there were an alarming 55 abortions per 100 live births. The growing economic desirability of a larger labor force prompted the government to express a new urgency about improving wages and social benefits. Thus since 1971, it has expanded the number of day nurseries, doubled grants available on the birth of a child to the equivalent of five weeks' pay for the average women, extended the period of maternity leave on full pay to six months, and increased the monthly supplement paid to every mother for the first two years after birth. The result has been four consecutive years of a rising birth rate in Czechoslovakia.[56]

Why be critical of these social reforms? In a situation of economic scarcity, state initiative in offering money payments for motherhood is similar to a threat of economic deprivation. These payments do not represent a substan-

[53] Lader, *Abortion*, p. 121.
[54] Ibid., p. 123.
[55] *The New York Times*, April 6, 1974.
[56] *Manchester Guardian* (Great Britain), December 28, 1972.

tial gain in the standard of living but are merely the minimum acceptable wage a woman will respond to. From the viewpoint of women, state policies that attempt to make us mothers one year and factory workers the next are simply another form of controlling our reproductive capacity by regulating our work role.

Poland further demonstrates the use of reforms to attempt to control women. The housing shortage alone has greatly depressed the birth rate. It was also a major factor in the wave of workers' rebellions in 1970. The origin of Poland's housing shortage lay in the government's early emphasis on developing capital industries at the expense of consumer needs. The consequent rapid industrialization caused a shift in population distribution from rural to urban areas. With the post–World War II baby boom, population in the cities soon outgrew available housing. Since the 60s, the birth rate has declined and the government has become quite concerned about housing conditions and the problems facing working mothers. According to one party official, "Lower population could not be tolerated within our plans for economic development. As it is, we have a labor shortage at certain times of the year. Therefore we had to begin thinking about models that would insure the growth of population." [57] What this tells women is that the conditions under which we must work and give birth mostly serve the needs of the economy. If Poland wants to develop its capital one year, then women must forgo sexual relations and the luxury of a private bedroom. If workers are too much in demand and become too militant, we must alleviate the "labor shortage" by producing more workers. We are then given homes and kitchens to return to.

In Rumania, the state went beyond social reforms and economic subsidies. Until 1966 it had the world's most liberal abortion law. No approval was required, nor were there any bureaucratic procedures. The estimated abortion rate was four abortions per live birth with some women having as many as twenty abortions during their reproductive period. In 1966 the law was abruptly reversed. Abortion was restricted to stringent medical reasons such as rape or incest or to women over 45 with four or more children. The importation of IUDs and pills was stopped. Divorce was made more difficult. As a result of these repressive measures against women, the crude birth rate more than doubled in the following year.[58]

Even in China, one of the socialist countries most respected by the Left, the State has had to turn to material rather than political incentives. Since the 1962 failure of the Great Leap Forward to reach target food supplies, family planning has been integral to the Chinese economy. In 1966, the Cultural Revolution led to greater freedom for the young. Marriage age declined and birth rates increased. Hence, in 1968, a campaign for family planning was started with renewed efforts to encourage late marriage and small families.[59] The past decade of steady growth in grain output ended in

[57] *The New York Times*, June 5, 1974.
[58] Postgate, London women's group.
[59] Ibid.

1972 with a decline in harvests. In order to meet the food needs of a growing population, China has resumed large-scale grain imports and has invested less capital on industrial goods for development. As fewer workers are needed, population control has become all the more essential to economic progress. The government has enforced strong restrictions on food rations for women with extra children and women with two children are being pressured to abort future pregnancies.[60]

Thus we see that the socialist "alternative" in which "birth control is always put in the context of the whole economic system" [61] shares several characteristics with the capitalist use of contraception. From the viewpoint of women, the issue in both cases still remains the issue of *our control*.

Within the women's movement we are beginning to redefine our strategy in relation to abortion and contraception. Recent advances in methods for determining the sex of the fetus; new and more efficient techniques of abortion and sterilization, along with the development of IUDs and hormonal sterilants have made government control of reproduction rates *through the woman* the dominant possibility. These technological advances have increased the potential for governments to use fertility control as a means of containing social rebellion. For women in the U.S. this has taken the form of coercive sterilization. As we have seen, during the 60s there was a growing militancy among women around the issue of welfare. Their struggles as mothers to increase their income from the government brought them face to face with coercive sterilization practices. At the same time their organizing experiences have defined the case for all women: insofar as the ultimate responsibility for child care and child support falls on women, we will struggle for the power to control not only the biological aspect of reproduction but the economic aspect as well.

[60] *Boston Globe*, October 24, 1973.
[61] Mass, *The Political Economy of Population Control*, p. 46.

chapter eight
medicine and social control*

—Barbara and John Ehrenreich

"All professions are conspiracies against the laity," said George Bernard Shaw in *The Doctor's Dilemma*. Although Barbara and John Ehrenreich do not believe that doctors are engaged in a conscious conspiracy, their look at doctors' practices in the United States leads them to conclude that doctors' power to affect even nonmedical aspects of the society has vastly expanded. By holding down their numbers while holding on to their power, doctors have increased their income spectacularly. Further, they have invaded the consciousness of Americans through extensive media coverage so that few people are free from some passive acquiescence in accepting the doctors' pronouncements.

The other chapters in this book focus more on corporate and state control of social welfare programs than on the workers who deliver the services. This chapter focuses on the professionals, and shows how the most prestigious and highly paid professionals in the United States have shaped a service through tightly organized pressure and control of the medical schools. Their power may be used to exclude some people from the services the doctors provide or to vastly increase the range of services offered to other people; both patterns involve reshuffling of the label "sick." Mie Watanabe's article shows both elements operating. Disciplinary control occurs when some doctors force sterilization on poor women; expansionary (cooptive) control occurs when some doctors enter eagerly into lucrative abortion practice.

This chapter argues from the assumption that class, sex, and race strongly influence people's attitudes and practices. Because doctors belong to the upper middle class and are predominantly White and male, they often help to perpetuate society's dominant ideology, thereby helping to reinforce existing class and caste patterns of dominance and submission. Most human-service professionals have faced the same charge, and there is a good deal of research evidence to document it.

* A preliminary version of this chapter appeared in *Social Policy*, May–June 1974; © Barbara and John Ehrenreich.

There are two sides to the coin of authoritarianism. Authority is legitimate to the extent that people accept it as legitimate. When people attribute magical powers to doctors—or to any authority—they give up some of their own autonomy. In *The Brothers Karamazov*, Dostoevesky had the Grand Inquisitor show how the Church maintained control over people by maintaining an aura of mystery and claiming ultimate authority. Doctors use the same elements of control; perhaps they have become our new priests.

The question most frequently addressed to angry groups of service consumers in the 60s was, "What do you people *really* want?" The initial answers could be condensed to one word: "More"—more educational opportunities, more health and mental health services, more welfare and social services. In time, the answers were tempered with the realization that "more" might be less than enough, and even "better" might not be good enough. What was the point of more schools, or even more teachers and equipment per school, if the fundamental mission of the schools was to socialize kids into capitalist values and (unappealing) work roles? Who wants a community mental health center, even an attractive and well-staffed one, if its ultimate prescription for mental health is acquiescence to oppression? As a radical analysis developed and deepened, it made it clear that the schools, the welfare agencies and the mental health and other social service systems were agencies of *social control.* "More" was not only not enough, it could be dangerous.

The one area of human services which escaped the 60s relatively unsmeared was medicine. It is true that radicals (ourselves included) bitterly castigated the medical system, but always more for what it did *not* do than for what it did. It did not offer high-quality, dignified medical care to the poor; it did not energetically expand preventive services; it did not lower the financial barriers to the care experienced by working-class people. Why not? The answer was simple enough: The medical system was too concerned with profits, power, and status to care much about services; these were merely a by-product of American's "number one growth industry"—health. Radical analysis tended to ignore the by-product and focus on the industry—its institutional contours, its relationship to government and the economy in general, etc.[1]

If there was a "politics of health" that went deeper than the political economy of the institutions and the gross inequities in the availability of care, it was not examined. Medical services themselves were seen as politically neutral: The need for them was biologically ordained; their precise content was technologically determined. Although all the visible abuses—profiteering, unjust distribution, the use of poor people as "teaching material," racism and sexism from doctors, and so forth—came under fire, the core of the system remained sacrosanct, out of bounds for social criticism.

[1] The most complete radical treatment of the health system is in *The American Health Empire*, a report from the Health Policy Advisory Center, prepared by Barbara and John Ehrenreich (New York: Random House, 1970).

There are two important exceptions—two areas where radical analysis has gone beyond a single-minded concern with availability and quality and begun to probe the ideological content of health services themselves. First there is the area of mental health. Early critiques of mental health services focused on their unavailability to poor and working-class people. Today, many radical psychiatrists are skeptical about the therapeutic value of conventional mental health services for anyone. They have arrived at the conclusion that mental health services operate directly to enforce oppressive sex and class roles, to reinforce individualism, and to promote the idea that however oppressive your situation is, your problems are "all in your head." [2]

The second area in which the health movement has broached the issue of the ideology of health care is the area of women's medical care. Faced with what some have described as "sexocidal" tendencies in medicine—evidenced by massive pharmaceutical experiments on women, excessive gynecological surgery, and so forth—it is not surprising that the overwhelming concern of the women's health movement is *survival*. As in the health movement in general, availability, cost, and quality are the central issues. At the same time, the ideological content of the services has not gone unexamined. Feminists point out that the treatment of women is often patriarchal to the point of medical irrationality. (For example, standard obstetrical procedure features the woman unconscious and/or strapped down to a table while the lordly obstetrician extracts the baby with forceps. There is considerable evidence that anesthesia, the supine position, and forceps are unhealthy for mother and baby.) The effect of this kind of treatment is to promote feelings of passivity and low self-worth on the part of women, hence to reinforce oppressed roles as wives and workers.[3]

But the issues raised by feminists and radical mental health workers have not been integrated into the mainstream of radical analysis of the medical system. They have been incorporated as qualifications, and little more: "We want *more*, but, if possible, without the sexism, racism, ideological manipulation, etc." Whether such a qualified expansion is possible, whether the ideologically objectionable features of the services can simply be "peeled off" the presumably neutral core, has not been examined. Answering such questions, it seems to us, is central to the framing of a truly socialist, feminist, and humanist vision of health care.

Our purpose here is to lay out a tentative approach to an understanding of the social control functions of the medical system. At the outset we want to make clear, first, that our approach is sociological, and not primarily medical or economic. We are not concerned with the biological impact of medical services, but with their social impact—how they are viewed by people, what expectations people bring to them, how their behavior or understanding of

---

[2] H. M. Ruitenbeck, ed., *Going Crazy* (New York: Bantam Books, 1972); and P. Chesler, *Women and Madness* (New York: Avon, 1972).

[3] Boston Women's Health Collective, *Our Bodies, Ourselves* (New York: Simon & Schuster, 1972); and *Health-Pac Bulletin*, May 1970.

social reality is affected by them. Thus we would not ask of a given service, or element of service, such as a chest X-ray, "Was it really necessary or helpful?" It might well be both necessary and helpful, but regardless of the answer, we are interested in a different set of questions: How was it experienced by the patient? What were the nature of the social interactions required for its performance? Though some may see this approach as narrow or blind to everything that is "good" in medicine, we see it as essential to making a fresh start in our analysis—to seeing medicine as something other than what the medical men themselves define it as. And except insofar as the financial transactions between doctor (or hospital) and patient directly affect the social relations between them, we shall not be concerned with the economics of health care, either.

Second, our description of the medical system as a system of social control is not, in itself, an attack on the medical system. *Any* social system is characterized by mechanisms of social control—mechanisms that ensure that members of the society follow the behavior patterns acceptable to the particular society (in particular, in the societies we are most familiar with, to the ruling classes of the society—but even a totally egalitarian society would have such mechanisms). Our concern here is not with the fact that the medical system functions as a system of social control *per se;* it is rather with the *content* of the social control exercised. To sum up our argument briefly, a capitalist health-care system operates to maintain and reinforce capitalist social relations.

Third, we should make it clear that to analyze something as a system of social control is not to view it as a conspiracy. We are not arguing that the health system is consciously designed to exercise social control, or that the social control functions of the health system somehow explain its structure and dynamics. To the contrary, we explain the social control functions as themselves a result of the institutional structure, organization, and economics of the health-care system.

Finally, we want to emphasize that our analysis is a tentative one, bordering in places on the purely speculative. The value of such a tentative beginning lies in the work which it stimulates others to do.

THE SOCIOLOGY OF MEDICINE

Doctors (and most of the public) view the medical system as a system for distributing technical expertise and intervention in the interest of improved biological fitness among the recipients. *Sociologists* view the medical system as a system of social relationships: "Sickness" is a *social role* (as opposed to "disease," which is a *biological state*) and it is the business of the medical system to control entry into sick roles and to define the behavior appropriate to them. In the medical view, the issue of social control never arises, unless one considers that making people fit or capable to perform their normal activities is in itself a form of social "control." In the sociological view, the medical system is, at least in a formal sense, a system of "social control"—simply because it defines roles, regulates entry into them, etc. Our interest here is not in academic formalisms—sociological or medical—but in the social and ideological impact of the medical system. We take some of the conclusions of academic sociology as a starting point for our analysis because they provide important insights into the fundamentally *political* issues that concern us: who is being "controlled," by whom, how, and in whose interests? And although such questions may not be of great concern to bourgeois sociology, we emphasize that they cannot even be framed within the *medical* description of the medical system which has so thoroughly dominated radical thinking up until now.

The two most important contributers to the sociological description of medicine are Talcott Parsons and Eliot Freidson.[4] We have no intention of summarizing, much less critiquing, their work, but we would like to briefly restate what we have found important in it. We consider them separately because their views, while in no way considered contradictory in sociological circles, do imply two apparently contradictory descriptions of the medical system and of the forms of social control it exerts.

Parsons' classic contribution to medical sociology is his description of the sick role. The characteristics of the sick role are: (1) The individual is not held responsible for his/her condition. (Sinners and criminals are responsible; sick people are not.) (2) Conditions defined as illness are seen as a legitimate basis for certain *exemptions* from normal responsibilities—"sick" people can stay home from work, be waited on, etc., depending on the severity of the incapacity. (3) The exemptions held out to sick persons are only *conditionally* legitimate, the prime condition being that the sick person recognize that sickness is an undesirable state and that he/she has an obligation to try to get well. (4) In our society, this is an obligation to seek competent help and to completely cooperate with the efforts of competent helpers in becoming well.

In Parsons' view the sick role is always a tempting one: It is not considered blameworthy and it offers a way out of normal responsibilities. Insofar as illness is motivated, "the motives which enter into illness as deviant behavior are partially identical with those entering into other types of deviance, such as crime and the breakdown of commitment to the values of society. . . ." So it is understandable that certain features of the social construction of sickness are set up to discourage people from using a sickness as a way of dropping out:

> Life has necessarily become more complex and has made greater demands on the
> typical individual. . . . The motivation to retreat into ill-health through mental or

[4] Talcott Parsons, *The Social System* (New York: Free Press, 1951), pp. 428–79; Eliot Freidson, *The Profession of Medicine* (New York: Dodd Mead & Co., 1970), esp. pp. 203–331; Talcott Parsons, "Definitions of Health and Illness in the Light of American Values and Social Structure," in E. Gartly Jaco, ed., *Patients, Physicians and Illness*, 2nd ed. (New York: Free Press, 1972), p. 107.

psychosomatic channels, has become accentuated and with it the importance of effective mechanisms for coping with those who do so retreat.

First, there is the fact that sickness is seen as undesirable:

> The stigmatizing of illness as undesirable and the mobilization of considerable resources of the community to combat illness is a reaffirmation of the valuation of health and a countervailing influence against the temptation for illness. . . . Thus the sick person is prevented from setting an example which others might be tempted to follow.

As an added precaution, the sick are insulated from each other and from the general public, and placed under the supervision of certain non-sick people (medical personnel):

> The essential reason for this insulation being important in the present context is not the need of the sick person for special "care" so much as it is that, motivationally as well as bacteriologically, illness may well be contagious.[5]

The picture of the American "sickness system" that emerges from Parsons' work, then, is like nothing so much as the American welfare system. Welfare too holds out exemptions, particularly from the requirement to seek gainful employment. But these exemptions are offered only to the "legitimately" poor (those certified as eligible) and they are only offered on the condition that the recipients recognize their state as undesirable and cooperate with "competent helpers" (social workers) to overcome the "character defects," "family pathology," etc., which have led to it. Like the sick role, the "welfare role" puts the recipient under the supervision of certain non-poor people (case-workers). And, even more obviously than in the case of sickness, a variety of measures (low payments, degrading procedures) are taken to make sure that the welfare role will not be too tempting to the mass of working people. Concern for the sick or poor, it seems, must always be held in check by the fearful possibility of *contagion*.[6]

Singularly absent from Parsons' description is any sense of agency. What determines the "social construction of sickness" he describes? In the homogeneous and seemingly middle-class America of Parsons' medical writings, the answer is simply "our values," and these appear to arise out of some deep cultural consensus. The first thing that strikes us as important

---

[5] Parsons, "Definitions of Health and Illness," pp. 118, 121. In Parsons' scheme, sickness poses something of a moral dilemma to American society which, he argues, has an unusually high regard for health and activism. For humanitarian reasons, we feel obliged to treat the sick well—but never so well, or so visibly well, that others will be tempted to seek the same treatment by joining the ranks of the "sick." One may wonder why a people who supposedly value activism and work so highly find sickness so alluring. Could they possibly be *oppressed* and feel that, in Parsons' words, "the way to deal with the frustrating aspects of the social system is 'for everybody to get sick' " (Parsons, *The Social System*, p. 477)? But oppression is not a dimension of Parsons' analysis. Borrowing from psychoanalytic theory, Parsons explains this anomaly in terms of American patterns of child-raising.

[6] Frances Fox Piven and Richard A. Cloward, *Regulating the Poor* (New York: Pantheon, 1971), pp. 33–36.

about Friedson's work is that he identifies the actual architects of our "social construction of sickness": It is the medical profession that defines illness in theory (i.e., defines which biological syndromes admit one to the sick roles and which can be considered as minor, psychosomatic, or otherwise ineligible for special treatment). And it is the doctors who identify illness in practice (determine who is eligible for sick roles), and undertake to supervise those identified as "sick."

> They [professionals] are not merely experts but incumbents in official positions. . . . Given the official status of the profession, what happens to the layman—that is, whether or not he will be recognized as "really" sick, what the sickness will be called, what treatment will be given him, how he will be required to act while ill, and what will happen to him after treatment—becomes a function of professional rather than lay decision. . . . Thus the behavior of the physician and others in the field of health constitutes the objectification, the empirical embodiment, of certain dominant values in a society.[7]

Where Parsons is concerned with a culturally diffuse "sickness system" (our term) Freidson is concerned with the actual medical system. He describes it as an agency of social control on a par with the legal system or organized religion. Each of these institutions is concerned with the prevention, detection, and management of social deviance—criminality in the case of the law, sin in the case of the church, sickness in the case of the medical system. In his understanding of deviance, Freidson makes a significant departure from Parsons. Parsons sees deviance as motivated behavior or deliberate idiosyncrasy—more a matter for psychiatry than for sociology to comprehend. Freidson's approach is operational; he describes deviance as a state *imputed* by the relevant officials: The courts label certain people as "murderers" or "shoplifters"; doctors label certain others as "cancer cases" or "neurotics." Once so labeled, the person is required to enter the social role appropriate to the label—to undergo certain types of treatment, to modify his or her behavior in ways seen as therapeutic, perhaps to abandon all other social roles and enter an institution filled with similarly labeled people (cancer ward, jail, mental hospital).

The aspect of the sick role which seemed to concern Parsons was the exemptions it entailed, and the allure these might exercise on the non-sick. The aspect of the sick role that concerns Freidson is the requirement that the sick person cooperate with the agencies and personnel set up to deal with his or her sickness. To enter the sick role is to enter a state of professional dominance:

> In essence, the process of treatment and care may be seen as a process which attempts to lead the patient to behave in the way considered appropriate to the illness which has been diagnosed, a process often called "management" by professionals. . . . Professional management generally functions *to remove from the patient his identity as an adult, self-determining person,* and to press him to serve the moral and social identity implied by the illness which is diagnosed [emphasis added].[8]

[7] Freidson, *The Profession of Medicine*, p. 304.
[8] Ibid., pp. 329, 330.

This is a remarkably cold-blooded description of the sick role, and one that raises serious political—if not moral—issues.

What does arouse Freidson's moral concern is not the power of the medical profession to manage the sick, but its power to define what is "sick." He describes the medical system as continually expanding its definition of sickness to embrace more and more forms of social deviance: Sin is going out of style along with the church; the courts are losing ground to the psychiatric establishment, and "the hospital is succeeding the church and the parliament as the archetypical institution of Western culture." [9] Drunkenness becomes "alcoholism"; "perversion" becomes "psychosis"; and so on as medicine expands its jurisdiction to cover more and more areas once reserved for law or religion:

> The consequence of the movement [expansion of medicine's jurisdiction], however, is the strengthening of a professionalized control institution that, in the name of the individual's good and of technical expertise, can remove from laymen the right to evaluate their own behavior and the behavior of their fellow—a fundamental right that is evidenced in a hard-won fight to interpret the Scriptures oneself, without regard to dogmatic authority, in religion and, the right to be judged by one's peers, in law.[10]

The picture of the medical system that emerges from Freidson's description is that of some vast, expansionist, and itself uncontrolled regulatory apparatus—forever advancing the frontiers of its jurisdiction and enfolding more and more citizens into its (always benevolent) supervision. Medical theory aggressively claims new territory as "sickness." Practicing physicians zealously recruit their patients into sick roles (lest they miss someone who turns out to be "really sick" after all). The ranks of the "sick" swell, but there is no way that this army of "deviants" can turn against the social order; each marches to a separate drummer, and submits to his or her own medical "management."

There is a world of difference between this and Parsons' vision of the medical system (or, to be fair, our extrapolation of his vision). The one is chary in its favors (exemptions); the other is recklessly indulgent. The one excites moral concern over what it may not do, whom it may not care for, in its caution lest "sickness" sap the moral fibre of the nation. The other excites concern for what it *does* do, whom it does care for, in its drive to be caretaker for more and more of the nation's ills.

We emphasize this difference in perspective not because we are interested in provoking an academic sociological debate where there was none before, but because the same apparent contradiction runs through the radical critiques of the medical system: On the one hand we blame the system for being too chary and exclusionary—"there are not enough services; what there are, are too costly, uninviting, etc." On the other hand we, to a lesser

---

[9] Philip Rieff, *Freud: The Mind of the Novelist* (Garden City: Doubleday, 1961), p. 360, cited in Friedson, *The Profession of Medicine*, p. 248.

[10] Freidson, *The Profession of Medicine*, p. 250.

extent, blame the system for being expansionist—claiming ever more areas for its jurisdiction and endlessly expanding its institutional apparatus. Nowhere is this contradiction closer to the surface than in the critiques of "medical empires." [11] Some empires were criticized for being "conservative" and failing to expand their services to needy communities. Others were criticized for being "expansionist" and seeking to expand their services—i.e., their "control" over community health resources. Some were criticized for having *both* tendencies.

We do not wish to make too much of this apparent inconsistency. As activists learned in the health movement, the medical system does have both exclusionary and expansionist faces, and neither is wholly benign, or even "neutral." In fact, we can now postulate that the expansionist and exclusionary aspects of the medical system, recognized by both academic sociologists and radical critics, correspond to two different forms of *social control* exerted by the medical system, which we shall call *disciplinary* social control and *cooptative* social control.

TYPES OF MEDICAL SOCIAL CONTROL

Disciplinary Control

This type of social control is exerted by exclusionary sectors of the medical system. Exclusionary sectors are characterized by high barriers to entry (high costs, geographical inaccesibility, etc.) and/or socially repellent treatment of those who do enter (discourtesy, extreme impersonality, racism, fragmentation of care, long waits, etc.). The impact of exclusionary sectors on the populations they are supposed to serve is to discourage entry into sick roles, either because of the visible barriers to entry or because of public knowledge of the treatment experienced by those who do enter (or, in some cases, both). In so doing, such services exert what we will call disciplinary social control in that they *encourage* people to maintain work or family responsibilities—no matter what subjective discomfort they may be experiencing.

Disciplinary social control operates primarily on those who are not "sick" (in the sociological, not the medical sense). At times, it has been used quite consciously to maintain industrial discipline in the work force. Foucault describes the combined poorhouses/insane asylums of eighteenth- and nineteenth-century Paris and London. These were maintained as *public*

[11] A concept advanced by the Health Policy Advisory Center to describe the increasing centralization of urban medical services around medical schools and major teaching hospitals. Strictly speaking, an "empire" would include the core controlling institution (medical school or teaching hospital) plus all its affiliated lesser hospitals and health centers of various types. Usually, though, the word "empire" has been used in reference to the core institution only. See *The American Health Empire*, prepared by Barbara and John Ehrenreich (New York: Random House, 1970), Chapters 3–6.

spectacles to remind the populace of what awaited them if they opted to drop out into pauperism or madness.[12] In much the same way today, exposés of conditions in state mental hospitals serve to discourage "madness" as an out, just as public knowledge of the indignities inflicted on welfare recipients serves to discourage willful unemployment. (Doctors also may function quite explicitly to keep people out of sick roles and in work roles rather than to detect and cure disease. Consider the company doctor, whose role is to pressure the injured worker to return to his station: production losses are minimized and the company saves on workman's compensation benefits. The widespread requirement of a "doctor's note" to excuse absence from work or school similarly reflects the anti-"malingering" function of the medical system.)

Cooptative Control

This kind of social control is exerted by expansionary sectors of the medical system. Expansionary sectors are characterized by relatively low barriers to entry, and acceptable, even sympathetic, treatment of those who do enter. Such services encourage people both to enter sick roles and to seek professional help in a variety of non-sick situations (for preventive care, contraceptive services, marital difficulties, etc.). In so doing they bring large numbers of people into the fold of *professional management* of various aspects of their lives. It is this situation of professional management—whether all-inclusive, as in the case of a cancer patient or partial—which allows for the exercise of cooptative control. It should be clear that cooptative control, unlike disciplinary control, operates on those who do gain entry into the system, to whatever degree. The important question, of course, is What is the nature and ideological content of cooptative control? In other words, what is the impact of professional management on the patient's ideology, self-image, acceptance of work and family roles, etc.? We will devote a major section of this paper to a discussion of these questions.

First, however, it is important to emphasize that the exclusionary and expansionist aspects of the medical system are often closely intermingled. A given agency, or even physician, may present exclusionary or expansionist faces at different times, in different situations, to different groups of patients. At the same time, as we all know, there are certain consistent patterns in the kind of care experienced by different groups in our society—classes, sexes, races, age groups. For example, the overwhelming historical experience of the poor is of an exclusionary system. Thus the different forms of social control we have distinguished are exerted differentially on different groups in society. History provides a striking illustration of the differential social control functions of the medical system.

Consider the kinds of medical care experienced by the urban poor and by

---

[12] Michel Foucault, *Madness and Civilization* (New York: Pantheon 1965), pp. 46–64.

the urban upper and upper middle classes in late nineteenth-century America. (This period is interesting not only because it provides such vivid contrasts but because this is the period of the formation of the American medical profession.) The urban poor—mostly first- and second-generation immigrant workers—faced a grossly exclusionary system. Aside from a few dispensaries located in the ghettos, professional out-patient care was virtually unavailable; doctors were not interested in serving people who could not pay, or could not pay well. Institutional care, in the few municipal hospitals of the time, was avoided for good reasons—sanitary conditions in the hospitals were atrocious; nursing care was minimal until quite late in the century; and medical science had little to offer anyway.

Professionally "legitimate" sick roles were simply not available to the poor. Grinding poverty and the brutality of employers meant that if you were sick enough not to work, you were probably sick enough to die, and conditions in the hospitals meant that if you were going to die, you were better off dying at home. *Disease*, of course, *was* readily available to the poor—TB, cholera, typhus and typhoid fevers, malnutrition, and untreated complications of childbirth were rampant. But without a social and medical system willing to identify the diseased and offer exemptions to them, disease does not become sickness—the diseased go right on working. Thus, to the extent that the nascent medical system of the time had any effect on the poor, it was to enforce industrial discipline.

Meanwhile, the urban upper classes—families of wealthy businessmen, bankers, etc.—faced a medical "system" that was expansionary to a degree experienced by very few Americans today. Relative to today, there was an *excess* of doctors serving the better-off. (At least it appeared so to the AMA at a time when doctors were reduced to running newspaper ads and other less-than-professional tactics to drum up business.) One of the medical profession's most successful business strategies was the exploitation of affluent women as patients. First, medical theory maintained that women—or at least "ladies"—were inherently sick; menstruation (with or without any irregularity), pregnancy, menopause, and puberty were described as morbid conditions requiring close medical management. To fill in the time between these reproductive crises, doctors found a host of vague disorders—"nerves," "chlorosis," "hysteria"—also requiring diligent treatment. (Medical neglect of poor women, who also suffered from the supposedly baneful effect of uterus and ovaries, was justified on the grounds that the poor were constitutionally tougher than the rich, consistent with their "coarser" natures.)

Sickness became so stylish among upper-class women that it is hard to say where the sick role ended and the approved social role of women began. Fainting and nervous delicacy were signs of good breeding; lengthy rest cures and visits to health spas were definitely "in"; invalidism was virtually a way of life for many; the doctor was an almost constant companion. The woman who yearned for a more active life ran into stern medical admonishments— higher education could cause the uterus to atrophy; political involvement, even voting, could be an invitation to hysteria. Rebelliousness was itself pathological, and indicated the need for a medically managed return to "normalcy."

Whether the doctors were motivated by greed, misogyny, or a benevolent concern for the "weaker sex" does not concern us here. There can be no question but that medicine operated as a key agency in the social control of women—enforcing passivity and a childlike dependency on men, particularly on doctors and on the husbands who paid the bills. It is true that these women *were objectively* dependent on men anyway; they had few rights and no means of self-support. But medical theory provided a "scientific" justification for their dependency; and medical practice served, in effect, as an intimate surveillance system—ready to detect female discontent when it was still at the stage of "nerves" or hysteria, and to intervene at once with a regime for "recovery." [13]

Thus the emerging medical system exerted two different kinds of social control on the two groups we have considered: Services for the poor served as a warning to the poor not to get "sick" (and possibly to the rich, as a warning not to get poor). This is what we have termed "disciplinary" control, and was aimed at the not-yet sick, the working poor. The wealthy, especially wealthy women, on the other hand, experienced what we term "cooptative" control. This form of control was latent in the services themselves, and directed at those labeled "sick" (a category which, in medical theory of the time, included all affluent women).

THE EVOLUTION OF THE MEDICAL SYSTEM

The differential pattern of social control which prevailed in the late nineteenth century cannot, of course, be simply extrapolated to the present. The class structure of society has changed dramatically; sex roles have changed in all social classes. Even more important, for our analysis, the medical system itself has undergone profound changes—not only since 1900, but since 1930. Two broad changes in the medical system seem particularly relevant: (1) The vast expansion of the system, in all dimensions; and (2) The rapid rise in status and class position of the medical profession. The first is related to an expansion of the cooptative social control exerted by the medical system; the second is related to changes in the ideological content of that control.

The expansion of the medical system since 1900, or even more strikingly, since 1930, needs little documentation. It can be measured with any parameter one wishes to apply—the absolute and relative amount of money spent on medical services, the number of people employed by the medical

[13] See B. Ehrenreich and D. English, *Complaints and Disorders: The Sexual Politics of Sickness* (Old Westbury, N.Y.: Feminist Press, 1973).

system, the amount of institutional resources devoted to medicine, or the public utilization of medical services.[14] Underneath what appears to be an amorphous mushrooming, we can distinguish three major dimensions of expansion:

1. An expansion in the *jurisdiction* of the medical system to include totally new types of services and functions, and services which were not formerly seen as "medical": family planning, abortions, in-patient obstetrical care, long-term care of the aged and disabled, community mental health services, marriage and sex counseling, cosmetic surgery, etc.

2. An expansion in the *number and kinds of services* available within the traditional jurisdiction of medicine, along with a marked increase in the efficacy of these services. Thanks to biomedical technology, the medical system at last has "something to offer." Very little is left to "nature's course" any more, or considered hopeless. There are antibiotics for infections, radiation and chemotherapy for cancer, antihistamines for allergies, psychic energizers for depression, and surgery for just about anything.

3. An expansion in the *availability* of medical care along class lines. Medical care, though certainly not yet a right, is far from being a luxury. Medicaid, Blue Cross, and a host of other programs have put medical care within the financial reach of large numbers of poor and working-class people who would formerly have stood completely outside the medical system.

We will not attempt to analyze all of the social implications of medicine's expansion in these three dimensions. But one thing seems clear: The expansion of the medical system has been accompanied by a deepening public *dependency* on that system, and this dependency now extends, in varying degrees, to all strata of society. In the first place, the development of medical technology has produced a fantastic rise in public expectations of what the medical system has to offer.[15] Medical "miracles"—from heart transplants to

[14] Per capita expenditures on health services and supplies, adjusted for the increase in the medical care component of the consumer price index, rose (in 1970 dollars) from $169.92 in 1950 to $315.83 in 1970, an 86% increase. This represented a jump from 4.6% of GNP to 7.1%. Utilization of virtually all kinds of services has risen rapidly, although not entirely synchronously for all types.

Out-of-hospital utilization of doctors rose from 2.6 visits per person per year in 1928–31 to 4.7 per year in 1958–59 and has stayed at about that level ever since. Hospital out-patient visits per capita increased 66% from 1962 to 1970 alone (541 visits per 1000 population to 899 visits per 1000 population). Out-patient psychiatric services (community mental health centers, day treatment services, clinics) increased 34.4% from 1955 to 1969 (2.3 visits/1000 population to 10.2 visits/1000).

Utilization of in-patient services has also increased sharply: annual general hospital admissions and mental hospital admissions per 1000 population more than doubled between 1940 and 1970 (general hospitals: 74 per 1000 population per year to 152 per 1000; mental hospitals: 1.4 per 1000 to 3.3 per 1000). The population of nursing homes increased from 491,000 to 850,000 (94%) from 1963 to 1969. (All data from *Statistical Abstract of the U.S.*, 1972, except physician utilization for 1928–31 cited in Odin W. Anderson and Ronald M. Anderson, "Patterns of Use of Health Services," in H. E. Freeman et al., eds., *Handbook of Medical Sociology* (Englewood Cliffs, N.J.: Prentice-Hall 1972).

[15] It is not, strictly speaking, the technology itself which inflates expectations, but the *advertising* of the technology. In the popular family and women's magazines, health and medical

kidney dialysis—promote the idea that almost any problem can be "cured." Headache? Take it to the doctor or take the pill that "doctors recommend." Recurrent cough? May be cancer, but don't delay, the doctor has a cure. There is nothing too trivial to take to the doctor, and nothing too serious to be cured. At least to the middle class, death itself becomes almost an accident—a failure of technique.

Second, advances in medical technology have helped to pave the way for the *jurisdictional* expansion of the medical system, and this in turn has led to a great broadening and diffusion of the public dependency on medicine. If medicine can "cure" anything from polio to TB, then why not dad's drinking problem, or mother's crankiness? The medical system is inexorably replacing lay sources of help (extended family members, neighbors, ministers) for problems ranging from how to handle a baby's cold to how to handle marital tensions or the burden of aged relatives. Even "Dear Abby," that steadfast holdout of lay wisdom, counsels all the really difficult cases to "see your family doctor." In part, this broadening dependency on medicine reflects real increases in the ability of medicine to deal with certain problems; in part it reflects basic changes in the pattern of American life: the breakdown of close-knit communities (especially for the recently suburbanized working class) and of extended families. The housewife isolated in an impersonal suburb may not *have* anyone to turn to except the doctor. But it is also true that doctors themselves encourage dependency by actively seeking to discredit lay advice and help—from chiropractic to "old wives' tales."

Health care is not, of course, the only human-service sector to expand in the last three decades; the educational system and the social welfare systems have grown apace. But the various service sectors differ markedly in the impact rapid growth has had on their professional workers. The numbers of teachers and social workers have expanded as rapidly as have the services themselves. Along with rapid growth in numbers has gone a substantial measure of what has been called "proletarianization": teachers' and social workers' work has become more routinized, and the teachers and social workers themselves have become subject to closer and closer scrutiny by superiors. As a corollary of being treated more and more like "workers" and less and less like "professionals," both groups have rapidly accepted organization into unions in the last decade, and have conducted numerous widely reported strikes.

The case of the doctors is altogether different. The unique political power, tight organization, and traditional autonomy of doctors has enabled them to

---

articles probably outnumber those on any other subject except marriage: "Researchers Claim New Pill Will Ease Tension Without Side Effects," "What You Should Know About Stomach Aches," etc. (A journal aimed at doctors recently ran a drug company ad for a new low-estrogen oral contraceptive: "Because her 'medical journals' alarm her about 'the pill' . . . and because she runs to you for her answer . . ." (*Medical World News*, January 11, 1974). Or look at TV: in a recent week in New York City, there were ten weekly shows, two daily shows, and two "specials" concerned with doctors or medicine, a total of fourteen hours of programming. The media both feed on and fan the public's fascination with medicine.

provide a greatly increased volume of services without significant increase in their own numbers. The doctor in solo practice has, as is well known, become a smaller and smaller component of the overall delivery of medicine; medical care delivery has increasingly shifted to institutions—the hospital, the clinic, the group practice, the community health center, and so forth. Within these institutional medical settings, the doctors represent a smaller and smaller proportion of all health workers. More and more of the tasks that traditionally would have been considered the doctors' are assigned instead to nurses, technicians, and administrators. But despite these changes, the doctors' power over the medical system remains virtually absolute. They have enormous administrative power within the institutional settings in which they practice. More important to our analysis, they remain the chief technical functionaries in the actual practice and public representations of medicine. It is still the medical profession which defies and identifies new diseases, diagnoses illness in individuals, and presides over the medical management of patients.

What is especially significant, the doctors have held on to their monopoly over communication with patients: Nurses, technicians, and others may chat, but they cannot comment on your X-rays, or reveal so much as your temperature. In the eyes of the patient, the contributions of all other workers are secondary—only the doctor has the power to cure, or to pronounce you incurable.

By holding down their numbers and holding on to their power within an expanding system, the doctors have greatly improved their own incomes and standing in the American class structure. Back at the turn of the century, there was widely considered (by the doctors at least) to be an excess of doctors. In rural areas and middle-class urban areas, doctors were certainly plentiful by today's standards. They often had good incomes, but few were wealthy men or men from wealthy backgrounds. Access to a career in medicine was relatively free compared to the present. As late as 1910, there were eight Black medical schools and a substantial number of schools catering to women. Scores of "diploma mills" offered the title "doctor," if not serious medical training, to all comers at moderate cost.

In the first two decades of this century, however, opportunities for nonwealthy and non-White medical students almost vanished. The AMA and a few large foundations (notably the Carnegie Foundation, which funded the famous Flexner Report on medical education and the Rockefeller Foundation, which helped to implement the recommendations of the Flexner Report) waged a successful campaign to eliminate the greater number of the nation's medical schools, in the name of quality medical education. The results of this campaign were: (1) Most of the schools catering to students other than upper-class White males were closed. This included all but two of the Black medical schools and all but one of the women's schools. (Flexner, in his report, bewailed the fact that any "crude boy or jaded clerk" had been able to seek medical training.) (2) The cost of medical education sharply increased as medical schools installed laboratories, new equipment, etc.

Again, poorer students were excluded. (3) A high school and college education became a prerequisite for medical training, again filtering out many prospective bright but poorer (or female or Black) students. (4) The actual number of medical schools dropped rapidly from 162 in 1906 to 95 in 1916 and 79 in 1924; the number of doctors practicing in the communities soon followed. In 1900 there were 173 doctors per 100,000 Americans. By 1920, there were only 137 and by 1930 only 125.[16]

From that time on until the late 60s, doctors were recruited primarily from upper- and upper-middle-class families. In 1967, for instance, 66 to 81 percent (depending on the category of medical school—public, private, etc.) of all medical students had fathers who were doctors, other professionals, or businessmen. As for practicing doctors, today 93 percent are men and more than 98 percent are White.[17]

And from the 1920s through the mid-60s, the AMA kept a tight lid on the nation's supply of doctors by what the *Journal of the AMA*'s editors referred to as "professional birth control"—strict limiting of the number of medical school places. (*n.b.*: We again emphasize that we are not concerned here with the technical impact of the reforms in medical education—i.e., whether or not they improved the quality of medical care, etc. We are concerned only with the sociological impact, which was to limit the number of doctors and to limit the sources of recruitment of doctors.)

The doctors did not reap the full benefits of their declining numbers until after the Depression was out of the way. Then, with doctor supply limited and demand for health care soaring, their incomes rose dramatically, and with their incomes, their social standing. Consider: In the late 1920s and 1930s, doctors' average incomes were about on a par with those of dentists and lawyers; they were slightly over twice the average family incomes of the period and two-thirds higher than those of college teachers. By the 1960s, they had far outdistanced the lawyers and dentists. Their median incomes ($41,500 in 1970) were more than four times those of the average family and three-and-a-half times those of college teachers. A study in 1967 showed that the median assets of doctors aged in their fifties was $134,400. By comparison, the median assets for families with the head of the family aged 45 to 54 was $10,847.[18]

Data on doctors' social standing is more fragmentary, but suggestive. Recent studies of occupational prestige have shown doctors at the very top, on a par with Supreme Court Justices. Comparison with earlier studies indicates a definite, though small increase in prestige from 1925 until the late

[16] U.S. Bureau of the Census, *Historical Statistics of the U.S., Colonial Times to 1957;* see also Rosemary Stevens, *American Medicine and the Public Interest* (New Haven: Yale University Press, 1971) for the full story of the turn of the century reforms.

[17] Occupational figures from R. Fein and G. Weber, *The Financing of Medical Education* (New York: McGraw-Hill, 1970); percentages of women and Blacks from U.S. Bureau of the Census, *Statistical Abstract of the United States, 1972.*

[18] Income figures from *Historical Statistics of the U.S., Colonial Times to 1957* and *Statistical Abstract of the United States 1972;* asset figures cited in Fein and Weber, *The Financing of Medical Education.*

40s at least. C. Wright Mills' study of class in a middle-sized city in the mid-40s indicated that with respect to class origins, whom they married, education, and job histories, "the free professionals [doctors and lawyers] are similar to the big business owners and executives" rather than to the small businessmen whose incomes they more closely approximate. The society pages of newspapers indicate the social acceptability of doctors as husbands to the daughters of the wealthy. G. William Domhoff's 1967 study of adult males listed in the *Social Register* (a guide to high society that represents the upper stratum of the upper class) revealed that no less than 8 percent of the adult males listed had the title "doctor" (presumably in almost all cases, MDs). This is a fifteenfold overrepresentation: doctors make up only about 0.55 percent of the adult male population as a whole. And a quick look at magazines aimed at doctors, such as *Medical Economics*, conveys a vivid impression of upper- and upper-middle-class lifestyles—country clubs, travel, heavy stock market involvement, etc.[19]

Whether we look at class origin, present incomes, assets, lifestyles, or patterns of social interaction, we are on safe grounds in saying that doctors are generally members of the American upper and upper-middle classes. Relative to the overwhelming majority of patients whether poor, "working-class," or "middle-class," they are distinctly upper class.

THE CONTENT OF COOPTATIVE SOCIAL CONTROL
BY THE MEDICAL SYSTEM TODAY

We have noted two major developments in the medical system since 1930: (1) An expansion of services in several dimensions, accompanied by a broadening and deepening public dependency on the medical system; (2) The lack of a proportional expansion in the numbers of the chief functionaries of the medical system, the doctors, accompanied by an absolute and relative improvement in the social position of doctors. Within the medical system, doctors remain the unquestioned elite, holding a monopoly on the key functions of diagnosis, defining of illness, management of illness, and communications with patients. Within the larger society, doctors are also an elite group, members of the politically, economically, and culturally domi-nant strata. We can now put these two developments together: The expanding public dependency on the medical system is a dependency on *White, upper-middle-* or *upper-class males.*

To put it another way: The expansion of services and of utilization means that more people have more contacts with socially advantaged White male professionals, over more "needs" and "problems," than ever before. What is

[19] R. W. Hodge, P. M. Siegel, and P. H. Rossi, "Occupational Prestige in the United States, 1925–63," *American Journal of Sociology,* 70 (1964), 286–302. C. Wright Mills, "The Middle Classes in Middle-Sized Cities," in C. Wright Mills, *Power, Politics and People* (New York: Oxford, 1967); G. William Domhoff, *Who Rules America?* (Englewood Cliffs, N.J.: Prentice-Hall, 1967).

the nature of these contacts? What is the character of the social relationships that arise? The outstanding features of the doctor-patient relationship as a social interaction are:

1. *Intimacy.* Patients are required to expose their bodies to detailed visual and manual probing, and to confide their deepest anxieties about their physical condition. In addition, the patient is usually urged to confide in the doctor about other personal matters that may be peripheral to the problem at hand—family relations, sexual relations, the use of drugs or alcohol, etc. The intimacy, of course, goes only one way: Doctors do not confide in their patients, nor do they undress. "Intimate" revelations may, of course, be essential to proper diagnosis and treatment. For our purposes, it is important to note that intimacy and personal trust cannot readily be restricted to the narrow imperatives of a particular episode of disease. Parsons has argued (correctly, we think) that

> through processes which are mostly unconscious the physician tends to acquire various types of projective significance as a person which may not be directly relevant to his specifically technical functions. . . . The generally accepted name for this phenomenon in psychiatric circles is "transference," the attribution to the physician of significances to the patient which are not "appropriate" to the realistic situation, but which derive from the psychological needs of the patient. For understandable reasons a particularly important class of these involves the attributes of parental role as experienced by the patient in childhood. . . . [Thus] the situation of medical practice is such as inevitable to "involve" the physician in the psychologically significant "private" affairs of his patients.[20]

2. *Authority.* Patients are required to submit to the medical management of their problems almost without question. The penalty for excessive questioning is usually a quick put-down—"Where did *you* go to medical school?" "What are you so anxious about?" (Anxiety is in itself pathological, so this rejoinder amounts to the diagnosis of a new illness.) And so on. The penalties for persistent questioning, outright criticism, or general uncooperativeness are more severe: First, the doctor may reject the patient—"You'll have to find someone else." (Sometimes the rejection is accompanied by dire warnings. For example, a doctor once rejected one of the writers, for questioning the necessity of further lab tests, with the statement, "I don't care if you die!" Fortunately, the condition was far from life-threatening.) Finally, the doctor may "blacklist" the patient among other doctors whom he knows or works with. But these penalties need seldom be invoked: Most patients accept the authoritarianism of the doctor and would be bewildered or even let down by more egalitarian treatment. What is especially interesting for our purposes is that the authoritarianism of the doctor-patient relationship increases as the social distance between doctor and patient increases. The degree of authoritarianism is greater for poor and working-class patients, non-White patients, female patients; and, as the class position of doctors advances, it becomes greater for everyone else, too.

[20] Talcott Parsons, *The Social System*, p. 453.

It should be stressed that these features of the doctor-patient relationship do not apply only to doctors and "sick" patients; people seeking preventive care, prenatal care, contraceptives or abortions, or cosmetic surgery all experience intimate and authoritarian relationships with doctors. To a lesser degree, so do people who are only indirectly involved in the encounter—parents of children needing care, children of aged parents. To enter a situation of professional dominance, you do not have to enter a sick role. In fact, you do not even have to be a patient.

Why do people submit to—in fact, struggle for access to—this kind of relationship, given that it is characterized by a degree of intimacy and authority that would be considered humiliating in any other social relationship? The obvious answer is that people expect to get immediate relief or help, and very often this expectation is met. There are effective contraceptives, antibiotics, surgical interventions, and so on. Cutting through the inflated advertising of medical miracles, and even correcting for iatrogenic effects, there *is* a valid body of biomedical technology, and the only available route to it is through a relationship of professional dominance. But, quite apart from the technology, the relationship itself has a kind of therapeutic value: If the doctor cannot solve your problem—and in a society characterized by insidious chronic disorders the likelihood is that he cannot "solve" it—he can at least manage it. The therapeutic value of professional dominance, from the patient's point of view, is that the problem becomes the *doctor's* problem. It is not for you to fret or question the treatment; it's in the doctor's hands now and "he ought to know what he's doing." The authoritarianism of the relationship fosters a magical transference of the problem from patient to doctor. (This transference phenomenon, not to be confused with the kind of transference Parsons discusses, is probably related to the inability of American medicine to deal adequately with problems that require the patient's willed participation in the cure—e.g., by giving up smoking. Patients expect to be cured, or at least to gain legitimate exemptions from work; they do not expect the doctor to impose new hardships.)

There are some crude similarities between the relationship of professional dominance and other relationships people enter into with powerful, socially advantaged others. Authoritarianism, rewards for submission, penalties for disobedience, and even "magical transference" ("I wouldn't want to be boss—or president, or foreman—think of all the responsibility") are common to such relationships. But the relationship one has with a doctor is also profoundly different from any other relationship one is likely to have with an authority figure, especially one who is of such elevated social class. It is a uniquely intimate and personal relationship. How many other important people are interested in you and concerned about you, even if only for a few minutes each month or year? And it is a manifestly benevolent relationship: Disobeying a teacher or boss might be seen as gutsy, but disobeying a doctor can only be construed as irrational.

To backtrack a little: We have said that an expansionary medical system is characterized by cooptative social control. In order to understand the ideological nature of that control, we have examined the social relationships required for the delivery of medical care. These are relationships of intimate dominance by a professional elite consisting overwhelmingly of White, upper- and upper-middle-class males. These relationships are tolerated, in fact sought after, for their technologically and psychologically therapeutic effects. It should be evident that such relationships, often bridging the most powerful and the least powerful social groups, are rich in possibilities for social control: First, they are ideal vehicles for the transmission of ideological messages from the socially dominant group, and we shall consider this possibility in a moment. But, at least as important, it seems to us, is the ideological impact of the relationship itself. A relationship of dominance and dependency, of intimacy and authority, between a person and a member of the upper class, can only act *to promote acquiescence to a social system built on class and sex-based inequalities in power.*

There is no conspiracy behind this. But neither is it true that ideological control of this type is a natural and inevitable concomitant of the delivery of medical services. It is possible—in fact it is easy—to imagine a highly technologically advanced medical system which engenders a very different sort of social relationship—one in which sickness is not an occasion for isolation of the individual and his or her subjection to medical "manage- ment," but for collective concern and mutual assistance; one in which the experience of the patient is not self-alienation but self-help; one in which helping roles are occupied by social equals, and being helped has no stigma of submission. Of course, such a system would still be exerting social control, but in an entirely different ideological direction—one of self-determination, and solidarity among equals.

Perhaps we can generalize and state that the social mechanisms which arise in any society for the care of dependent persons—children, the aged, the handicapped, the ill—must always operate in the direction of social cohesion. (In fact, the existence of such mechanisms is one of the defining characteris- tics of a "society.") The question is, cohesion to whom, to what groups? In pretechnological situations, the social mechanisms for illness and other forms of dependency commonly involve the formation or tightening of bonds between individuals of similar social status—local midwife and pregnant women, grandmother and sick child, etc. In particular, such relationships often centered in and helped strengthen the family. By contrast, the situation in the U.S. is that not only disease, but a growing number of other conditions call for the formation of primary social bonds to members of the upper classes. The effect is certainly to promote social cohesion, only in this case it is cohesion between social groups whose ultimate interests are not the same.[21]

There is another aspect of cooptative social control we have alluded to: the

---

[21] In at least one country that is seeking to develop a technically modern medical system, China, the State has made it a conscious policy to diminish the social distance between medical personnel and the people. In China, we would suggest, the social organization of medicine operates to promote cohesion within the working classes and the nation. See Joshua Horn, *Away With All Pests* (New York: Monthly Review Press, 1970).

use of the doctor-patient relationship for the transmission of overt ideological messages. This is probably the most familiar type of social control exercised by the medical system—the racist and sexist put-downs, digs about a patient's lifestyle, etc.—but it is extremely difficult to pin down or document. The well-known confidentiality of the doctor-patient relationship (which is essential for the intimacy) has precluded any systematic studies of the social interaction that goes on. Furthermore, some of the most interesting ideological messages probably come through thoroughly disguised as technical directives or advice. All we can do here is to give some examples of the types of messages communicated by doctors, without attempting to establish their prevalence or impact. We distinguish three broad types of messages:

1. Messages that are completely unrelated to the technical requirements of the encounter. This would include comments by the doctor on elections, legislation, or any other broad public issues. Although this use of a doctor's time may seem highly improbable to those of us unaccustomed to clinic care, it is apparently not that unusual. AM-PAC (the AMA's Political Action Committee) unabashedly recommends that doctors make good use of their working hours to inform patients about public issues and candidates.[22] In the AMA's all-out fight against Medicare and pro-Medicare political candidates a few years ago, doctors resorted to such tactics as putting political flyers in with their bills, lecturing their patients before healing them, and threatening to drop politically uncongenial patients.[23]

2. Messages that are related to the technical aspects of the encounter, but that are patently gratuitous. For example, a Black woman we know complained of weakness and tiredness; she was told by the doctor that "colored people are always lazy." Most of our knowledge about this kind of message comes from the women's movement, in which women have made a point of sharing with each other their experiences with doctors. Again, we can only be anecdotal. One woman had a doctor tell her that her breasts were "too small," and then say, "Oh well, as long as your husband is satisfied . . ." Another woman, a teacher, was advised to douche every day because "professional women should always douche." In addition to these kinds of messages, which have the obvious effect of reinforcing the patient's sense of sexual or racial inferiority, doctors also transmit a great deal of conventional morality on such subjects as sex and drugs. In fact, some parents rely on the doctor to introduce their teenagers to these subjects. Doctors are important arbiters of what is moral (usually represented as what is "normal") in sexual activity, drug use, and drinking.

3. Messages disguised as technical communications. This category is potentially limitless. Who, especially among lay people, is able to distinguish between technically necessary and relevant communications and covert social opinions? For example, women's self-help groups report that a great many

[22] "How the Opinion Maker Makes Opinion in Politics," leaflet from the American Medical Political Action Committee (ca. 1973).

[23] Richard Harris, *A Sacred Trust* (Baltimore: Penguin, 1969).

women are told that their uteruses are "tipped"—an apparently neutral observation which, by suggesting abnormalities of reproductive function, has the invariable effect of reinforcing feelings of inadequacy. However, in their own work, the self-help groups have discovered that most uteruses are tipped to one degree or another, including those of women who have successfully borne children. To take another case, pediatricians frequently counsel parents (in books written for the public as well as in office communications) not to put small children in day-care centers on the grounds that the children will catch too many infectious diseases. This advice obviously acts to discourage mothers from working, but it is scientifically unfounded: There are no studies in the English language medical literature showing significantly higher morbidity among children in day-care centers.[24] More generally, the actual treatment given by doctors to poor patients may differ from that given to middle-class and wealthy patients. One form of medical care, psychiatric treatment, is known to vary with class—the more affluent patients get psychotherapy while the less affluent are more likely to be treated with drugs. And differential attitudes of doctors toward patients of different socioeconomic class have been documented. There are certainly grounds for speculation, at least, that the actual technical medical treatment of the poor may be a factor in strengthening the feelings of "low self-worth" which many sociologists claim to detect in the poor—i.e., that the medical system reinforces the sense of class inferiority in those of lower-class position when they use its services.

The point is that the doctor-patient relationship is an ideal one for the transmission of almost any kind of message that doctors may feel inclined to convey. Given the intimacy and authoritarianism built into the relationship, and the prestige and presumed expertise of the doctor, the patient is likely to take such messages much more seriously than he or she would from other people. Whether there is any consistent content to these medical messages is a matter for further investigation. Certainly in the case of women's medical care there seems to be consistent bias toward sexism. It is tempting to speculate that medical messages in general may consistently reflect the attitudes of the social group to which doctors belong. If so, we would have to regard the medical system as a significant vehicle of communication between the upper classes and the general public.[25]

[24] Based on a review of the *Cumulative Index Medicus*, the standard index of medical literature, for the years 1963–1973 inclusive.

[25] There are several reasons to hypothesize a consistent, class-oriented content:

1. The intense socialization of doctors as students and interns and residents probably produces a certain uniformity of attitudes. It is interesting that certain features of their socialization—repeated sleeplessness and interrogations—resemble the supposed "brainwashing" of POW's.

2. At least *moral* uniformity is rigidly imposed on practising doctors by a system of peer surveillance which doctors would find intolerable if applied to their technical performance.

3. The AMA provides doctors with pamphlets, lecture outlines, and the like, offering, at least, to "think" for the busy doctor on a variety of social issues.

CLASS DIFFERENCES IN THE SOCIAL CONTROL
IMPACT OF THE MEDICAL SYSTEM

We have spent so much time analyzing the nature of the cooptative control
exerted by the medical system because the expansionary nature of the present
system makes this kind of control more important than it has been at any
other time in our history. But disciplinary social control is still an extremely
important social factor. The two kinds of control—cooptative and disciplinary—affect different groups of people in different ways and in different
proportions. In fact, the exact mix of cooptative and disciplinary control
experienced by different groups has been changing very rapidly. The result of
these changes has been in many cases the very opposite of "social
control"—public dissatisfaction and even upheaval.

We will confine our discussion to two very broad economic groups, largely
omitting the dimensions of age, sex, and race: (1) What we will call the
"medical poor"—people who are "medically indigent" though not necessarily on Medicaid or welfare. In the big cities, this group is made up
predominately of non-Whites and the elderly of all races. Their major sources
of care are institutional—hospital wards, clinics, and emergency rooms. (2)
What we will call the "medical middle class"—working-class people, blue-
and white-collar, who are not medically indigent but who feel the effects of
rapidly rising medical costs. Their major source of primary care is the private
physician in group or solo practice.[26] (Above these two groups are wealthier
groups, upper-middle and upper class, who do not concern us as subjects of
social control. They experience no barriers to medical care and, in fact, form
the market for luxury care. They are in roughly the same social classes as
physicians.)

The Medical Poor

Historically the poor and the near-poor were simply excluded from the
medical system by their inability to pay. Even in urban areas where charity

---

4. Doctors are fairly uniformly upper-middle or upper class. Especially in smaller cities,
   they are members of the local ruling class, associating with local businessmen, bankers,
   lawyers, etc. and presumably sharing moral and political attitudes with them.

[26] Note: These broad categories gloss over some important differences in medical experience.
Among the poor, there are major differences between the young and the elderly, the urban and
the rural, and probably between the working poor and welfare recipients. In the "medical
middle" we should probably distinguish between a poorer and less urban group receiving most of
its care from GPs and a more prosperous, urban group which is plugged into the network of
specialists.
The "medical poor" and the "medical middle class" together comprise the working
class—nonsupervisory wage and salary workers. Our division of the working class into two
components reflects the complex internal stratification of the working class, which, in terms of
medical care as well as of many other criteria, is not homogeneous. The impact of different
patterns of medical care for different sectors of the working class in *maintaining* the internal
stratification of the class remains to be explored more thoroughly.

services were available, the poor showed considerably lower utilization rates than middle-class people—a difference made all the more striking by the fact that the poor have always had much higher *disease* rates than other groups. Utilization by the poor picked up somewhat in the 60s but there remain serious gaps: The Black poor underutilize services even when they are free or financed by Medicaid, and the poor of all ethnic groups underutilize preventive services (immunizations, annual check-ups, cancer screening, etc.), again, even when these services are free.[27] To explain the persistence of underutilization even after financial barriers are removed, it has become fashionable to invoke a peculiar mind-set among the poor—they lack "future orientation," or they regard their bodies as machines "to be worn out but not repaired";[28] they are "alienated" or poorly "integrated" socially.[29]

A far simpler, though less comforting explanation is that most of the services available to the poor are so unappealing that they actively discourage utilization. The picture of the bottom half of the two-class medical system has been painted often enough—the decaying public health centers presided over by equally decaying municipal doctors, the crowded clinic waiting rooms patrolled by security guards, the open wards with twenty or more beds staffed by a single practical nurse, and in some cases an active contingent of vermin—and so on. Medicaid or no, such services are a painful deterrent to getting sick, and even to seeking the care that should prevent sickness. We would say that the services for the poor are constructed, wittingly or unwittingly, to exercise disciplinary social control.[30]

But there has been, in the last ten years, a significant expansion of services for the poor beyond the traditional clinic/ward type. This expansion has brought the poor, for the first time, into the sphere of cooptative social control by the medical system. In addition to the general class-bridging effects discussed above, cooptative control has taken some very specific and overt forms in the case of the poor. Consider the forms which this expansion of services has taken:

[27] William C. Richardson, "Poverty, Illness and the Use of Health Services in the United States," in Jaco, *Patients, Physicians, and Illness*, pp. 240–49; Anderson and Anderson, "Patterns of Use of Health Services"; Rashi Fein, *The Doctor Shortage: An Economic Diagnosis* (Washington, D.C.: Brookings Institution, 1967).

[28] Daniel Rosenblatt and Edward A. Suchman, "The Underutilization of Medical-Care Services by Blue-Collarites," in Arthur B. Shostak and William Gomberg, eds., *Blue-Collar World* (New York: Prentice-Hall, 1964).

[29] Philip M. Moody and Robert M. Gray, "Social Class, Social Integration, and the Use of Preventive Health Services," in Jaco, *Patients, Physicians, and Illness*, pp. 250–61.

[30] Other immediate sources of underutilization of services include the costs of transportation and of taking time off from work, inconveniently located services, racism and simple rudeness from hospital workers, maintenance of "folk healing" traditions, and lack of knowledge about health facilities and about health itself.

More fundamentally, it is notable that this one segment of the working class is excluded from medical care far more often than the other segments. The reasons for this, we would speculate, lie in part, at least, in the lower value our society places on the lives of economically marginally productive people, and in part on the "need" to instill values of "industrial" work discipline in peoples of more recent rural origin (as many urban slum dwellers are).

First, health services for the poor have not expanded uniformly. Certain specialized services, particularly birth control and out-patient mental health services, have expanded out of proportion to the expansion of general health services. For many ghetto residents, a simple infection still means a grim day spent at a hospital clinic, while for problems of fecundity or psychoneurosis there may be well-appointed centers equipped with interpreters, outreach workers, and baby-sitting services. This disproportionate concern with birth control and mental hygiene has been directly interpreted in Third World communities as a social control effort. Black militants have denounced ghetto birth control services as "genocidal," and have suggested that the mental health services represent a refined police surveillance system. Whether one considers birth control and mental health services to be desirable or not, it is clear that they do have the alleged effects—reduction of birth rates and more efficient detection of social deviants.

Second, there has been some expansion of general medical services in the form of comprehensive medical centers—government-financed group practices for the poor. These "neighborhood" or "community" health centers, as they are called, were designed to provide the poor with the kind of personal, continuous relationships with doctors which do not usually occur in the clinic setting. To the extent that this aim has been met (and it should be pointed out that many community health centers are little more than small-scale versions of the impersonal clinics in the sponsoring hospital), the community health centers are settings for the cooptative control of the poor as individuals, bringing them into relationships of professional dominance. In addition, the community health centers in many cases represented an attempt to control the poor *collectively*. At the most obvious level, many centers were created with the explicitly cooptative aim of cooling out a hostile community. The Watts community gained a center a year after the 1965 riot, and countless "Martin Luther King Health Centers" dot the land.

The community health centers also exert direct community control in an even more conventional sense. As institutions with budgets ranging from $2 million on up, they are often the most important economic centers in their localities. They have become, in many cases, key centers of political patronage, offering scores of unskilled and semiskilled jobs to the friends of local power brokers (Democratic party heavies, OEO officials, and a whole raft of other minor bosses resentfully termed "poverty pimps"). For example, the Hunts Point Multi-Service Center in the South Bronx—a health center *cum* housing, legal, and social services—was the launching pad for Democratic City Councilman and local party boss Ramon Velez.[31] His center, and dozens like it, have served as nuclei for the reconstruction of Democratic machines in the cities. It seems likely that this was the conscious intent of the Democratic administrations of the 60s when they designed that cornucopia of scant services and lush patronage called the "War on Poverty."[32]

[31] *The New York Times*, November 19, 1973, p. 37.
[32] See, Piven and Cloward, *Regulating the Poor*, pp. 250–84.

On a less obvious level, the community health centers have had a *culturally* destructive effect. Fanon might have described them as outposts of the White man's culture planted in "the colonies" to undermine the cultural identity of the oppressed. Whether or not this was the intent, it was probably an important effect. The Black, Puerto Rican, and Chicano target populations of most centers have (or did have) rich traditions of folk medicine which were integral to community structure—*curanderos*, botanical healers, spiritualists, not to mention skilled aunts and grandmothers. If professional medicine was to make significant inroads, it was essential that the community health centers discredit, destroy, or coopt the prevailing folkways. The doctors worked on this directly, and the most ambitiously cooptative centers employed anthropologists and other social scientists to assist them.

Professionals in the community health centers "movement" often felt themselves working uphill against community resistance or indifference. Underutilization was a widespread problem, especially in the early years. Accustomed to an exclusionary medical system, poor people tended to view these new expansionary enterprises with suspicion. Ever more cooptative tactics were employed to "win the hearts and minds of the people": the employment of local people to do outreach work, the addition of training programs for semiprofessional medical jobs, the creation of community advisory boards. (In the view of many medical progressives, such methods were not only appealing come-ons; they were therapeutic in themselves, helping to break through the "social pathology" of the ghetto.) The most ambitious and "sensitive" centers presented uniformly Black or Brown faces to the community (though the doctors and directors were still White); they virtually dragnetted their catchment areas for patients; they sent out trained community workers to track down appointment-breakers. The result, in a number of cases, was soon *overutilization*, and with it a rapid decay of the amenities which had distinguished these centers from mere clinics.

With the community health center movement, the advertising of professional medicine far exceeded its ability to deliver. Federal funds began to wane as early as 1968, and few doctors are Schweitzer-like enough to enter grantless ghettos. But, as is well known by now, expections had been raised. If there was a life-giving center for Watts, why not for Hough, or south Chicago, or Bedford-Stuyvesant? In fact, the same may be said for all the tentative expansions of the medical system into the ghettos. To the extent that they did touch the hearts and the minds of the people they raised dangerous and unmeetable expectations. If mental health meant peace of mind, then why didn't the community mental health center do something about slum landlords? If the hospital and its outreach center stood for health, what were they doing about garbage in the streets? In the end, the medical approach to the problems of the ghetto succeeded only in putting the heat on the medical institutions of the ghetto—for *all* of the problems of the ghetto.

The Medical Middle Class

It is this group, far more than the poor, that experienced the medical expansion of the 40s through 60s. Here we find the fastest-rising utilization rates and the skyrocketing expenditures. Health insurance, whether in the form of a hard-won fringe benefit or an expensive private purchase, has made the increased consumption possible. Rising expectations have made it necessary. Members of this group, both blue- and white-collar, are better educated than ever before, more attuned to the benefits of technology, more accepting of professional expertise. And it is here that we find the TV medical drama viewers, the readers of doctor novels, diet books, and sex manuals. Here are the weight-watchers and cholesterol watchers—anxious about the seven earliest signs of cancer, and anxious about anxiety itself. Here, much more than among the poor today or the working class a generation ago, it is expected that birth, death, and any extremes of experience (pain, madness) will be overseen by physicians and sequestered in institutions. There are scattered pockets of cultural resistance—to mental health services among older blue-collar people, to family limitation services among some Catholic groups—but these are largely vestigial. The general orientation has been to rush headlong into the expanding medical system with whatever money one has, and get as much as one can take.

However, there is a very serious and growing exclusionary trend countering this rush to consumption. We have already emphasized the failure of the medical profession to expand numerically in proportion to the demand for medical services. For our medical middle class, this does not yet mean that doctors themselves are in short supply, but it does mean that doctors' *time* is getting scarce. Private practitioners have been increasing their patient loads without proportionately increasing their working time. For the individual patient, this means longer waits for appointments (four to six weeks is not unusual for a specialist), longer waiting times at the office, shorter, more impersonal encounters with the doctor, and, of course, no house calls at all. One may well ask what is left of the celebrated doctor-patient relationship when ten or fifteen minutes is allotted per patient and part of this time is spent with a nurse or medical assistant who takes histories, weighs the patient, gives instructions on prescribed regimens, etc. The suburban doctor's office is becoming no less an impersonal mill than the urban out-patient clinic.[33]

With the exclusionary trends in the care received by the medical middle class, disciplinary social control comes into operation. Long waits and frustrating encounters with doctors lead to the common feeling that "I don't want to bother the doctor." Even in the more educated strata of the working class, people are not fully utilizing preventive services such as Pap tests, breast

---

[33] In the large and reputedly "excellent" suburban group practice we use, an affiliate of New York's Health Insurance Plan, ten minutes are allotted for each pediatric and gynecological visit, and the time for annual check-ups has recently been cut from thirty minutes to fifteen minutes.

exams, and vaccinations, nor are they reliably bringing the "first signs" of various diseases to medical attention. From a public health point of view, the results are discouraging: Diseases that are preventable or curable if caught early continue to be major killers. But people are only responding to the clear message *not* to bother the doctor—to keep on the job.[34]

There is every indication that the exclusionary trends in the care received by the medical middle class are the wave of the future. In fact, it is government policy to augment them, but by different means. "HMOs" (Health Maintenance Organizations) and "PSROs" (Professional Standards Review Organizations)—widely misinterpreted as consumer "victories"—are actually devices to reduce medical expenditures by reducing utilization of medical services.[35] HMOs sound like an expansion of services, something like community health centers for the medical middle class. In reality they are financial arrangements to provide participating doctors with incentives to curb utilization (particularly of expensive hospital services). HMOs can, in fact, substantially reduce costs without lowering the overall quality of care provided. But the HMO financial arrangement has the potential, at least, to permit doctors to profit personally from excessive underutilization; fragmentary evidence suggests that this may have happened in some HMOs.[36] PSROs sound like an effort to make doctors accountable to the public by forcing them to monitor each others' services. But the only thing that will really be monitored is utilization (was this lab test or this hospital admission really necessary, etc.)—not quality. These reforms are efforts to discipline the demanding public, with the doctors serving as the disciplinary agents.

CONCLUSION

In the last section we have attempted to dissect the uneasy mix of expansionary and exclusionary tendencies in the medical experience of poor

[34] A very significant medical tendency which we suspect is related to the time pressure on the private practitioner is that of diagnosing physical complaints as psychosomatic. The evidence for this is indirect, but impressive: (1) Private practitioners themselves commonly estimate that at least 50% of the cases they see are "psychosomatic." (2) Studies of prescribing habits of doctors show that tranquilizers are the most commonly prescribed drug. A psychosomatic diagnosis—medically accurate or not—clearly amounts to a diagnosis of *malingering.*

[35] Both HMOs and PSROs are the children of Nixon Administration legislation. The former are provided for in the Health Maintenance Organization Act of 1973 and the latter in the Social Security Act Amendments of 1972. The immediate origins of both programs are in government concern over the fantastically rapid rise in government health-care expenditures in the years since 1965. We are indebted to Harry Becker for our interpretation of these programs.

[36] See, for instance, *Medical World News*, June 5, 1973, pp. 17–19; and the California Council for Health Plan Alternatives "Evaluation Report" on the California Medical Group, prepared for Teamsters and Food Employers Security Trust Fund, Los Angeles (mimeo, 1972). Studies of the Kaiser plans have suggested that the HMO mechanism leads to sharp declines in the accessibility of services resulting in considerable tendencies for subscribers to the plans to seek out-of-plan care, substantial differences in utilization by socioeconomic status, and so forth (see *Health-PAC Bulletin*, November 1973).

and working-class people. We have endeavored to show that both tendencies, both types of systems, exert social control and operate to maintain the status quo.

The exclusionary and expansionary tendencies arise in part from the internal dynamics of the medical system, but, as should be apparent to anyone who follows public policy in health, they are also shaped by the overt intervention of the ruling class. One element of the ruling class—the one that held sway over public policy during the Kennedy and Johnson years—is expansionist, and favors increased public spending to promote further expansion. The other, which was represented by the Nixon Administration, is exclusionary and favors government intervention to curb what are viewed as the "excesses" of the 60s.

The two groups are, of course, the groups usually distinguished as the "liberal" and "conservative" elements of the ruling class. Their different approaches to the medical system mirror their approaches to social control in general. The liberals, for example, favor rehabilitation of criminals, medical care for addicts, and less authoritarian structures of work and education. The conservatives favor punitive treatment of criminals, addicts, and other deviants, and even more authoritarianism in the family, the job, and the schools. One group seeks to manage discontent through cooptation; the other through repression. One believes that the structure of society can be held together by ideological persuasion: the other puts its trust ultimately only in force. To repeat what is almost a truism, but represents a central radical understanding of the 60s: Neither group is about to remove the fundamental inequities that are the sources of discontent. And neither group trusts the people to be unmanipulated and unpoliced—nor have they any reason to.

On the whole, the radical approach to health has been little more than an amplified echo of the liberal, expansionist faction of the ruling class. Radicals have simply demanded that medical services be more readily available to all, with the qualification that it should be technically high-quality care, delivered with dignity and without racism or sexism.

It is time that we transcended the argument in these terms. It is time that we got off the single axis of "more" or "less" and began to ask "more" of what, for what purpose, to what effect? The only way to do this is to free *ourselves* from the medical mystification that confines us to seeing medical care as something wholly ordained by technology—a "commodity" whose social nature cannot be examined because it is believed to have none.[37]

---

[37] Equally, we must free ourselves from the economic mystification of health care, which confines us to seeing the health-care system as little more than a system through which doctors, drug companies, insurance companies, etc. extract profits from the sick. In this article we have ignored economic approaches to the medical system. Instead we have described the medical system as a system of social relationships. The economic and sociological approaches are not alternatives, but complementary. The economic approach can be used to explain the development of the medical system and to make predictions about its future development. This is because profits (or at least the minimization of costs) are major motivations in the development of the system. But it cannot explain the *experience* of medical care, or the political implications of that experience for the larger social system. Conversely, the sociological approach we have taken

We have tried to make a start in this direction. But the more serious tasks lie ahead. If the medical system is understood as something more than a system for distributing a "commodity," if it is understood as a system of direct *social relationships*, then the question becomes: What kinds of social relationships do we want a medical system to foster? How can we design a system so that the social relationships it engenders promote *socialist* relationships in society in general?

The task we are posing is not just an exercise in utopian engineering. It is not the same as asking how would one design an electrical power system under socialism, or how would one manage the water supply. The medical system itself has deluded us into thinking that the problems addressed by medicine are indeed "medical" or "technical" problems—that they are properly the preserve of specialists and experts who stand outside culture and politics. But the problems which our society relegates to the medical system—the care of the disabled and dependent, the management of reproduction, individual suffering, and death—are no less than some of the central problems which confront any human society. Medicine has allowed us to evade them too long.

---

cannot explain the development of the medical system. The officials of the medical system are not motivated by a desire to exert ideological control in the interests of the larger capitalist system, and it would be ridiculous to imagine that they are. But the kind of approach we have taken may help point the way to an understanding of the cultural and political *impact* of the medical system on the larger society. And, though it may not help us to predict anything, it can help us to understand what kind of an ideological function a medical system might serve within a socialist society.

To say that the two approaches are complementary is to say that they must co-exist in our understanding or that understanding will be limited and superficial. A purely economic approach is often defended as the only "correct" Marxist approach. It is argued that the only Marxist understanding of capitalist society is an understanding in terms of the exchange of commodities. But it was Marx who insisted that under capitalism, the relationships between commodities, or between people and commodities, obscure and mystify the underlying relationships between people. We must not allow ourselves to be mystified *especially* when examining a sector of the economy in which the "commodity" is not a material thing, but is in fact a direct human encounter.

The danger of the purely economic approach is not only that it leads to faulty analysis, but that it leads to a programmatic strategy which is basically economistic in nature. The only demand becomes "more"; the only challenge to capitalism is to produce "more" within the framework of an irrational and oppressive system.

serving the rich, punishing the poor: welfare for the wealthy through criminal justice*

—Estelle Disch

Why do we have a chapter on criminal justice in a book on welfare, when most people know that neither society nor criminals are helped very much by the criminal justice system? Again we come back to our definition of "social welfare" and the social services, and we remind the reader that our definition is broad. The criminal and juvenile justice system is a service system staffed by service workers. It is *supposed* to promote the general welfare, even though it apparently does not deliver safety to society, nor does it "rehabilitate" most of the recipients of service.

Street crimes represent the other face of a system whose laws, made by property holders, show more concern for property than for working people's welfare. Most of the law-makers seek to protect the existing arrangements of property and private profits, and the people who own little or nothing do what they can to survive.

State and local governments spend about as much on "law and order" as they do on social welfare programs that meet people's survival needs—income maintenance, housing, health care. During the War on Poverty of the 1960s, the federal government spent some money to combat poverty. It lost the war and turned to "law and order," cutting back on poverty programs and increasing law enforcement programs.

There are two major ways to deal with social unrest. One way takes the route of repression; the other takes the route of guaranteeing people that their basic survival needs will be met, and that they will have a share of power and influence over society's institutions. The way of repression threatens everyone's safety, because the influence of a police state spreads so pervasively. The way of equalizing resources and power protects us all from the crimes of both the rich and the poor.

* I want to thank Edwin M. Schur for first introducing me to the larger issues in criminal justice; Jack Spence, John Conklin, Howard Zinn, Roslyn Zinn, and Marvin Mandell for critically reading an earlier draft of this chapter; and my mother, Helen Perkins Disch, for teaching me that it is not a crime for women to work.

Our beliefs are shaped by words. We are taught that some people are criminals and others are not, and we treat people accordingly. The people who shape the categories shape the society. Estelle Disch helps us to redefine our words and reconsider "welfare."

At a time in history when crime rates are rising, when inmates are struggling for humane treatment, when politicians are lacing speeches with cries for law and order, and when the public is feeling intensely about crime, it is useful to look at the American system of criminal justice. It is my contention that the services rendered by the criminal justice system—namely, deterrence, justice, and rehabilitation—are designed to punish the poor and protect the rich, creating a system of "justice welfare" for the rich similar to the welfare afforded wealthy Americans through our system of tax loopholes.[1]

Ideally, the criminal justice system serves both the public and the accused in numerous ways: by enforcing the ideal of "equal treatment before the law," the public and the accused are served by "justice"; by offering rehabilitation services, the accused and the public are served by successful rehabilitation—the former criminal lives a better life, and crime rates go down; and by punishing criminals, society is served by the deterrent effect of fear of punishment in the law-abiding population.

Unfortunately, the service offered falls far short of these ideals. Part of the reason lies in the double bind in which this service system finds itself: it is designed to both punish and treat a single set of individuals. It is not surprising that a lot of mistrust surrounds a service system that simultaneously says, "You are bad" and "You are worth saving." In other service systems, where the aspect of punishment is more subtle, consumers of the service can be more quietly manipulated into accepting what doctors or social workers might want them to do.

A larger reason for the failure of this service system, however, lies in its relationship to the wider social and economic structure of which it is a part. The criminal justice system has been created by wealthy American men, and is being used not for the control of crime but rather for the control of low-income "criminals." As will be demonstrated in the sections that follow, economic bias pervades the services rendered (or not rendered). Deterrence, justice, and rehabilitation will each be discussed in this context. Then, some of the effects of the overall system will be discussed in the final section.

DETERRENCE

The concept of deterrence raises complicated questions having to do with *who* is deterred from *what behaviors* by *what means*. Our criminal justice system does

[1] Philip M. Stern describes this welfare program in "Uncle Sam's Welfare Program—For the Rich," *The New York Times Magazine* April 16, 1972, reprinted in Jerome Skolnick and Elliott Currie, *Crisis in American Institutions* (Boston: Little, Brown and Co., 1973), pp. 40–51.

do a lot of deterring in some areas, but has done little to curb rising rates of street crime and has, in fact, *encouraged* criminal behavior by its nonprosecution of white-collar criminals. Both street crime and white-collar crime[2] will be discussed here as they relate to deterrence.

Our present system of criminal justice is failing to curb the rate of street crime. The *rates* of this kind of crime are increasing, and the effectiveness of the crime control system is not improving fast enough to deal with crime growth. In a statement to police chiefs on August 27, 1974, United States Attorney General William B. Saxbe reported that crime rates increased 6 percent in 1973 and 15 percent in the first quarter of 1974.[3] In spite of the fact that the Law Enforcement Assistance Administration (LEAA) has made funds available for more effective law enforcement over the past few years, crime rates continue to rise.

One reason for the failure of law enforcers to curb crime rates lies in the fact that the high rates are not the "fault" of inadequate police and court work; the problem is too large to be solved with increased arrests and punishments. For instance, in 1972, only 21 percent of the serious crimes known to the police (as reported in the FBI *Uniform Crime Reports*) were "cleared" by arrest (that is, someone was *arrested* for the crime, but not necessarily convicted): 82 percent of murders, 57 percent of forcible rapes, 66 percent of aggravated assaults, 30 percent of robberies, 19 percent of burglaries, 20 percent of larcenies ($50 and over), and 17 percent of auto thefts were cleared. Because the latter three crimes accounted for about 86 percent of the serious crimes known, it is clear that an overwhelmingly large proportion of crimes against property went unpunished.[4]

Attorney General Saxbe, in the speech referred to above, offered a typically inadequate solution to the crime rate. He proposed to increase deterrence by coming down hard on multiple offenders, most of whom are from inner-city, low-income neighborhoods:

> . . . the starting point in dealing with them [criminals] is to increase the odds against them. We must make certain that the odds are on society's side, and that when somebody commits a crime he is going to be caught. After he is caught he is going to face the prospect of certain and sure justice. And after he is convicted he is going to be placed in prison.[5]

Deterrence of the sort proposed by Saxbe—$3 million for special prosecutors in ten cities—raises serious questions. First, it is baffling to consider the possibility of a police force large enough to detect and arrest the people responsible for the approximately 4.5 million known serious crimes for

---

[2] White-collar crime includes crimes against bureaucracies by individuals (embezzlement, theft) and crimes against the public by large and small businesses (fraud, price-fixing), and by politicians.

[3] Robert L. Ward, "Saxbe Plans Program to Fight Soaring Crime," *The Boston Globe*, 206, No. 59 (August 27, 1974), 8.

[4] Data source: U.S. Federal Bureau of Investigation, *Uniform Crime Reports for the United States—1972* (Washington, D.C.: U.S. Government Printing Office, 1973), p. 31.

[5] In Ward, "Saxbe Plans Program," p. 8.

which no one was arrested in 1972. Second, the cost to taxpayers to support the additional courts, prisons, and accompanying personnel would be incredibly high. And finally, there is serious debate as to whether or not increased law enforcement work would be an effective deterrent, even if we wanted to spend the money on such efforts.

Social scientists have argued over the effectiveness of increased police work and punishment. Some argue that increased probability of being caught and punished *is* an effective deterrent.[6] Others argue that increased probabilities of being caught are effective deterrents, but that the severity of punishment doesn't make much difference.[7] Still others argue that efforts like those proposed by Saxbe might show no effects.[8] Indeed, the effects of sending larger numbers of people to prison are questionable when we consider recidivism rates (see below under "Rehabilitation"), and the studies of capital punishment as a deterrent to homicide suggest that there is no relationship between rates of homicide and whether or not a state utilizes the death penalty.[9]

The differential effects of various sanctions on deterring crime become even more complicated when deterrence is explored in broader economic terms. For instance, among shoplifters studied by Mary Owen Cameron, some of whom were middle-class and didn't otherwise see themselves as criminals, detection and the threat of punishment seemed to be an effective deterrent against further shoplifting.[10] Howard Becker, in reviewing Cameron's book, suggested that the fear of being caught and punished was an effective deterrent for middle-class potential criminals.[11] In general, however, we lack systematic data on the role of deterrence in the behavior of middle-class and wealthy Americans. Although there are many studies comparing groups of low-income criminals with noncriminals (especially among children), there are not comparable studies examining motivational differences between, say, corporate executives who fix prices and those who don't; or childhood experiences of businessmen who engage in fraudulent advertising and those who don't.

One reason for our lack of information about wealthy criminals,[12] and of

[6] Gordon Tullock, "Does Punishment Deter Crime?" *The Public Interest*, No. 36 (Summer 1974), 109; and Don C. Gibbons, *Society, Crime and Criminal Careers*, 2nd ed. (Englewood Cliffs, N.J.: Prentice-Hall, 1973), pp. 452–53.

[7] Ibid. p. 453.

[8] Edwin M. Schur, *Our Criminal Society* (Englewood Cliffs, N.J.: Prentice-Hall, 1969), p. 189.

[9] For a summary of some of the sociological literature on the death penalty, see Gibbons, *Society, Crime, and Criminal Careers*, pp. 455–57; Richard Quinney, *The Social Reality of Crime* (Boston: Little, Brown, 1970), pp. 184–90.

[10] Mary Owen Cameron, *The Booster and the Snitch* (New York: The Free Press, 1964), pp. 159–70.

[11] Preview of Cameron, in *American Journal of Sociology*, 70 (March 1965), 635–36.

[12] The terms "wealthy, criminal," "white-collar criminal," etc., are used interchangeably in this paper. The terms refer to people committing crimes against bureaucracies (employee theft of goods, embezzlement, tax evasion, etc.) and crimes against the public by small and large businesses, and by politicians (fraudulent advertising, marketing of harmful drugs, dishonest appliance repair, illegal war-making, etc.). It includes both Sutherland's concept of white-collar

information on the effectiveness of criminal sanctions in deterring criminal behavior among that group of people, is the inherent protection offered to wealthy criminals under our system of "justice." We are reluctant both to define certain unethical corporate practices as "criminal" and to prosecute wealthy offenders when they do break the criminal law. Wendell Berge, assistant to the head of the Anti-Trust Division of the Department of Justice, defended this position in 1940:

> While civil penalties may be as severe in their financial effects as criminal penalties, yet they do not involve the stigma that attends indictment and conviction. Most of the defendants in anti-trust cases are not criminals in the usual sense. There is no inherent reason why anti-trust enforcement requires branding them as such.[13]

The small number of suits brought against wealthy law-breakers has several implications, some of which will be pursued later, related to the effects on public images of criminals. In terms of deterrence, however, there is an ironic twist of justice when we look at crimes committed by the rich. In an area of crime control in which criminal sanctions might well be extremely effective, there are very few sanctions. In his discussion of "respectable" crime, Edwin Schur concludes:

> Quite simply, a strong case can be made for clamping down on white-collar crime and related offenses. The direct cost of such crime to society is substantial; the indirect cost in terms of promoting a climate of fraud may also be great, and these are offenses that can in some considerable measure effectively be curbed by criminal law.[14]

The irony, to Schur, is that we aim law enforcement effort "at offenses against which . . . the criminal law may have little deterrent effect."[15]

If we were to bring harsher penalties to white-collar criminals, we would then have to consider the correctional system and its potential deterrent effects on the individuals punished. As will be discussed below, prisons have a poor record for rehabilitating low-income people. On the other hand, there is one study of white-collar tax evaders which indicated that they had an extremely low recidivism rate.[16] It is again ironical that the correctional

---

crime (crimes by people in respectable positions) and Geis' concept of upperworld crime (crimes by people in economically powerful positions, regardless of whether or not they are "respectable"). See Edwin H. Sutherland, *White Collar Crime* (New York: Holt, Rinehart and Winston, 1961); Gilbert Geis, "Upperworld Crime," in Abraham S. Blumberg, ed., *Current Perspectives on Criminal Behavior* (New York: Alfred Knopf, Inc., 1974), pp. 114–37.

[13] Sutherland, *White Collar Crime*, p. 43.

[14] Schur, *Our Criminal Society*, pp. 189–90.

[15] Ibid., p. 189.

[16] Robert W. Winslow, *Crime in a Free Society: Selections from the President's Commission on Law Enforcement and Administration of Justice* (Belmont, Cal.: Dickenson Publishing Co., 1968), p. 181. See also Geis, "Upperworld Crime," pp. 132–33, for a discussion of the possible effects of criminal sanctions. The recidivism rate refers to the proportion of inmates returning to prison after a prior incarceration. It is usually computed by following the official records of individuals released from some aspect of the correctional system and tabulating what proportion of them are locked up again within six months, a year, or several years.

system may well work best for those groups which it is least apt to serve under our present law enforcement system. Its deterrent effect, then, is minimal for wealthy criminals.

There are some general things that can be said about the effectiveness of deterrence across class lines. There are certain kinds of crime from which both the wealthy and the poor are deterred by virtue of our economic structure. The poor are deterred from antitrust violations and other kinds of fraud which take a lot of capital to engage in (like fraudulent advertising, fraudulent home appliance repair, etc.); the rich and middle class (with the exception of increasing rates of middle-class delinquency) seem deterred from the kinds of street crime most often engaged in by low-income citizens—perhaps because of the threat of losing face in their communities, perhaps because more community or psychiatric support is available to wealthy kids who seem headed in delinquent directions, or perhaps because wealthier people have access to other kinds of money crimes that are less likely to be enforced.[17] Overall, this system of deterrence provides a service to the rich; because criminal charges are seldom pressed against them, they effectively continue their money crimes in relative peace. Law enforcement is largely directed against the poor (however ineffectively), and the larger causes of crime—like economic need and widespread alienation—are ignored.

JUSTICE

"Crime" is a vague word. Technically, it refers to all behavior proscribed by the criminal law. A "criminal" or juvenile "delinquent" is someone who has been caught, arrested, tried, and found guilty of criminal (or delinquent) behavior. Because our system of justice is based on the assumption that people are innocent until proven guilty, we often assume that citizens who have not been proven guilty are indeed innocent, and that those who *have* been proven guilty of crimes are the *real* criminals of our society.

According to surveys of cross-sections of the population, however, nearly all citizens of the United States are potential criminals. In a survey conducted in the forties, 91 percent of the 1,700 respondents admitted that they had committed acts for which they might have been sent to jail or prison at least once in their lifetimes.[18] In a study among young people (ages 13 to 16), 88 percent admitted to having committed acts for which they could have been judged delinquent, yet only 9 percent of this group was detected. Of those detected, only 4 percent received police records, and only 2 percent were judged "delinquent" [19] (the juvenile justice system's euphemism for "guilty").

[17] Because of the large numbers of unsolved crimes, however, we cannot say with certainty that *no* wealthy and middle-class people are contributing to the high rates of crimes known to the police as reported in the FBI Index.

[18] James S. Wallerstein and Clement Wyle, "Our Law-Abiding Lawbreakers," *Probation*, 25 (April 1947), 107–12.

[19] Jay R. Williams and Martin Gold, "From Delinquent Behavior to Official Delinquency,"

Finally, a survey of 10,000 households revealed that persons in the households had been victims of crime much more often than reported to the FBI for its Uniform Crime Reports. When clustered together, property crimes were mentioned in the survey more than twice as often as they appear in the Uniform Crime Reports; crimes against the person occurred nearly twice as often as reported.[20]

These data demonstrate that there is much more crime than we hear about; that there is more crime than we would ever have time to process through arrest, trial, and punishment, even if we wanted to do so; and that crime occurs at all social class levels—that it is *not* intrinsically and isolatedly located among lower-class citizens. Social class and the occurrence of crime, however, is a complicated matter. It would be simple to assert that poor people and rich people, Blacks and Whites, and men and women commit all crimes at the same rate, and that only the poor, Blacks, and males get caught. What seems to be the reality, however, is that low-income people in cities are more apt to commit some of the crimes that frighten the public the most (murder, rape, armed robbery). Simultaneously, rich people tend to commit other kinds of crimes—like producing and selling harmful drugs—which, because of their "hiddenness," tend to frighten the public less, and therefore go unpunished. There is heavy public pressure to wage war on the most personally "frightening" crimes.[21]

Public fear of crime is a result of many factors. While there is cross-culturally shared fear of being robbed at knifepoint, or assaulted, raped, or murdered, the public has not been taught to actively fear the potentially failing brakes of a school bus or automobile, or the potentially harmful effects of a new drug. It is therefore difficult to separate intrinsic human fear from "taught" fear. It is likely that we could learn to fear the corporate consumer products much more if we had full knowledge of the facts behind production. That would mean, of course, that the advertising industry would have to collude with the public instead of with corporate interests—an unlikely possibility. It would mean, very likely, a broadened definition of the word crime.

Other factors enter into the socioeconomic distribution of labeled criminals. First, people at different socioeconomic levels have differential access to money crimes. It takes a high-level white-collar job to embezzle funds; it takes access to high-level corporate decision making to fix prices. Because most reported FBI Index crimes are property crimes (86 percent of the reported serious crimes mentioned earlier in this paper are property crimes), it seems reasonable to assume that if poorer Americans had access to the large sums of money that wealthier Americans do, they wouldn't have to commit

---

Social Problems, 20, No. 2 (1972), 209–29. There is some indication that kids overreport their delinquent behavior, but even considering that, a lot of it goes unreported.

[20] President's Commission on Law Enforcement and Administration of Justice, *The Challenge of Crime in a Free Society* (Washington, D.C.: U.S. Government Printing Office, 1967), p. 21.

[21] Thorsten Sellin and Marvin E. Wolfgang, *The Measurement of Delinquency* (New York: John Wiley & Sons, 1964).

robbery, burglary, and larceny at such high rates; instead, they could contribute to embezzlement rates or price-fixing rates.

A second factor closely tied to the relationship between social class and crime is the focus of resources of the law enforcement agencies. Without unlimited law enforcement resources, choices are made as to which laws to enforce and which to ignore. It is clear that resources are heavily focused on the kinds of crime that occur in city streets rather than in corporate offices. Thus it *looks* as though criminals are primarily young, male, and disproportionately non-White from low-income neighborhoods, even though there are many wealthy, older, male and female White law-breakers.

Finally, within the criminal justice process itself there are a lot of data to support the assertion that poor people, now-Whites, and young people are discriminated against when it comes to arrest, trial, and sentencing—contributing to the failure of justice.[22] There are, in contrast, some recent studies which suggest that there is no discrimination, but in the wake of years of studies to the contrary, these new data must be weighed carefully. In either case, there is almost no data to support discrimination *in favor of* non-Whites, or males, or low-income citizens. If the criminal justice system were indeed "just," it seems reasonable to expect equal rates of discrimination on both sides of the balance.[23] On the discrimination side, the following kinds of data are reported. Piliavin and Briar found that

> Older juveniles, members of known delinquent gangs, Negroes, youths with well-oiled hair, black jackets, and soiled denims or jeans (the presumed uniform of

[22] Sexist bias in the criminal justice system will not be explored in this paper, in large part because the situation of women *vis à vis* the criminal justice system is difficult to assess. In the case of laws that discriminate against women—such as laws against abortion and prostitution—the sexist bias of the law is relatively clear; in fact, if "victimless" crimes were to become legal (drunkenness, prostitution, drug use), an estimated 50 to 80% of the women currently in jail would be released. On the other hand, there is some evidence to indicate that women get much "softer" treatment by law enforcement officials than men do, and that if there were true equal treatment before the law there would be a smaller discrepancy between the numbers of men and women in prisons. The possibility that women "get off easy" in the criminal system must be considered in a wider context, however. For instance, Phyllis Chessler, in *Women and Madness*, asserts that "in 1964, the number of American women being psychiatrically 'serviced' began to suddenly, or at least, measurably increase. Adult female patients rapidly exceeded the number of adult male patients [in asylums]. There were significantly more women being 'helped' than their existence in the population at large would allow us to predict." (New York: Avon Books, 1972, p. 55.) It is likely that there are many women who, if male, would have gone to prison, but are in mental institutions instead. To assert this with confidence, however, we would need systematic data on the lives of groups of men and women, following their careers in "deviant" and "nondeviant" behavior, and then tracing the official and unofficial sanctions levied against their nonapproved behavior.

[23] For studies that found no class discrimination, see Travis Hirschi, *Causes of Delinquency* (Berkeley and Los Angeles: University of California Press, 1969). Hirschi found that a key element in being adjudicated delinquent was the presence or absence of a meaningful authority figure in the child's life, rather than the social class of the child. See also D. J. Black and A. J. Reiss, Jr., "Patterns of Behavior in Police and Citizen Transactions," section 1 of *Studies of Crime and Law Enforcement in Major Metropolitan Areas*, Vol. II (Washington, D.C.: U.S. Government Printing Office, 1967).

"tough" boys), and boys who in their interactions with officers did not manifest what were considered to be appropriate signs of respect tended to receive the more severe dispositions.[24]

Thus, the chances of being arrested were higher among boys whose images and behavior police didn't like—even though data supports the assertion that large numbers of White, younger, differently dressed kids were *also* committing delinquent acts.

This kind of discrimination is not confined to poor, urban children. Mary Owen Cameron, in the study of shoplifting and shoplifters in Chicago referred to above, found similar patterns of law enforcement among a group of largely female adults representing a cross-section of the socioeconomic population. While noting that most offenders are never brought to the police, she mentions some of the conditions which affect who gets caught by store detectives and, after being caught, who receives a criminal record and who doesn't: racial biases of detectives lead them to scrutinize Blacks more carefully; detectives are hesitant to confront "respectable" people; young people are scrutinized because they're assumed to be theft-prone; Black shoplifters, while found in about the same proportion as in the Chicago population, are more likely sent to the police, and those Black women convicted in court are more apt to receive harsher penalties than White female shoplifters.[25]

Finally, it is widely known that the chances of getting a "not guilty" disposition are often dependent upon factors like personal appearance, race, prior record, sex, work and school history, and whether or not the defendant has a private lawyer. It is also widely known that poor people do not have private lawyers, and that public defenders are overworked and underpaid, and therefore do poor legal work for their clients.[26]

Data describing arrested persons and inmate populations lend support to the above assertions that discrimination on the basis of social class enters into the series of decisions which send only *some* law-breakers to prison. After describing the population of persons arrested, the President's Commission made this conclusion:

> The picture that emerges from this data is of a group of young adult males who
> come from disorganized families, who have had limited access to educational and

---

[24] Irving Piliavin and Scott Briar, "Police Encounters with Juveniles," *American Journal of Sociology*, 69 (September 1964), 206–14; reprinted in Earl Rubington and Martin S. Weinberg, *Deviance: The Interactionist Perspective* (New York: Macmillan, 1968).

[25] Cameron, *The Booster and the Snitch*, pp. 24–32, 136–44, 91–96.

[26] For a moving, interesting account of what happens when poor Black kids get *good* legal services, see Lois Forer, *No One Will Lissen* (New York: Grosset & Dunlap, 1970). This book documents a federally funded project to bring legal services to an inner-city neighborhood in Philadelphia. For some evidence supporting the assertion that discrimination occurs in court, see Richard Harris, "Annals of Law: In Criminal Court—II," *New Yorker Magazine*, April 21, 1973; and "Annals of Law: In Criminal Court—I," *New Yorker Magazine*, April 14, 1973. Also see Stephen R. Bing and S. Stephen Rosenfield, *The Quality of Justice in the Lower Criminal Courts of Metropolitan Boston* (Boston: Lawyers' Committee for Civil Rights Under Law, 1970).

occupational opportunities, and who have been frequently involved in difficulties with the police and the courts, both as juveniles and adults.[27]

A similar picture emerges when characteristics of prisoners are examined. Inmates have less education than the general population (8.6 years as contrasted with 10.6 years), are more apt to be laborers (23.9 percent as contrasted with 5.1 percent in the general population), are less apt to have high-status occupations (5.8 percent as contrasted with 20.6 percent in the general population), etc.[28]

It is likely that the frequency of "serious" crime (as defined by the FBI Index) is heavily concentrated in the lower class. However, the fact that our social structure funnels only certain citizens into the lower socioeconomic ranks (those born there), and then funnels members of primarily that group into prisons, is an economic reality.

There is a serious effect of class discrimination, beyond the injustice applied to certain individuals: we learn that certain people are "criminals" and, by implication, learn that other people are *not* criminals (with occasional exceptions—like Nixon, Agnew et al.). With the help of the mass media and many criminologists, we develop stereotypes of criminals based on the kinds of people who are in jail. In an article summing up some of the criminological literature, Eugene Doleschal and Nora Klapmuts conclude:

> This very selective bias in the legal system means that most studies of crime and the offender take as their starting point a stereotype of the "criminal" that is a social and legal artifact.[29]

Although the criminal justice system is being overburdened with the cases of low-income, essentially politically powerless "criminals," there is blindness to the everyday violence of corporate power, and everyday middle-class crime. Our tunnel-visioned approach to crime allows wealthy criminals to support their money addictions while law enforcement resources and attention focus on the kinds of poor people who, also in search of money, commit the FBI Index Crimes and ultimately go to prison. If we explore crimes like price fixing, tax evasion, illegal war-making, illegal campaign tactics, fraud (by, for instance, auto repair people), monopolies, etc., we find that the specialists for these kinds of crimes are found among the middle class and the rich. It takes a lot of political and economic power to engage in the kinds of crimes that corporations commit so successfully and quietly. It takes mass media amenable to these "quiet" crimes to block from open public view the kinds of crimes the automobile manufacturers, drug companies, and other large corporations commit annually. It takes more capital than the average poor person has to engage in business fraud such as illegal automobile or home appliance repair—crimes which often victimizes the average citizen.[30]

---

[27] President's Commission on Law Enforcement and Administration of Justice, *The Challenge of Crime in a Free Society*, p. 47.

[28] Ibid., p. 45.

[29] "Toward a New Criminology," *Crime and Delinquency Literature*, 5. No. 4 (December 1973), 613. This article offers an efficient summary of the discrimination process in criminal justice.

[30] For some data on fraudulent repair practices, see *The Repairman Will Get You If You Don't*

A number of values contribute to the perpetuation of this class-biased justice. One is a hesitancy among law enforcement personnel to arrest and prosecute people like themselves or like those who pay their salaries. Another value is a tendency to deny that "crime" has been committed when the criminals are not singly identifiable and when the crime is easily overlooked. (For instance, when Bon Vivant Vichysoisse killed a person, newspapers reported that federal inspectors had been overlooking the crime of filth in the plants. Inspection means confronting illegal health conditions head-on, rather than denying them.) And finally, there is a lack of any kind of caring about the consumer. As Schur puts it:

> Whether the offense involves income tax evasion by an individual or misrepresentation in the prospectus for a stock offering, improper labeling of drugs or collusive agreement to overprice in a particular industrial market, *a philosophy of contempt for or manipulation of individuals at least subtly colors the behavior* . . . [and] the citizenry becomes largely inured to deceptive practice, conditioned to uncritical responses to appeals and deals, *with each potential "victim" of fraud himself prepared to capitalize on whatever fraudulent opportunities present themselves.* [Italics mine—E. D.][31]

A classic exception to the refusal to bring criminal sanctions against top executives occurred when price fixing among the big electrical companies was exposed.[32] In exchange for fixing prices, rigging bids, etc., on electrical equipment valued at over $1.7 billion annually for a number of years, seven top executives received thirty days in jail. There are pressures against heavy criminal sanctions, even when the costs to the public are high.[33]

There are other economic values inherent in decisions as to how to punish corporate criminals, as illustrated by the case of the production of MER/29, an anti-cholesterol drug, by the William S. Merrell Company. The side effects of MER/29 included cataracts, nausea, loss of hair, changes in hair color, dryness of skin, and other symptoms—all this with a demonstrated failure to significantly reduce cholesterol levels. A judge in one of the civil suits brought against the company supported a lower money settlement than the jury recommended, on the basis that the company might be subjected to "extraordinary financial strain" if all the injured patients sued the company.[34] The judge referred to "innocent stockholders suffering extinction of their investments for a single management sin," in making his decision.[35] He seemed to overlook the history of the case: The company lied to the Food and

Watch Out (Garden City, N.Y.: Doubleday, Doran and Co., Inc., 1942), pp. 53–184, cited in Winslow, *Crime in a Free Society*, p. 177.

[31] Schur, *Our Criminal Society*, p. 170.

[32] Richard Austin Smith, "The Incredible Electrical Conspiracy—Part I," *Fortune*, LXIII, No. 4 (April 1961), 132–37, 170, 172, 175–76, 179–80; and "The Incredible Electrical Conspiracy—Part II," LXIII, No. 5 (May 1961), 161–64, 210, 212, 217–18, 221–22, 224.

[33] For a more detailed discussion of this case, see Schur, *Our Criminal Society*, pp. 160–61; and Winslow, *Crime in a Free Society*, pp. 185–88.

[34] Stanford J. Unger, "Get Away with What You Can," in Robert Heilbroner et al., *In the Name of Profit: Case Studies in Corporate Irresponsibility* (Garden City, N.Y.: Doubleday, 1972), p. 124.

[35] Ibid., p. 124.

Drug Administration and to doctors in order to get the drug approved for sale. Three defendants got six months probation (they could have gotten up to five years in prison and $10,000 fines each), and the corporation (Merrell and the parent corporation) was fined $80,000. Stanford Unger, in reporting the case, concludes:

> If the crime is not one of obvious violence [he doesn't define "obvious violence"] and the defendants are white gentlemen of pleasant demeanor and apparent good will, their punishment shall be mild.[36]

The concept of "violence" referred to by Unger is another aspect of our blind approach to crime. Even though traffic deaths occur about five times as often as homicide, and even though mechanical failures in cars are blamed for large numbers of traffic deaths, there is incredibly successful resistance by the automobile manufacturers to offer safer vehicles. Because the violence of shoddy machinery occurs without an individual's name attached to it, the violence goes uncounted, and unpunished.[37] Colman McCarthy describes corporate blindness to its effects on human beings:

> . . . the vice-presidents are free to measure the company's success not by the consumer's voice . . . but by sales reports. . . . When profits aren't up . . . or when management thinks they can be better, a decision is inevitably made in favor of cheapening the product. When the result of such a decision may be death, the ethical numbness encouraged by the profit system becomes grimly apparent.[38]

Examples of corporate irresponsibility and greed are numerous. What is crucial here, however, is that they do not do their work in a vacuum; there is explicit and implicit support for their behavior in the lack of punishment and in the *kind* of punishment the corporations and their executives receive when they are occasionally brought to trial. Clearly, it is all right to be greedy if you are rich (but not quite as greedy as Nixon tried to be), and it is immoral to be greedy if you are poor; if poor, you will likely be punished for stealing, whenever the law enforcement process is sharp enough to catch up with you, even though the economic losses due to white-collar crime and corporate crime are far greater than those due to robberies and burglaries.

REHABILITATION

We know from the preceding sections that primarily poor people are sent to prison. Within the prison experience, and within treatment programs generally (parole, probation, etc.), the "service" given is a failure. For many years correctional "experts" have been attempting to lower recidivism

---

[36] Ibid., p. 123.

[37] See Ralph Nader, *Unsafe at Any Speed* (New York: Grossman, 1965); and Colman McCarthy, "Deciding to Cheapen the Product," in Heilbroner et al., *In the Name of Profit*, pp. 32–59.

[38] McCarthy, "Deciding to Cheapen the Product," p. 59.

rates—which are as high as 80 percent for serious offenders[39]—through "innovative" programs both within prisons and in the community. As a result, low-income inmates have become subjects of experimental reform again and again—usually under the guise of humanitarian motives. The motives appear humanitarian because they appear in a narrow context—correctional officials are encouraged to make *their* part of the criminal justice system effective, which often has meant interjecting humanitarian elements into the punishment structure. For instance, the following represent attempts to alter the life-disaster rates of people processed by the criminal justice system: (1) new programs within prisons such as psychotherapy, therapeutic communities, educational and vocational training; (2) wider community-based services to adults and, especially, juveniles; (3) increased transitional steps out of the prison system, such as prerelease centers, work-release programs, furloughs, and halfway houses; and (4) court-based pretrial "diversion" programs aimed at keeping offenders out of prison.

All these efforts seem to be helping a few *individuals* without altering the wider picture. Evaluation research, following up inmates who have experienced some of these innovative programs reflect various rates of failure, ranging from an occasionally significant lowering of the recidivism rate, to having no effect on the recidivism rate. In a recent study in California, inmates were randomly assigned to several different treatment modes in prison in an effort to evaluate which worked best. The results demonstrated that all the prison programs were equally ineffective.[40]

Community-based programs seem to have somewhat more success, but are still inadequate to affect the rates of crime. In a summary of many correctional programs of different types—community-based and prison-based—Robert Martinson concluded that one of the best effects some of the programs have is to not make things *worse:*

> . . . a great many of the programs designed to rehabilitate them [criminals and delinquents] at least did not make them do *worse.* And if these programs did not show the advantages of actually rehabilitating, some of them did have the advantage of being less onerous to the offender himself without seeming to pose increased danger to the community. . . . The implication is clear: that if we can't do more for (and to) offenders, at least we can safely do less.[41]

In most studies the recidivism rate is one of the most accessible measures of success or failure. Other effects of the justice experience, especially effects upon the more personal aspects of people's lives—such as their ability to work

[39] Ramsey Clark, *Crime in America* (New York: Simon & Schuster, 1970). Clark estimated that 80% of felons would return to prison. In studies of recidivism in Massachusetts, about 68% of those released from the maximum security prison were recidivists. The rates are about 55% for medium- and minimum-security prisons. Lower rates usually refer to special groups of offenders, or all offenders together—not just serious offenders.

[40] Gene G. Kassebaum, David J. Ward, and Daniel M. Wilmer, *Prison Treatment and Parole Survival* (New York: Wiley & Sons, 1971).

[41] "What Works?—Questions and Answers About Prison Reform," *The Public Interest*, No. 35 (Spring 1974), 48.

and their feelings about themselves, their families, and society—are more difficult to measure and more often go unnoticed. Descriptive writings about prison life, however, reflect the enraging, degrading experience that it is.[42] Difficult to evaluate, these more human aspects of prison life have often been ignored by social scientists. Because it seems that the more personal effects are overwhelmingly negative, it makes sense that they have been examined less often, given that most correctional research is conducted with the permission of departments of correction—groups that have a vested interest in repressing information about prison brutality.

The implications of this double failure—the failure to reduce crime in the society and the failure to treat human beings in a humane way—are deeply felt in the way ex-offenders see themselves and in the way society sees them. The judicial system selects certain people to be processed and labeled "criminal." One effect of this label seems to be a self-perpetuating career in crime.[43] It seems that once a person is labeled, the probabilities of getting un-labeled, or re-labeled are small. There are no formal mechanisms in our social or legal structure for rewarding "rehabilitated" criminals—no "welcome back" ceremonies saying that a person has paid his or her debt and is forgiven.[44] Instead, the former inmate meets a hostile environment where jobs are scarce and living expensive. The now-labeled criminal is asked again to conform to social norms for which there are few rewards except for the chance to avoid prison the next time.

The class issues here should be clear: only the poor are experimented with in the correctional system, while the rich are ignored; the "service" rendered is a failure when evaluated on its own terms; and as long as correctional experts focus on their own domain, the wider society, including its wealthy criminals, will not be seen as a factor in the failure. Without a wider look at the causes of crime, correctional officials will continue to experiment with ways of significantly lowering recidivism rates and wonder why even those efforts fail.

In summary, then, the "welfare" the rich receive through criminal justice has serious effects on the rest of society. One of these effects is the

[42] Leonard J. Berry and Jamie Shalleck, eds., *Prison* (New York: Grossman Publishers, 1972); Angela Davis and Other Political Prisoners, *If They Come in the Morning* (New York: The Third Press, 1971); Emma Goldman, *Living My Life*, Vols. 1 and 2 (New York: Dover Publications, Inc., 1970); George Jackson, *Soledad Brother* (New York: Bantam Books, 1970); David M. Peterson and Marcello Truzzi, *Criminal Life: Views from the Inside* (Englewood Cliffs, N.J.: Prentice-Hall, Inc., 1972), pp. 135–185, etc.

[43] The sociological literature on the labeling of deviance discusses this effect. See Edwin M. Schur, *Labeling Deviant Behavior* (New York: Harper & Row, 1971) for a comprehensive summary of the literature; Rubington and Weinberg, *Deviance: The Interactionist Perspective*, and the second edition of this book (1973); also on the self-fulfilling prophecy, see Robert Rosenthal and Lenore Jacobsen, *Pygmalion in the Classroom* (New York: Holt, Rinehart & Winston, 1968).

[44] See writers who discuss the role of deviance as a force for group cohesion: Lewis A. Coser, *The Functions of Social Conflict* (New York: The Free Press, 1956); Kai Erikson, *Wayward Puritans* (New York: Wiley & Sons, 1966); Edwin Schur, *Labeling Deviant Behavior*, pp. 146–48.

discrimination against members of the population who happened to have been born non-White or poor. By virtue of this selectiveness within the criminal justice system, certain people are chosen by the system to be its public "criminals." The people chosen get little or no "correctional" help; they are processed, punished (via street supervision on probation, or via prison and parole), and returned to "society"—as if prisons were not part of society—with few additional economic skills or good feelings about themselves or the system that sent them to prison or "treatment" in the first place. Because their options for economic survival have not increased, and because the discriminatory process which decided to punish them in the first place has not changed—and, in fact, is now biased against them because they are now known as "bad actors"—the likelihood of their entering the criminal justice process again is high.

EFFECTS OF "JUSTICE WELFARE": SERVING THE RICH

Many social critics and social theorists have attempted to explain why crime and the criminal justice system exist as they do. Conservatives, for instance, have taken a specialized approach to crime control—focusing all their attention on labeled criminals and calling for better law enforcement techniques while denying the broader social picture that surrounds people who go to prison.[45] They support the public stereotype of the criminal, call for law and order, and rest blame for crime on identified and yet-to-be-identified criminals. Because their theory of cause is based on "sick" individuals, their mode of treatment is the individually oriented system of more efficient law enforcement, punishment, and, sometimes, rehabilitation programs. This approach has widened police power and training in various cities, and has sometimes funded prison programs. It has not been successful in reducing crime.

Liberals and radicals have taken a wider look at crime as a symptom of social conditions. They define the society, rather than the individual criminal, as the "patient" and suggest changes ranging from massive preventive community-level programs to economic and social reorganization of the entire society.[46] Edwin M. Schur, for instance, in his book *Our Criminal*

---

[45] For a longer discussion of the Nixon strategy on crime, see Richard Harris, *Justice* (New York: Avon Books, 1969, 1970); for a summary of liberal and conservative perspectives on innovation in criminal justice, see Walter B. Miller, "Ideology and Criminal Justice Policy: Some Current Issues," *The Journal of Criminal Law and Criminology*, 64, No. 2 (June 1973), 139–62.

[46] Edwin M. Schur, *Radical Nonintervention* (Englewood Cliffs, N.J.: Prentice-Hall, Inc., 1973); David M. Gordon, "Class and the Economics of Crime," an abridged version of an essay in James Weaver, ed., *Political Economy: Radical and Orthodox Approaches* (Boston: Allyn & Bacon, 1972) and in David M. Gordon, *Problems in Political Economy: An Urban Perspective* (Washington, D.C.: Heath, 1971), p. 58; Nora Klapmuts, "Diversion from the Justice System," *Crime and Delinquency Literature*, 6, No. 1 (March 1974), 108–31.

Society, describes ways he feels our entire society is criminal, by virtue of its unequal distribution of wealth, its perpetration of mass violence abroad, its racism, etc., and suggests that without major changes in these larger crimes, we cannot expect changes in the rates of more narrowly defined street crimes.[47]

Robert Merton, in his famous typology of deviant behavior, theorizes that crime is one result of frustrated wants.[48] His discussion suggests that all Americans are taught to want wealth and power (goals), and that hard work and education (means) are the approved ways of becoming wealthy and powerful. Most people, however, never become as wealthy or powerful as they would like to be, in part because the approved means don't "work." Merton thinks that this disjunction between goals and means causes "anomie" and suggests several ways people can adapt to this condition. One of these adaptations is "innovation"—finding and utilizing alternative (illegal) means to the goals.[49] Given the economic reality that massive amounts of wealth are concentrated in the hands of a relatively small number of powerful Americans, and given that even those wealthy Americans compete among themselves to attain greater and greater amounts of wealth and power (à la Watergate), it is no surprise that our society is filled with "innovators"— people wanting to make a few extra dollars, who are limited to illegal ways of doing so, because the legal ways don't work well enough to suit them.

David M. Gordon, a radical economist, offers a similar explanation for crime:

> Driven by the fear of economic insecurity and by a competitive desire to gain some of the goods unequally distributed throughout the society, many individuals will eventually become "criminals." [50]

He asserts that ghetto crime, organized crime, and corporate crime are all motivated by economic survival, and that what makes them different from one another are the class-based variations in *access* to different kinds of crime, and to different kinds of sanctions, some of which have been elaborated above.[51] Gordon thinks that the American system of criminal justice is a result of capitalism, and suggests that only a massive economic reorganization of the society would change the crime situation.

Many aspects of the criminal justice establishment support the power structure in the United States. First, the tendency to blame or reward individuals for their own failures or successes vis à vis the criminal justice system supports the individually oriented achievement ethic so dominant in our society. By teaching individual criminals that they are personal failures rather than symptoms of a failing society, the system subtly and effectively

---

[47] Pp. 229–38.
[48] "Social Structure and Anomie," *Social Theory and Social Structure*, rev. and enlarged ed. (Glencoe, Ill.: The Free Press, 1957), pp. 131–60.
[49] Ibid., pp. 141–47.
[50] *Problems in Political Economy*, p. 58.
[51] Ibid., pp. 58–60.

immobilizes any political energy they might otherwise have. In Merton's typology of deviant behavior mentioned above, rebellion is one possible response to a state of anomie.[52] It seems that it is to a political system's advantage to *encourage* (overtly or tacitly) individual forms of deviation—crime, drug addiction, alcoholism, or blind acceptance of the status quo—rather than risk collective forms of deviation which might lead to rebellion, establishment of new values, and new distributions of wealth and power.[53]

Another way the criminal justice system serves the rich is by supporting the illusion that crime in America is the product of a small (but growing) group of "criminals," thus protecting the rich from being discovered as criminals. It wages war on crime, presenting an *appearance* of dealing with the problem; newspapers and magazines are laced with stories of criminals who have been located by the law enforcement process. It provides a convenient focus for crime concerns, and offers only limited information to the public concerning corporate crime or crimes against the public by politicians. (Watergate has been a refreshing relief in an otherwise relatively barren field of information.) It prosecutes primarily poor criminals while wealthy potential criminals go about their corporate-level manipulations of the consumer and the economy in peace. It helps us focus on violence in the streets of American cities as the "real" crime (the most serious crime), while we ignore links between the American corporate structure and mass violence abroad (Vietnam, Cambodia, Latin America, etc.). In effect, it provides a shield against a clearer, broader look at crime. Poor criminals become scapegoats.

Finally, there is a huge economic establishment which depends upon crime for its sustenance. In 1965 we spent $4.2 billion on police, prisons, and courts. Changes in the emphasis of law enforcement efforts would very likely shake up that system. In an edited autobiography of a professional thief, Bill Chambliss reports that "we find the thief and law enforcement agencies entering into a symbiotic relationship in which each group aids the other for the benefit of both. The 'public' is unaware." [54] With reference to the economic interdependency between insurance companies and crime, he says:

> Like the law encorcement agencies, insurance companies need a useful level of theft within every community; a level of theft that keeps business and the general population sufficiently alarmed that they will pay the premiums on their insurance but a level that is not so outlandishly high that the premiums charged in order to make a profit do not interfere with the insurance companies' ability to sell policies.[55]

[52] "Social Structure and Anomie," p. 147.

[53] For example, when inmates begin organizing for civil rights and increased power within prisons, the leaders are often sent to "the hole" (solitary confinement) or "shipped out" to another prison in order to break up the group's solidarity and weaken the pressure for change.

[54] Bill Chambliss, ed., *Boxman: A Professional Thief's Journey* (New York: Harper & Row, 1972), pp. 170–71.

[55] Ibid., p. 171

Thus, there is a giant business and governmental network which depends upon the existence of crime and law enforcement as they are presently constituted (including interests like the manufacturers of safes, uniforms, weapons, etc.). It is not likely that this group would willingly give up the power it has, in the interests of justice or crime control: probation officers, prison guards, and correctional administrators want to keep their jobs, even if they are failing to aid the stated goals of the criminal justice system.

The criminal justice system is an effective means of controlling and punishing the poor by helping to keep them powerless while powerful people enjoy the privilege of protection from criminal sanctions. Larger numbers of people are becoming aware of these realities of criminal justice: sociologists, economists, and political scientists are looking more carefully at the wider structures within which crime is found;[56] groups like the American Friends Service Committee have been experimenting with new ways to bring justice to people's lives through court monitoring, community-level mediation sessions between police and citizens, observing in prisons, etc.; and inmates are beginning to see the world in political terms. The writings of Angela Davis, George Jackson, The American Friends Service Committee, and the sociologists in search of a "new criminology" are encouraging. Although the realities they present are incredibly discouraging, the movement of people in change-oriented directions lends a bit of optimism in this otherwise bleak picture.[57]

[56] For some refreshing sociological literature, see Ian Taylor, Paul Walton, and Jack Young *The New Criminology: For a Social Theology of Deviance* (New York: Harper & Row, 1973); Eugene Doleschal and Nora Klapmuts, "Toward a New Criminology"; Richard Quinney, *Criminal Justice in America: A Critical Understanding* (Boston: Little, Brown and Co., 1974).

[57] For an inspiring look at struggle, see Howard Zinn, *SNCC: The New Abolitionists* (Boston: Beacon Press, 1964); *Justice in Everyday Life: How it Really Works* (New York: Morrow, 1974).

Are people on welfare getting a free ride through life?

Or are they "paying" for social services in ways that would be abhorrent and unacceptable to other segments of society?

Welfare in America: Controlling the "Dangerous Classes" explains how social welfare services are often designed not to help the poor but to keep them in their place. Betty Reid Mandell and other contributors provide graphic evidence that our welfare system is characterized by such fundamental inequities as—

- Control of social services by elite boards of trustees sometimes motivated more by corporate politics than by the needs of the poor

- Treatment from medical service personnel in clinics and hospitals that often demeans and degrades the poor

- Discriminatory sterilization and abortion procedures that are practiced under the guise of population control

- A criminal-justice system that usually serves the rich and scapegoats the poor

- Foster-care and adoption programs that seriously neglect the emotional and psychological needs of poor children.